Male Call

New Americanists

A SERIES EDITED BY DONALD E. PEASE

MALE CALL

BECOMING JACK LONDON

Jonathan Auerbach

Duke University Press   Durham and London   1996

© 1996 Duke University Press

All rights reserved   Printed in the United States of America

on acid-free paper ∞

Designed by Cherie H.Westmoreland

Typeset in Plantin with Pabst display by Keystone Typesetters, Inc.

Frontispiece/cover art: Wolf-head logo designed in 1904 by
Ernest James Cross for use on Jack London's bookplates. Courtesy of
I. Milo Shepard and Kenwood Vineyards.

Library of Congress Cataloguing-in-Publication Data
appear on the last printed page of this book.

To my father and

the memory of my mother:

Good Comrades

Contents

Acknowledgments

This project began when Lenny Cassuto invited me to deliver a twenty-minute talk on Jack London (subject open) for an American Literature Association symposium held in November 1993 in Cabo San Lucas, Mexico. Once I accepted, a long-standing, albeit mild, interest in *The Call of the Wild* and a more sudden interest in a mild winter resort quickly started to excite each other. Only later, when the talk expanded into an article and then a book (my own efforts to make it into print), did I realize how closely my initial mixture of motives—a package deal, so to speak—was in keeping with Jack London's pragmatic approach to publishing. I thank Lenny for extending the invitation and for subsequently reading drafts of individual chapters.

Other colleagues and friends who offered much-needed advice include Bob Levine, Neil Fraistat, David Wyatt, Linda Kauffman, Charles Caramello, Vincent Carretta, Don Pease, Amy Kaplan, Jerome McGann, Martha Banta, Barbara Hochman, and Eric Sundquist. I am also grateful for the insights provided by members of a Dartmouth College humanities institute in which I participated in spring 1993. I was subsequently able to pursue this project thanks to a semester's leave granted for spring 1994 by the University of Maryland, College Park General Research Board, as well as a Fletcher Jones Fellowship awarded by the Henry E. Huntington Library, San Marino, California, for an invaluable month's stay during summer 1994 to research its vast Jack London holdings.

In addition to the Huntington Library and especially its Jack London curator, Sue Hodson, I also appreciate the help I received from other libraries, including the Merrill Library at Utah State University, the Bancroft Library at University of California, Berkeley, the Baker Library at Dartmouth College, the Alderman Library at the University of Virginia, the Library of Congress, and the University of Maryland Interlibrary

Loan Department, which was able to track down the only existing newspaper copy of London's 1893 initial appearance in print.

For permission to reproduce previously unpublished Jack London material, I thank the Huntington Library and the Utah State University Library, as well as I. Milo Shepard, who kindly granted me access to the Jack London Collections at these libraries, as well as permission to use the wolf's-head logo for this book. Thanks also to *American Literature*, which published an earlier version of Chapter 3 on *The Call of the Wild* (67 [March 1995]: 52–76). Finally, I thank the various readers and editors working for Duke University Press, Reynolds Smith and Joe Becker, as well as Nancy Malone for her superb copyediting.

Introduction

In the recent movie *American Heart*, a down-and-out former convict (played by Jeff Bridges) urges his teenage son to keep off the streets and stay in school, giving him a copy of Jack London's *The Sea-Wolf* to betoken the promise of unlikely success in America. In a *New York Times* interview (2 January 1994), President Clinton's perennial accuser (and fellow Arkansan) Cliff Jackson holds back tears while offering the figure of Jack London as the source for his own inspirational rise from a childhood far more deprived than the president's. And in a *San Francisco Examiner* article (18 April 1994) published some ninety-nine years after he had first appeared in the very same newspaper in 1895, Jack London's account of the 1906 earthquake is excerpted, along with a brief narrative of his life and a drawing of his profile. First-person testimony, biography, and a sketch of a handsome, perpetually young face: a century after his initial emergence in print, Jack London continues to reappear in virtually the identical format.

Such examples testify to the enduring popular appeal of London, who remains today the most widely read American author in the world.[1] Along the lines of Greil Marcus's engaging study *Dead Elvis*, it might be tempting to analyze the remarkable staying power of "Dead Jack" as a cultural icon. But I am more interested in examining how London wrote to become a romantic folk hero in the first place—a fame all the more extraordinary considering the tremendous disadvantages he had to overcome to make his mark in the world. As my examples suggest, the writer's triumph over poverty—cultural as much as economic—became the very personal parable, told and retold, that served to sustain success for London, who early on discovered how he could be his own best subject.

Most discussions of London begin by listing his many occupations— tramp, oyster pirate, sailor, gold prospector, socialist, and laundryman, among others—with the assumption that such colorful experiences were channeled directly into his naturalist writing. To understand his fiction, in this view, we retrace his travels in the Yukon or aboard the *Snark*. But I want to reconstruct another sort of journey by suggesting that the single occupation that London from early on most cared about—in fact the only calling that allowed him to make sense of himself—was that of professional writer. Instead of treating his writing as a kind of afterthought to his adventures, I propose instead to begin to understand the formidable power of London's work in terms of turn-of-the-century institutions of publishing itself—the collective process of composing, typing, sending, rejecting, editing, revising, negotiating, publicizing, interviewing—what London called "getting into print."

More than any other American writer of his time, London entered the profession of letters completely lacking cultural capital—education, social connections, and access to the centers of publishing; more than any of his contemporaries, he also understood how success in twentieth-century magazine and book production so depended on symbolic capital—mass marketing, self-promotion, and the projection of an exciting name. Conceiving himself as a bold, powerful, glamorous figure who cared about his audience, London continually worked hard in his life and writing to make himself interesting, to encourage his readers to "find his strong personality in his works," as one of his early reviews put it.[2] London's brilliance was to see how such interest could be accrued by the very poverty of his beginnings, how an absence of cultural capital could itself be converted into symbolic coin.[3]

Put off, perhaps, by so open a striving for popularity, academic critics have for the most part not been very kind to Jack London, leaving the field to a relatively small band of loyalists. These keepers of the flame have tended to make their case somewhat defensively in three related ways: along conventional New Critical formalist lines; by way of various ideological analyses of London's thinking on now fashionable topics (race, class, gender), often with the goal of proving that London was not really such a racist or that he really did respect women despite his macho posturing; and/or, most pervasive, in terms of the brief but highly charged life that London led. Formalism and biography, we have been told, tend to be incompatible. But in the case of London studies, they have become mutually reinforcing, investing the scenes of London's life and analogous scenes he imagined in his writing with a special, reciprocal fascination, as if the fiction needed biographical glossing to continue to have currency.

Although much important work on London has been done during the last two decades, formalism, ideological analysis, and biography have not proven to be fully satisfying for interpreting his writing. Despite the best efforts to make a case for his formal excellence, such claims tend to downplay what I take to be one of the very sources of his power—his passionate, awkward, hyperbolic, and frequently overwrought prose style and plotting. More recent revisionist attempts to make London a significant thinker strike me as also a bit ill-conceived. Inspired largely by popularized accounts of great ideas, London was inclined to indulge in philosophical speculation that frequently reveals on closer examination a fairly conventional grasp of Spencer, Darwin, Nietzsche, or Marx. Even when London rises above such familiar thinking, as in his detailed rendering of the capitalist state's hegemony in *The Iron Heel* (1908), to take one truly remarkable example, these acute political insights are curiously framed by way of glamour. Understanding how radical ideas need to be made appealing for the mass market, London invents an attractive hero (named Ernest Everhard, transparently enough) who acts as a larger-than-life object of adoration for his wife, the first-person narrator of the novel. By so imagining events and ideas in terms of his own objectified celebrity, London means to enhance and focus the narrative's power for an audience with preconceived expectations about him—expectations that from the start of London's public life profoundly shaped his literary representations.

As I shall argue throughout this study, London's importance lies less in abstracted ideas or formal precision than in his masterful striving to keep readers interested by offering himself as the ever present, energetic subject of his writing. In this regard London's biography is crucial, but only when treated as the prime source of the writer's rhetorical appeal, not an explanation or motivation for his work itself. From the start of his career London himself grasped the importance of linking his life to his work. As early as 1893, at the age of seventeen, he forges this link and breaks into print for the first time by winning top prize in a San Francisco newspaper writing contest for his submission "Story of a Typhoon Off the Coast of Japan."

Here I am less interested in the contents of the story than the editorial apparatus surrounding its publication in the newspaper. Headlined "Word-Pictures Done by Young People," London's story is accompanied by an attractive drawing of the young author and prefaced by the editorial board's explanation for its choices. "Mr. London had the advantage" over the second-place winner, the editor remarks, "inasmuch as he described something he had seen, whereas Miss Ryan's pen was prompted only by imagination." But how could the judges know this? Along with his submission, London decided to attach a cover letter, which was reprinted by the admiring editor: "This is neither an imaginary sketch nor a copy from a traveler's note-book, but an actual storm through which the sealing schooner Sophie Sutherland passed off the coast of Japan, I being before the mast as a boat-puller." The editor then goes on to quote London's mother, who delivered the story in person to the newspaper office: " 'John has often wished he could write about what he has seen.' " London's sketch thus wins first prize not strictly by virtue of its "intrinsic" merits—a concept that London was one of the first to call into question—but rather because the aspiring author recognized that his writing needed a context for its publication: adventure story, authenticating cover letter, and personal testimony from the proud mother. (The father for London would always be absent, as we shall see.) The appeal of the sketch depends on his newspaper readers' belief that it derived from actual experience—a factual "advantage" that London willingly offered as the autobiographical story behind his exciting story.[4]

Taking their lead from the author himself, London's subsequent readers have continued to have some difficulty distinguishing between the writer and his writing. As this representative anecdote suggests, both London and his turn-of-the-century audience drew on long-standing conventions of reading that assumed mimetic fidelity as the ground for literature. London actively modified and exploited such conventions, we will see in the next chapter, to affirm more specifically the author's centrality in manufacturing veracity—a process that resulted in a kind of

Male Call

feedback loop between London and his public. During the years since his dramatic death in 1916, this feedback loop has tended to accelerate, with critics still inclined to interpret his stories transparently by way of his experiences and vice versa. London's ten months in the Yukon become the basis for analyzing ten years worth of fiction about the Northland, while his complex attitudes toward fame and the marketplace are continually glossed by invoking the same half-dozen passages from *Martin Eden*. All these readings presuppose that the ultimate referent for understanding London remains his life, as Alfred Kazin succinctly noted over fifty years ago: "The greatest story he ever wrote was the story he lived."[5]

Currently there are two to three times as many biographies of London as book-length critical examinations of his work; I cannot think of another American author, canonical or otherwise, for whom this holds true. The pull toward biography in London studies has been so strong, in fact, that it is difficult to conceive of a way of critically interpreting his work that does not assume the concept of a personal career as the organizing principle of analysis. Whether the emphasis falls on his socialism, his Klondike tales, or later fiction set in Hawaii, reading his writing at times quickly gives way to chronological descriptions of his life, with plot summary all too often substituting for textual analysis, as if meaning were self-evident, simply the factual documentation of London's personal experience. In the face of what by any measure was a truly extraordinary life, starstruck critics run the risk of becoming a bit paralyzed when it comes to examining his writing.[6]

The figure of the writer looms so large and so powerfully in London's case that it threatens to engulf both cultural contexts and literary texts. Jack London understood the power of authorial authenticity best of all, but there's no reason why his readers must continue to take him on the terms he fashioned for himself from the material conditions of his apprenticeship. My own study thus begins by trying to question the assumptions and means by which he popularly construed himself. Focusing in the next chapter on the turn-of-the-century practice of magazine and book publishing, I argue that for London the writer's "self" does not so much serve as the basis for literary success and reputation as it is a consequence of the very quest for public approval. Authenticity, in other words, remains an effect of writing and not its cause. In subsequent chapters I will look at a series of overlapping institutions and issues such as race, work, and marriage through which London sought in his early writing to publicize a trademark personality that could attract a mass market of loyal followers.[7]

By attending closely to the broader cultural implications of Jack London's making, I mean to contribute to an ongoing set of revisions by critics such as June Howard, Walter Benn Michaels, and Mark Seltzer, whose important books on American literary naturalism have recently challenged an entire set of presuppositions associated with the genre. From Zola on, "naturalism" has been conceived as fundamentally grounded in deterministic laws of environment or "nature," defined in opposition to culture and/or as the biological basis for human behavior, what is commonly called "human nature." The naturalist novelist as surrogate scientist coolly observes and analyzes these inevitable facts of nature. Set in the primitive wilderness of the frozen North, city ghettos, or exotic seas; self-consciously infused with the evolutionist rhetoric of Herbert Spencer; and drawing on the adventuring author's elemental manhood, Jack London's writings have become perfect grist for a certain kind of critical mill—a romantic model that runs all the more smoothly by treating his life experience as a kind of validating second nature spontaneously called up during the writing process.

Yet as my brief interrogation of London's imprinted "self" has already suggested, what counts for nature in literary naturalism may no longer be so obvious. Offering an ideological analysis of the genre, June Howard reinterprets nature-culture binarism along class lines, demonstrating how social struggle and historical contradiction at the turn of the century are formally displaced or misrecognized by naturalist narratives as natural. By so insisting that naturalism works to polarize the categories of brute and spectator, Howard tends to reinscribe an equally fixed opposition between helpless character and privileged observer/novelist—a too absolute division between sign and sign producer that London's texts, particularly his dog stories, continually cast into doubt. Howard's study remains crucial for showing how naturalism's preoccupations with force and fate serve to express the middle-class fear of proletarianization. But her bottom-line Marxist commitment to the explanatory power of

Male Call

social class finally leads her simply to replace one set of rigid antinomies with another.[8]

For Walter Benn Michaels, social class is less the issue than how the market under the logic of naturalism tends by way of closed circuits of exchange to dissolve various sorts of ostensible contradiction—between persons and corporations, economies of gold and those of silver, properties of nature and cultural property. He includes among these turn-of-the-century exchanges the apparent opposition between writing as a form of production and its self-consumption by the writer. Pursuing a notion of identity as depending on a kind of internal difference, Michaels associates naturalism with a particular thematics of representation in which writing, understood as such, can neither be reduced to its material marks nor transcend its materiality, just as the writer's person is neither identical with body nor independent of it.[9]

Taking up the arguments of Michaels, Mark Seltzer has more recently presented a provocative, more dynamic model that accounts for the genre's preoccupation with its own materiality by demonstrating how American literary naturalism emerges from the complex tensions or "relays" between market culture (which Michaels assumes as a totality) and machine culture. Concentrating on the changing technology of writing at the turn of the century (which Michaels hardly discusses), Seltzer seeks to shift the terms of the discussion from what he calls Michaels's logic of equivalence to an analysis of how such equivalence is actively made. Naturalism is "unnatural" precisely in that it registers the "miscegenation of nature and culture"—figured specifically in London, according to Seltzer, as the wolf-dog, a man covered in fur.[10]

My work is indebted to these three key studies, which I will discuss in more detail in subsequent chapters. But considering how Jack London sought to make himself the hero of his own writing affords us a somewhat different way to think about American literary naturalism in general. A vital factor for understanding the writer's (continuing) mass appeal, London's celebrity construction serves to introduce another set of cultural contexts that both complements and complicates the operative critical categories of social class (Howard), market culture (Michaels), and machine culture (Seltzer). Rather than assume that naturalist literary production is strictly a matter of class, self-generated, or generated in conjunction with machines, I will examine how London conceived of his own production from the moment of composition as entailing a system of publication/publicity that functioned to confer prestige. Although status is partly activated by certain social, economic, and technological conditions, it carries its own logic. London's work as an author is less a question of identifying or possessing himself per se than of struggling to gain public recognition and power: the self as charismatically construed and traded in relation to others.

Moving in this way from the writer's marking of self to the writer's marketing of self, I hope to avoid a reductive tendency to treat naturalist texts as deconstructive exercises with no other referent than writing. I will argue that in addition to being about himself, Jack London's stories and novels intensely engage some of the most pressing concerns of his time: professionalism, race, labor, the social underclass, marriage, and sexuality. But insofar as these concerns served mainly to represent the writer, they cannot be construed as directly constituting the thematic "content" of his work. Rather, they offered London a set of cultural formations by which he sought to make himself somebody in print as well as by that very print. To the extent that my emphasis falls on London's own acts of self-representation, this book is neither a reception study discussing how various readers built his reputation over the years nor a full-blown examination of these turn-of-the-century cultural formations in their own right.

From early on, London's primary identity was that of professional writer. In the various guises of white man on trail, working dog, undercover social reformer, sociology professor, and effete bookworm turned sailor, London—in his first decade's short stories, essays, and novels, whether set at sea, in the blank Yukon wilderness, or brutish slums— vividly replayed over and over his intense drive for popular validation as a man of letters. In all these guises and settings, London conceived of such approval as a quest for mastery, which in turn he saw throughout his life as the measure of his masculinity. In his early work to 1904, manhood itself would increasingly come to reside for London in his body, the corporeal source of his authority and integrity as a writer. To be anything less than man and master was to be a slave. But slavery had less to do with economics than with power: subjugation by formalized institutions and structures that thwarted personal agency and yet also curiously seemed to make individuality possible.

Put another way, Jack London tended to define himself as a marginalized outsider against the very structures that he somehow also wanted to control. What at first glance looks like a standard social Darwinist trope that London often cited—"master or be mastered"—thus turns out on closer examination to teach the author, via a series of shifting naturalist scenarios, quite a different, more unusual motto—master *and* be mastered (or, be mastered *to* master). In a melodramatic early letter to his sweetheart Mabel Applegarth written at the very start of his career (late 1898), for example, London insisted that his burning calling as a writer was so strong that "if I were a woman I would prostitute myself to all men but that I would succeed—in short, I will."[11] The reasoning that would cast success in terms of prostitution (an equation resisted only by London's strategic invoking of gender) suggests a rather complex understanding of power that deserves extended attention beyond familiar commonplaces about American naturalism.

To make this somewhat abstract discussion of mastery a bit more concrete, let me consider briefly London's fascination with lycanthropy. As is well known, Jack London had a "thing" for wolves, signing letters to his wife Charmian and his intimate friend George Sterling "Wolf," naming his dream ranch home "Wolf House," and in 1904 soliciting the design of a wolf-head logo (shown on the frontispiece of this book) that appeared on his library bookplates (his literary property) as a kind of personal authorial logo—a standardized, exclusive, and recognizable identity. In his narratives the animal appears frequently, serving to epitomize, as many have noted, the tension in London between his desire for independence (the lone wolf) and his desire to be part of a collective whole (the wolf as a pack animal).[12] As I will make clear, in London the male "wolf" figures in a wide range of turn-of-the-century contexts that have little to do with the archetypal patterns or the ostensible wilds of naturalism: ideologies of Anglo-Saxon supremacy; the strife between labor and capital; and, perhaps most striking in *The Sea-Wolf* (published the same year that his logo was created), the practice of working-class sailors, prisoners, and hoboes who sexually preyed on other men. My point here is simply that as a tangible emblem of the author's self-possession, the material sign of the wolf enabled London to see and project himself—to embody, gather together, unify, and command an otherwise fragmentary set of cultural markings that could speak to his deepest psychic needs.

Given London's colossal ambitions (measured in part by his professed willingness to prostitute himself), his absorption with power, and his self-figuration as "Wolf," it is no wonder that biography has proved to be such a seductive approach to his work. Although I briefly consider certain psychoanalytic implications of his life, discussing his complex attraction to his socialist collaborator Anna Strunsky or speculating on his troubled, unending search to replace his lost father, for the most part I steer clear of such temptations, which tend to diminish the specific historical dimensions of his writing. Another approach would be to treat turn-of-the-century American naturalism as a set of discourses and practices governed by laws and logic that may make certain allowances for the concept of individual autonomy but without fully granting the power of personality. In this hard-line version of cultural studies, the subjectivity of any given author (as measured by literary style, for example) tends to count for little, so that to single out and praise London's texts as "interesting" or "compelling" risks falling into the same pattern of hero worship that I have set out to interrogate.

But London's work *is* interesting and important, I would insist, not by virtue of his literary genius or his profundity as a thinker on topics such as race or sexuality but rather because of his persistence in representing himself precisely in relationship to these urgent cultural matters. In his articulate account of nineteenth-century American "cultures of letters," Richard Brodhead has called for a new kind of critical practice that attends to the dynamics between personal agency and historical contingency:

The history of literary access, conceived as the history of the processes by which literary writing has had different cultural places made for it, and so has had different groups placed in different proximities *to* it; the history of access, conceived at the same time as the history of the acts—successful, failed, and partially achieved—by which potential authors have made themselves into authors within the opportunities and obstructions of particular social situations: this is the history we need to begin to compose if we would understand the relation of the whole of humanity to the whole field of letters.[13]

In this view, which informs my own critical assumptions, discrete individuals at particular historical moments actualize themselves as certain kinds of authors as they are reciprocally actualized by particular institutions. Writers make themselves and are made within certain multiply available cultural contexts. To begin to appreciate how such a social practice worked in the case of Jack London, I return for the remainder of this introduction to the crucial question of publication—how and when author and public intersect or realize each other. Following Mark Seltzer's influential arguments about the confusion between bodies and machines in turn-of-the-century naturalism, we can see that London's sense of the materiality of writing does begin with the conditions of composition, from brain to pen to typewriter. In this regard his reply to a query by his friend and fan Cloudesley Johns about the clumsy structure of one of his early Northland stories ("In a Far Country") is quite revealing: "I permit too short a period—One to fifteen minutes—to elapse between the long-hand and the final MS. You see, I am groping, groping, groping for my own particular style, for the style which should be mine but which I have not yet found."[14]

Here, personal style—an aesthetic matter of formal textual analysis, one would assume—is for London largely a function of the tangible mechanisms by which type is generated: the relation of man, hand, time, and machine, as if a different relation or ratio would produce a qualitatively different literary style. In other references to his typewriting, London uses an input/output metaphor, imagining the typing machine as interface between the person of the author composing by longhand and the final outcome as text, with revision taking place, London claimed, only during the process of typing itself.[15] Finalized by typing, the submitted manuscript then turns into print once it is published.

Such a mechanistic model for writing is complicated by London's internalization of the market at a very precise moment in the production process. In an astonishing reply to another Johns query about the genesis of a story's key phrase that we will examine again ("the White Silence seemed to sneer"), London explains: "No; at the moment I get a good phrase I am not thinking of how much it will fetch in the market, but when I sit down to write I am; and all the time I am writing, deep down, underneath the whole business, is that same commercial spirit. I don't think I would write very much if I didn't have to."[16]

Perhaps intended to shock his high-minded friend, London's explanation suggests how the mechanical production of writing, following the nonmaterial stage of thinking (invention), immediately enters into the larger commercial system that entails consumption as well as production. From the start London writes to be read by a public. The machine of writing is thus less the individual's typewriter (as Seltzer suggests) than the impersonal machine of the literary field itself, the mysterious process of sending writing out into the world and receiving writing back (mostly stereotyped rejection slips) that London so vividly invoked in his 1903 advice essay "Getting into Print" (to be discussed in the next chapter). Production becomes materialized as the mechanics of typing, and consumption finally means simply selling, but the interplay between writing and reading remains London's primary interest.

Midway between production and consumption is delivery: how writing reaches and returns from the distant editorial horizon, how names are made. This is one of London's prime concerns throughout his early writing, whether Northland short stories, *The Call of the Wild*, socialist exposés, letters on love, or sea novels—a concern that will serve as one thematic thread for my study. London understands the circulation of writing quite literally as mailing, the transmission of letters, a metaphoric activity that resonates powerfully throughout his early work. Conceived as a specific kind of labor, delivering mail operates in at least three distinct but related ways for London.

First, as we might have suspected, there is a clear autobiographical dimension: mail delivery as Jack London's alternative profession, a potential vocation he never actualized. In October 1898, days after he had sent out his first batch of Yukon stories, London took the civil service examination for mail carrier, a hedge against what was beginning to look like a failed writing career. By the time the results came in early 1899 (he had the top score), the aspiring author had been saved by two legendary magazine acceptances, a primal scene I will examine in the next chapter. He decided to reject the mail carrier offer lest his freedom as an independent "brain worker" be curtailed if he took a full-time salaried position. Yet he continued to contemplate the job of delivering mail, especially since his intimate correspondent Cloudesley Johns was working from 1895 to 1901 as an assistant postmaster in a small California desert town.

What, if anything, does this have to do with London's early writing? In the Northland narratives (which I discuss in chapters 2 and 3), the heroic endeavors of men and dogs in the wilderness do not center on gold mining and speculation—London's ostensible motive for going to the Klondike in 1897—but rather on delivering letters to distant outposts of progress. As dedicated civil servants, officials of the government, these commissioned agents are already positioned within a complex communications network that demands only that they distribute letters, not try to make them, open them, or read them. London's ideal author works hard and gains fame to the extent that he can carry letters without worrying about the significance of their contents. Framing a long epistle to Johns that is usually noted for its virulent race theories, London seems equally excited by "the stamp question": who pays if he sends an overweight letter with insufficient postage to postmaster Johns. Reasoning out this "stamp problem" to a tedious extreme (three paragraphs), London concludes that no individual has to pay, because the costs are absorbed by the government, a preexisting, if shadowy, authority that underwrites the circulation of mail.[17]

The second sense of mailing bears more directly on London's realized vocation as a popular writer for magazines—his ambition to succeed as a "postmaster" of another sort. As London recounted retrospectively, he spent much of his apprenticeship years sending out stories, receiving rejections, and sending them out again and again. One biographer jokes that he spent so much time at the post office during 1899–1900 that he might as well have worked there after all.[18] Not only are his early letters to friends filled with references to the costly materials of his craft (stamps, envelopes, typing paper, and typing machine, sometimes pawned), but they also included his published magazine articles and tales as well as those of other writers, many of which he clipped and sent along with his correspondence. Through letters, London and his friends thus generated a kind of circulating library, allowing print to be shared among the members of a professional community of writers—a community that materialized for London by way of his relentlessly literal rendering of the channels of publication.

London more pointedly acknowledged those letter channels in the elaborate system he used for tracking his writing through the postal system. Ever the careful professional, London kept detailed records from the start of his career, noting a manuscript's initial date of "outing," its follow-up "trailing," return, acceptance, word count, publication, dunning, payment, or "retirement" (no publication). As an early notebook entry on "The White Silence" makes clear, London even went so far in some of these early records as to log the total number of miles "traveled" by his writing as it crisscrossed the nation via mail in search of acceptance (see figure 1). Of particular interest here is London's fixation on trailing, those reminders he wrote repeatedly to magazine editors who were guilty of the "editorial crime" of not bothering to return or respond to his work. As we shall see, this scenario of trailing—letters in pursuit of letters—is enacted over and over again in the Northland fiction itself. For London, the determination displayed while on trail (whether in the Yukon or hounding editors) was as important to his self-esteem as the actual results of such pursuit.[19]

The impulse to document his mailing activity so thoroughly speaks to London's commitment to writing as a profession requiring regimentation and self-mastery. London's attempts to access and gain control over this professional print culture date roughly from spring 1897 (just before he left for the Yukon), when he began saving rejection slips from magazine editors at the same time as he began recording submissions of his work.[20] Thumbing through these hundreds and hundreds of rejection slips, mostly typed form letters and cards (on file at the Huntington Library), one cannot help but contemplate the remarkable cast of mind that would lead London to register his failure so meticulously, as if to say, "Someday, I'll show you."

To so store up failure against eventual success certainly has its logic. Clearly the threat of anonymity, a kind of social death, profoundly motivated Jack London's lifelong craving for recognition, his need for vindication in the eyes of others. But for London (as we will see most graphically with *The Sea-Wolf*), it is the punishment itself that proves the man: manhood defined more by the ability to take a beating rather than give

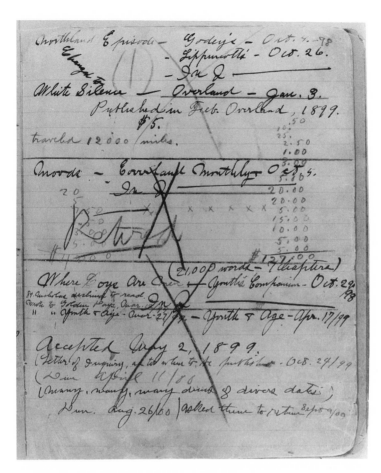

Figure 1. A page from London's "Magazine Sales No. 1 (1898 to May 1900)" records submission and acceptance dates, word counts, and pay for three early pieces of writing. The phrase "traveled 12000 miles" under his entry for "The White Silence" (originally titled "Northland Episode") refers to the cross-country distance the manuscript logged in the mails before it was accepted. The large numeral one in parenthesis indicates London's decision to make this story lead off his first collected volume, *The Son of the Wolf.* "Retired," written across the second entry, "Moods," means that London failed to place this unknown story (or poem). The entry for "Where Boys Are Men" records London's many unsuccessful attempts – "duns" – to get paid for his work after it had been accepted for publication. Courtesy of the Utah State University Library.

one. In London's work, masculinity and mastery are intimately linked concepts operating in complex, contradictory ways that London himself closely associated with his professional practice as a writer. In an early letter to his new friend Anna Strunsky, for instance, he enclosed an emended clipping of an article sent by a fellow literary aspirant (Johns), remarking, "I sometimes make and receive war through the mails in the form of bombarding and being bombarded by magazines and all sorts of erratic literature."[21]

The phrase "making and receiving war through the mails" suggests yet another dimension to mail—as a punning homonym for "male." That is, delivering letters for London quickly came to serve as a severe test of his manhood, part of the larger naturalist project of his contemporaries such as Frank Norris and Stephen Crane to masculinize writing and enhance its status as a professional vocation by wresting it from a nineteenth-century feminine, sentimental literary tradition.[22] Mail is made male primarily by means of a strenuous morality, what London would refer to as the "code of the Yukon." As we shall see, that code has less to do with the primitive wilderness than the discipline of writing or, more accurate, the discipline required to get yourself into print, to make your mark in public.

This mail/male pun informs much of London's early work, as one brief example will help make clear. Set in the Yukon, London's first novel, *A Daughter of the Snows* (published October 1902), organizes an otherwise rambling string of episodes by means of a love triangle, bold New Woman and her two rival suitors—a conventional plot that London would employ in far more interesting ways in *The Sea-Wolf.* The rivalry is eventually resolved by a pair of trials: an elaborate courtroom scene (so much for uncivilized wilderness), where the charismatic adventurer and journalist Gregory St. Vincent is exposed as a coward and a fraud; and a trial of action, where the more diffident suitor, Vance Corliss, proves himself by riding dangerous rapids to rescue a dying man.

During these two trials, the question of letters suddenly takes on importance. A kind of would-be Jack London, St. Vincent is shamed into confessing that his wondrous first-person adventure stories were borrowed from an 1807 Russian diary, presumably a faint echo of the Russian's annotated nautical book in Conrad's *Heart of Darkness* (1899).

While his cowardice ostensively concerns his breaking the Yukon code of "food and blanket" (his refusal to save a comrade's life), St. Vincent is equally damned and unmanned for the crime of being unauthentic—for speaking from prior texts and not from his direct experience.

Conversely, Vance Corliss abandons his bookish nature to take heroic action, but it is action that the playful heroine Frona Welse immediately wants to photograph and get into print as *Through Darkest Alaska*. The narrative's self-conscious fixation with documentation (literary or otherwise) takes an even more curious turn when we discover that the gaunt stranger whom Corliss has struggled to save is a half-dead mail carrier. At his rescue he feebly whispers that he is delivering "despatches . . . from the Outside"—letters, we learn on the very last page of the novel, bearing "important news" for Frona's father. The (real) male saves the mail for his lover's father, a domineering "captain of industry and a splendid monopolist."[23] Seemingly coming out of nowhere, the small plot detail of the mail carrier thus makes sense only when placed in a larger group of linked associations: moral law, manhood, the rule of the (capitalist) father, and letters.

Such a complex cluster of associations points to the overdetermined quality of London's writing. Given the slipperiness of his cultural figurations, an approach that divides his work into neat categories (Yukon experience, socialism, Hawaii tales, and so on) organized by the notion of a coherent personal career simply won't do. Yet literary analysis from a strictly formalist perspective seems equally limiting, for London himself recognized the value of trademarking his name and experience by working his "self" into print. The point here is not to banish biography but to see how London learns to incorporate and publish himself in his work. After he had attained a certain degree of success, in fact, it might be argued that he did not write to live, as he contended, but rather courted adventure mainly to have something to write about, a reasonable strategy for a famous author who repeatedly confessed from early on his inability to invent plots. Having encouraged and been encouraged by loyal readers (including editors) to treat his texts as allegories for his life, London then used adventure as the occasion for more writing.[24]

Using the trope of mail/male delivery to help direct this study, my method has been to concentrate on a smaller slice of London's corpus (his first decade of writing), in part because I want to test the still prevailing assumption among many academic critics that London's work cannot bear close scrutiny, in part because my approach to cultural studies keeps the individual author and his literary texts at the center of attention. Given London's tendency in his early writing to fuse his own quest for celebrity with other subjects (American Indians, dogs, the unemployed poor), his representations need to be untangled and examined with some care. Each of the following six chapters offers some semblance of categorical difference by fixing primarily on a single book or on collections of stories. But I have tried to unsettle such categories, comparing a band of elderly red men[25] in one story with a band of socialist revolutionaries in another or juxtaposing London's collaborative effort to write an epistolary novel on love against his depiction of city slums.

Such connections serve to generate a set of thematic threads running throughout this study that might seem to stray from my overriding thesis of "mail call." But while this thesis provides a conceptual framework, it does not strictly drive all my discussions of London's writing. In each chapter I pursue strong local arguments that link up with one another in perhaps unexpected ways. A glance at the strange love play between master and dog in *The Call of the Wild*, for instance, subsequently takes on additional significance in the light of the homoerotic tension between captain and mate in *The Sea-Wolf*. The formation of mail/male is designed to be coherent but capacious enough to do justice to London's own shifting self-interests. Although I begin by emphasizing the "mail" side of the pun, I gradually devote more and more of my attention to seeing how the "male" works, keeping in mind that publication and masculinity for London both entailed certain culturally specific acts of submission.

My basic argument runs that in his earliest professional writing (1898–1902), London sought to position himself as a man of letters within a rapidly expanding publishing field and the analogous "field" of the Yukon territory by developing new models of authorship (chapter 1) and totemic kinship (chapter 2) in relation to mass-market capitalism. Such models led London in his subsequent books (1902–4) to explore more specifically questions of manhood and mastery in terms of work, politics, and social class (chapters 3 and 4) and in the more private, domestic contexts of heterosexual and homoerotic love (chapters 5 and 6). This early quest to promote and prove himself culminates, I argue, in London's graphic rendering of the male body in relation to other male bodies. Stopping with the publication of *The Sea-Wolf* (whose magazine serialization in 1904 helped to secure his national reputation), I will be reading London's various self-representations as a mediating ground between his texts and the material conditions by which they were produced.

Whereas London's early advice essays about publishing (mostly written 1899–1903) and *The Sea-Wolf* (1904) represent logical beginning and end points, respectively, to frame a discussion of London's rise to fame, my middle chapters focus on a trio of London's books (*The Call of the Wild*, *The People of the Abyss*, and *The Kempton-Wace Letters*) that were each published in the remarkable year 1903—an extraordinarily rich year for understanding modern America, as Tom Lutz has shown in his valuable cultural study of neurasthenia.[26] Given the highly concentrated nature of London's work during this year, I have chosen not to arrange these three chapters chronologically by dates of either composition or publication (differences of only a few months), preferring instead an order that will allow me to highlight certain important thematic clusters—illiteracy, tramping, anti-Semitism, to cite just three—that serve to connect London's seemingly disparate representations of social marginalization. Thus I move from the question of writing and publishing to consider in turn the interrelated ideologies of race (the Northland stories), labor (*The Call of the Wild*), socialism (*The People of the Abyss*), marriage (*The Kempton-Wace Letters*), and sexuality (*The Sea-Wolf*), closing with a brief overview of the remaining decade of London's career once he had attained celebrity.

That London was able to gain the fame that he so desired should give us pause. Although at times he came close to appreciating how his "self" might be a function of his publishing and not the other way around, for the most part London clung to rather traditional notions of personhood, work, and literature. We therefore should not be so quick to label his brand of American naturalism self-consciously postmodern, since it is precisely his powerful romantic projection as manly hero that has continued to attract so many readers worldwide. His early work in particular reveals a fascinating, sometimes exasperating mixture of transparency and opacity, with opacity perhaps winning out in the end, one might argue. Although much has been made of the experimental aspects of London's later writing, especially in relation to Jungian psychology, much of his work after 1904, however interesting, strikes me as conservative, in the specific literal sense that once he became popular, London possessed an identity, a life's story, that he then felt compelled to conserve. My epilogue suggests that no matter how hard he tried to break free from celebrity and return to a more private set of self-definitions, London was fixed by fame.[27]

Hence my decision to focus on his early writing. London wrote an enormous amount in twenty years, including some powerful and important works late in his life. In defense of celebrity, as early as 1901 London himself had insisted to his friend Cloudesley Johns that it was just as strenuous for a writer with a name to keep it as it was for the unknown writer to get one. Yet over and over again London would harken back to his apprenticeship years, as if the struggle to gain recognition was in fact more important than the subsequent recognition. For London (and for me), how names and standards are maintained is perhaps a less interesting question than how they are constructed in the first place. The author's initial getting into print remains crucial: how Jack London wrote to become "Jack London."

The Question of a Name

"WANTED—Any kind of work; will typewrite reasonably, receive and deliver same." So stated the notice placed 4–11 January 1899 by Jack London in the *Oakland Tribune*'s "Situations Wanted—Male" classified section.[1]

A few months before the start of the twentieth century, a young working-class writer came across a newly published book entitled *500 Places to Sell Manuscripts* (1899). Part of a fledgling American industry promoting and marketing the production of literature, this book was compiled by James Knapp Reeve, also the founder of *The Editor*, a recently established magazine that billed itself as a "journal of information for literary workers." "Feeling rather nervy one day," as he wrote his fellow aspirant Cloudesley Johns, Jack London sent *The Editor* "a skit of 1700 words of advice to young authors," choosing the magazine, his letter to Johns suggests, because it was listed in Reeve's book as promising to "pay liberally."[2] That a twenty-three-year-old author with no books and less than fifteen published stories to his credit at the time would presume to give advice to other young writers is nervy indeed, a bold confidence validated by *The Editor*'s decision to go ahead and publish London's "skit of 1700 words," which he gave the impressive title "On the Writer's Philosophy of Life" (October 1899).

"On the Writer's Philosophy of Life" was the first of several advice essays published between 1900 and 1903—crucial documents for understanding Jack London's attitude toward writing. Along with his early letters to Cloudesley Johns (to whom he wrote almost one hundred times during this period), these essays are particularly revealing for a writer who was never especially given to theorizing about his craft. The fact that London published the piece to make money (only five dollars, as it turned out) does not negate his advice but serves to confirm it, for the essay itself is preoccupied with market considerations: not simply how or what to write but how to write in a way that will get you published—London's lifelong focus. At this early stage of the young literary worker's apprenticeship, London's advice seems mainly self-addressed, a kind of thinking out loud about his chances. Although sometimes couched in ironic humor, these strategic plans remain noteworthy for displaying the still relatively unknown author's uncanny ability to locate himself and his prospective readers within the emerging literature industry.

As Christopher Wilson and other critics have pointed out, from early on London unromantically viewed writing as a kind of labor that used the brain rather than the body, so that his repeated insistence in this essay that the writer develop a "working philosophy" really amounts instead to developing a philosophy of work.[3] Anyone who has spent any time reading London's early letters to Johns and other aspiring authors will be struck by how such shoptalk is continually phrased in terms of word counts, routinized production timetables, rates of pay, regimented daily writing schedules—a kind of literary Taylorism.

London's actual writing practice in this early stage of his career was largely derived from his reading of other people's advice: essays published in the identical sort of trade journals where he had managed to place his "philosophy of life" piece. For example, in London's copy of the April 1895 issue of *The Writer*, one of the first and most prominent of these periodicals (begun in 1887), we find an article entitled "My Record of Manuscripts," which described a system for documenting submissions that London himself would begin using a few years later (1898) on his return from the Yukon (see figure 1).[4] Subtitled, like *The Editor*, "A Monthly Magazine to Interest and Help All Literary Workers," *The Writer* offered its readers an astonishing array of practical tips, from how to avoid writer's cramp, to buying paper economically and methods for enclosing stamps with submissions, counting words, preventing typewriter keys from locking, and preserving newspaper clippings. The magazine also provided personal testimonials by successful writers ("How to Make Writing Pay"), formulas for short story composition, warnings about plagiarism, and a "Personal Gossip about Authors" column.

What *The Writer* studiously avoided, quite remarkably, was virtually any talk about the *content* of literature—the kinds of earnest discussions

Male Call

about the ethical responsibilities of the artist, romance versus realism, poetic technique, and so on that filled the pages of the *Atlantic Monthly*, *Harper's*, and *Scribner's*. Although such established middle-class magazines were still devoted to arbitrating taste along the lines of a nineteenth-century, belle lettres model (however updated by a focus on realism), these new "how-to" professional journals quite literally treated publishing primarily as manufacture, a largely mechanical process to be studied, broken down into its component parts (paper, stamps, typewriters) and component skills, and then duplicated. Sending the same kind of advice to those periodicals that he was also reading for useful hints, London thus helped early on to recycle a new kind of information aimed at "literary workers" like himself.

Insofar as this writing about writing focused on the technological and institutional conditions by which words materialized and circulated in print, these trade journals and directories in effect served to shadow both established and newer mass-circulation middlebrow magazines (such as *McClure's*), casting into relief what the self-evident "literature" of these other magazines generally refused or neglected to admit in their own pages. London's aim in perusing *The Writer* was not only to publish more advice for it but also to use this professional information to break into magazines with a wider readership, who were not aspiring writers themselves. Gaining such an audience depended on London's rather particularized awareness of his initial working medium: popular mass-circulation magazines. Yet instead of simply rehashing the practical tips that he himself was taking, London began to understand in these essays how this mass market required a different way of thinking about the figure of the author—a new way of construing the writer's person in relation to the market.

"On the Writer's Philosophy of Life" represents London's initial attempt to develop such a model of authorship. His advice opens as we might expect, clearing a space between the "literary hack" on the one hand and "genius" on the other. "You are no genius," London briskly informs his reader, not because genius/inspiration no longer exists (to be replaced by hard work and calculation), but more pointedly because "if you were you would not be reading these lines." Geniuses do not peruse *The Editor* looking for helpful information—nor, presumably, do they submit advice for such trade journals either. Instead, London and his readers more modestly represent writers with "ambitions and ideals" seeking "distinction" in their chosen "field." Such distinction, London next remarks in anticipation of his reader, depends on "being original" and "constantly strengthening that originality." Having raised the specter of literary tradition that had burdened writers from the Romantics on, London just as quickly tends to diminish this anxiety of influence by asserting that "you cannot expect to become original by following the blazed trail of another."[5] Viewing authorship primarily as a professional field where success counts more than immortality, London sidesteps traditional assumptions about literary vocation that insist on some dialectical tension between originality and imitation.

In bluntly giving his advice, London also pays little attention to a related Emersonian double bind: how to authorize or teach or formalize a self-reliance that cannot be imposed upon. London seems oblivious to these paradoxes, his concept of originality leading him to a more curious and perhaps more modern sort of problem. For London, writers do not "become original" by each being themselves, marching to their own drummers, but rather by putting "the stamp of 'self' upon their work—a trade mark of far greater value than copyright" (8). Such a "stamp of personality of individual view" (10), London finally suggests, functions as "a philosophy of life," the "yardstick" by which "every permanently successful writer" (8) measures the world and is measured by it. Philosophy here is not primarily an abstracted or systematic way of thinking but something London would continually forge from his enormous intellectual energy and curiosity to make himself—to make his person in print—cohere as a published writer.

Setting off "self" with quotation marks, Jack London boldly accepts as a starting premise for literary success what few if any authors before him would or could allow: that originality does not originate in the a priori inviolate person of the individual but must be "stamped" or imprinted with the defining "trade mark" of selfhood and thereby given "value" in the marketplace. Success in the market means personal validation, the "stamp" of approval conferred during the process of getting into print. But where did the writer's validating stamp come from? Although "intellectual giants" like Shakespeare possessed an "individual standard" that puts them beyond comparison ("each was himself"), these "permanently successful" masters, London insists, were not born great but "somehow, from the world and its traditions . . . acquired something which their fellows did not." That vague "something" London defines simply as "something to say," which in turn depends on "thinking thoughts which the world would like to hear" (9).

In his subsequent advice essays, London's efforts to locate and define literary greatness would continue to depend on his trying to resolve the ostensible tension between self-mastery and the market's mastery of the writer—to break down the apparent opposition between artistic autonomy and popular appeal. Here his advice still retains traces of traditional Romantic notions of inspired creativity, a self by which and through which transcendental expression is enacted. But by immediately removing himself and his fellow professional aspirants from the category of genius, London is left to rehearse or simulate such artistic activity by way of sheer diligence: a "working philosophy" whose "strong central thread" helps to project the figure of the writer in the world apart from his or her particular writing. Just as trade journals like *The Editor* and *The Writer* tended to treat literary content as an afterthought deriving from the material means of production and publication, so too does London, extending this logic, construe authorship itself as primarily a procedural matter. For London, these authorial procedures have less to do with compositional practice per se than with the set of attitudes or habits of mind that the disciplined professional must study and cultivate in hopes of capturing the attention of the public.

Key to this reconceiving of the author is London's emphasis on trademark, a concept that not only foregrounds writing as a kind of commercial manufacture but, more crucial, also emphasizes the writer's potential as a corporate entity. London seeks to maintain some control over the delivery of letters by suggesting to his fellow aspirants how they can each claim a standardized "self" as a material but mobile sign that is part of a larger market structure even as it continues to stand for the individual. Embodying publication itself, the person of the author would carry far more weight than his or her specific written work: a unifying trademark, applied to various products across the board (the corpus of writing) as opposed to a single copyright laying claim to an individual piece of work. If the writer's "self" is a detachable logo, marked again and again in the material act of writing for a public, then the primary task is to market it as your own.

To conceive of originality as corporate and stamped—uniformly unique—carries us well beyond the problematics or poetics of celebrity as experienced by Romantics such as Lord Byron.[6] Closer to home, we might be inclined to view London's assumptions about authorship in the light of Ben Franklin's or Walt Whitman's efforts at self-promotion, Poe's parodic debunking of artistic endeavor in "The Philosophy of Composition" and "How to Write a Blackwood's Article," Fanny Fern's construction of the writer's public persona in her newspaper columns and *Ruth Hall*, or Melville's bitter satire on the publishing industry in the seventeenth chapter of *Pierre*. Jack London is certainly not the first author to treat writing as a form of production in the capitalistic marketplace or to appreciate how such a market turns the author into a kind of commodity. Yet I would still maintain some critical distinction: here the issue is neither the threat of debasement nor the need to revise the public, literary self to accommodate and exploit the expectations and demands of a particular audience. London's initial piece of advice implies that even to gain any niche in this new kind of mass market, the author's "person" must be commercially deployed from the start, well before reception becomes a concern. Unavailable to antebellum authors, a trade directory such as *500 Places to Sell Manuscripts*—arranged by mutually exclusive generic categories—explicitly functioned to organize the literary field as well as the workers operating within it. The author is not so much compromised by institutions of publishing as generated from them.[7]

Perhaps the closest analog for London's construction of authorship in "On the Writer's Philosophy of Life" can be found in the life and work of Mark Twain, who as early as 1873 sought unsuccessfully to trademark his invented pen name as a way of protecting his writing against theft in the marketplace. Punning on the commercial trading of "Mark," Twain was primarily interested in establishing his personal trademark in lieu of an international copyright agreement that was years away from acceptance. By the time Twain came to write *A Connecticut Yankee in King Arthur's Court* (1889), the concept of trademark had begun to resonate beyond strictly legal matters to express Twain's complex appreciation of his own celebrity and theatricality: as his stand-in Hank Morgan observes while considering the "reputation" of a rival "new magician," "a man can keep his trade-mark current in such a country, but he can't sit around and do it; he has got to be on deck and attending to business, right along." The performer's trademark thus serves to sustain a previously secured reputation in constant need of maintenance for a volatile market and a fickle public.[8]

But why not invent the very grounds for approval as well? London's own effort from the start of his career to incorporate and authorize himself, via a validating "stamp of personality," speaks to certain changes in trademark law taking place near the turn of the century. In 1898, a year before London published this essay, President McKinley empowered a commission to revise patent and trademark statutes in response to a series of Supreme Court cases (starting with the 1890 *Minnesota Rate* case) that redefined property to include the concept of "goodwill": a corporation's nonmaterial assets such as its anticipated earning power, national recognition, and potential value when sold. Submitted in 1900, the commission's report proposed a bill (passed in 1905) that turned registered trademarks into the legal signs of such corporate goodwill. A trademark now could function as an exclusive, permanent symbol signifying a set of intangible expectations above and beyond what a company physically owned and made. Possessing a clear but mysterious potential value to be measured at the moment of market exchange, such newly consecrated arbitrary markers—Ivory Soap, Uneeda Biscuits, Coca-Cola, and so on—allowed Jack London to think about the potential goodwill of his own (brand) name as he first sought to circulate himself as a national man of letters. If corporations were beginning to assume the attributes of persons (thanks to court rulings on trusts during the 1880s), then perhaps authors, by way of a magical naming, could be made to resemble corporations.[9]

As I have suggested, London's interest in trademarking, as opposed to the more familiar notion of copyrighting, is part of a larger impulse in these advice essays to develop a new model for authorship in relation to the mass market. For the first time, the International Copyright Law of 1891 finally assured that newly published American authors would receive a royalty or strict percentage of book sales. Although such a scheme still kept publishers in control of the selection, editing, production, and distribution of writing, at least the author could participate freely in the market by assuming a direct share of profit or loss. For London, as for Twain and James, this arrangement was certainly preferable to alternative models in place toward the end of the nineteenth century: a factory model resembling wage slavery, for instance, by which writers working anonymously for publishing houses were paid piecemeal to churn out dime novels at an incredibly rapid rate.[10] London was equally suspicious of a more financially secure journalistic model: working as a salaried staff editor or writer for a national magazine or newspaper. Early on he was approached by both *McClure's* and *Cosmopolitan* with such offers, but the letters sent from *Cosmopolitan* editor John Brisben Walker (starting 13 December 1900) indicate that London was concerned about losing his freedom under such a proposal as well as his right to take a direct cut of the sales of his writing, which had the potential for enormous gains.[11] Although as a freelancer London agreed in 1901 to write a series of articles for the *San Francisco Examiner*, his motives for doing so had less to do with making money from journalism, as we shall see, than with positioning himself for subsequent magazine and book publication.

London clearly valued his independence as a writer. Such autonomy was also crucial for authors such as William Dean Howells, who sought to preserve creative integrity by developing a model of "the man of letters as a man of business." In the well-known 1891 essay of the same title and in others, Howells conceived of the writer laboring in the capitalist marketplace as essentially a freelance commercial artisan.[12] But Jack London had something else in mind. By pushing copyright in the direction of trademark, he sought to reconceive relations between publisher and author in a way that would allow the writer to become more of an entrepreneur in the capitalist market—to function in effect as head of his personal corporation, complete with a recognizable business logo of its own. Even when his individual magazine pieces failed to earn him sufficient money, London continued to operate in this mode because it helped him sustain the impression that he was personally directing his business in the market. By imagining his "stamp of self" as a trademark unifying his discrete texts, London grasped how his name—projecting magical goodwill—

might partially bypass the mediating role of publishers who might otherwise wholly determine his commercial fate.

As his subsequent advice articles to beginners made clear, London would become more and more interested in analyzing the multiple roles of the author within the field of publishing. In chapter 4 I will directly examine London's socialism, suggesting how his quirky Marxist perspective on monopoly capitalism enabled him to understand the market well enough to succeed in it. But such a perspective can be partially inferred by a careful reading of London's advice itself. A pair of essays—each published in December 1900, about a year after "On the Writer's Philosophy of Life"—point to London's growing interest in combining entrepreneurial and corporate models of authorship—to trademark himself, in effect, for national mass consumption. In the earlier "Philosophy of Life" essay London assumes a perfect match between a writer and her or his audience, in large part because many of the readers of this particular magazine were aspiring writers just like London. "Originality" can automatically translate into success, or rather the reverse: the fact that "publishers and public have clamored" for the "ware" of certain writers means for London that by definition these writers have "conquered originality" (8), as he oddly puts it, as if literature were a battle, and originality, an enemy to be defeated.

Dislodged from the writer's person or literary tradition, originality is thus simply read backward from popularity itself. After publishing more than a dozen additional stories and his first book (*The Son of the Wolf*) and receiving 108 rejections from publishers (compared with 266 in 1899), by the end of 1900 London might have been in a better position to ponder the complex institutional mediations between production and consumption in ways that complicated his earlier confidence in the writer's self-advertising.[13] Again, London's prime motive for submitting these two articles about writing is to make money, bragging to Cloudesley Johns earlier in the year that "I have stuck *Munsey's* with a thirty-two hundred word essay ["First Aid to Rising Authors"]."[14] This acceptance was all the sweeter in that it came from an influential publisher who had previously made a habit of rejecting London. But pecuniary motives do not undermine London's advice or lessen his sense of integrity, for he would repeatedly take some pains to defend his ideas against Johns's criticisms of such essays.

For London, the thirst for money (to satisfy what he often called "belly-need") and his intense desire for recognition and respect, as well as the principles by which he professed to live, are not mutually exclusive categories. An overly simplistic and moralistic view that takes for granted London's co-optation and/or victimization by the mass market will risk reinstating a set of reductive binary oppositions that have plagued literary critics and scholars for years: "high" versus "low" culture; authentic inner self and false exterior; aesthetic as opposed to commercial motives; literature (timeless art) versus transitory journalism. London's significance was to see from the start of his career how these oppositions were beginning to lose their distinct definitions in the new century.

Although London himself sometimes distinguished between his "hackwork" and his "serious" writing, he always located the key difference in terms of "ambition," so that these categories were not fixed, formal, or generic but rather fluid, subject to the interplay between the individual writer and his objectified, material desires.[15] As London insisted near the end of his "First Aid" essay: "Because we happen to be mercenarily inclined, there is no reason why we should lose our self respect. A man material enough of soul to work for his living is not, in consequence, so utterly bad as to be incapable of choice."[16] Subsuming questions of money, status, and ideals under the single matter of choice, London affirms his faith in his own talent as an emerging author to play the literary field by positioning himself within it in relation to its various literary workers—publishers, editors, literary agents, readers, and other writers. However naïve or overly optimistic London may have been about his ability to put himself at the center of all these power exchanges, his preoccupation with (literally) making a name for himself allowed him to conceive of the relation between production and consumption in terms other than strict rational calculation.[17]

Rather than speculate directly about the psychological dimensions of London's ambition, I am more interested here in examining the more tangible evidence by which that ambition can be gauged. Thanks to those detailed records that London kept from early on, we are in a position to see precisely how he learned to play the writer's market. "The

Strange Experience of a Misogynist," for instance, one of the very first stories he entered in his 1898–1900 notebook "Magazine Sales No. 1," tells the curious tale of a young man who wakes up to discover that women have vanished from the face of the earth.[18] What makes the story so interesting is that London's emphasis falls on how the absence of women affects labor relations, not simply love relations. If the contents of the story are striking, London's aspirations for it were even more so: before "retiring" the typed manuscript as unpublished, he sent it out successively to three of the most important magazines in the country—*Harper's*, *Century*, and *Scribner's*—all of which, not surprisingly, rejected London's social fantasy.

That London would try to start at the top speaks eloquently to his burning hunger for prestige. Repeatedly encountering rejection, London quickly learned that success was not so easy in this market; to note just one statistic cited by the editor of *The Writer* (William H. Hills), during 1890 the *Ladies Home Journal* took only 497 manuscripts out of 15,000 submitted—an acceptance rate of 3–4 percent.[19] While in his early years London was certainly honing his craft as a short story writer, perhaps more crucial, he was also honing the craft of magazine submission—where to send his manuscripts once he had composed them. Looking closely at the various destinations and dates of these submissions gives us one means to measure London's ambitions, the values he placed on his work. From the beginning of his career London understood these personal values (appraising both writer and writing) in relation to the importance (or lack thereof) placed by editors who read his work.

For example, London's records for the short story "Siwash" indicate that he sent the manuscript to five nationally known periodicals, oscillating between more staid, respectable middle-class publications (*Harper's Monthly*, *Scribner's*, *Atlantic*) and newer, mass-circulation, ten-cent magazines (*McClure's*, *Cosmopolitan*) before trying a lesser-known journal specializing in sports and recreation (*Outing*) and then yet another, still smaller one—*New Magazine*—which "passed over" (sent) the story to *Ainslee's*, where it finally appeared in print.[20] While a certain amount of contingency exists in this manuscript's frustrating quest for acceptance, its final destination in a recently established five-cent publisher of sensationalistic stories did in fact make more sense than London's other seven choices, given his relative obscurity when he began sending out the story (15 November 1899) and the story's provocative subject matter—a strong American Indian heroine (see my next chapter for a discussion of the story).

More to the point, perhaps, is that London never gave up on the story, despite his uncertainty about how it was to realize its value, that is, where it most properly belonged. Increasingly differentiated, late-nineteenth-century American cultures of letters gave aspiring authors myriad institutional venues for publication, but they also multiplied the risk of working at generic cross-purposes, increasing in turn the risk of an authorial identity crisis.[21] Was Jack London to be a *Scribner's* regular (like Henry James and Edith Wharton) or work for *McClure's*? Hence the need for a unifying trademark that would enable London to be "himself" wherever he appeared in print. Perplexed by the fate of magazine stories such as "Siwash," London would begin to use his advice essays to work out his own confusing experience of submitting manuscripts to various publishers.

The essays "First Aid to Rising Authors" and "The Question of a Name" both take off where London's earlier article left off by ruthlessly, if playfully, continuing to demystify writing as anything but a form of labor under capitalism. The tone of these essays is complex, seeking to outrage (one of London's telltale characteristics) by way of a mocking irony that veils a deeper set of anxieties about the writing game. The "First Aid" piece, for example, takes the writer's motives as its subject, "analyzing that ambition which leads men to make commodities of their written thoughts, and to send them forth, like turnips and cabbages, to be bought and sold."[22] Moving in this forthright, if tongue-in-cheek, manner from the question of originality to the question of ambition, London again seeks to define a particular space for his kind of writing not simply by clearing away abstractions such as "genius," as in the earlier essay, but also by excluding particular kinds of institutionalized writing and writers as well: "specialist" professionals such as doctors, professors, and historians; and amateur dabblers "removed from the struggle of existence." What remains are two classes of writers—selfless idealists who have messages, and the materialists, "clay born creatures like you and me." When it comes to assessing the motives of the materialist,

London suddenly shifts from a first-person account to remark, "Ask the editors, the publishers, the booksellers, the reading public, and the answer will be 'Cash' " (25).

That ambition is driven by cash is less surprising than the fact that for London ambition itself is socially constructed, located within a very specific network of institutionalized relations "rushing us into print." The writer and his or her ambition hover midway between subject and object, at once making and being made into print. Following a long, amusing rehearsal of his material and bourgeois wants (nice houses, pianos, good steaks, tobacco—all examples of the general proposition that "the world owes us something, and we intend dunning until we get it"), London goes on to "decide what part of us is the best to put on paper" (27). But by "us" London means the "stamp of self" now expressed mainly in terms of literary genre (fiction, poetry, essay, and so on), whereas "best" refers to "which pays the best." In a series of notes London jotted down two years later (1902) for an article comparing the writing of novels with that of short stories, we discover the same sort of slippage in London's thinking about value: unlike novels, he muses, short stories are more difficult for an author because they require that "every word must count—no padding—(& here's the rub, for he's paid by length, not strength)."[23] What begins as an analysis of aesthetic principles ("le mot juste") quickly gives way to a consideration of economic laws that transform a disembodied author motivated by transcendent ideals into a laborer working in a particular market. Words "count" and writing "pays" in two very different ways that threaten to undermine each other.

Constantly aware of being a literary worker operating in a very particular set of economic laws, London nevertheless cared more about publishing's validation—the fact that "the world owes us something"—than money per se, as I have been suggesting. The challenge for London was to pay attention always to the material meaning of value without letting it swallow up his ambition to "be a Somebody," as he expressed his desire for approval in "The Question of a Name." These generic distinctions based on pay rates enable him to mobilize and deploy compartmentalized writing selves, freeing his trademark personality to oversee the market's validating process. London has so internalized publishing practice that his advice here sounds more like the wisdom of an editor than a fellow writer, a testimony to the ease with which he is able to assume multiple positions within the literary field.[24]

In the other late-1900 essay—"The Question of a Name" (published in *The Writer*)—such positional multiplicity becomes a way for London to bridge a disjuncture between production and consumption that was beginning to trouble him. In "First Aid," London's playful equating of literary genre with parts of self allows him to treat authorial production and market consumption as if this exchange were a continuous unbroken circuit, like the "circulating library" he advises his readers to consult to feel "the pulse of the market." But "The Question of a Name" opens by probing the vexed relation between what gets written and what gets read: "Every first-class magazine is overwhelmed with material (good material), of which it cannot use a tithe; and it will reject an unknown's work, which may possess a value of say, two, and for which it would have paid a price of, say one, and in place of it accept a known's work with a value of one, for which it will pay a price of ten."[25] Here, the writer's best and the market's best don't necessarily match up, as London's distinction between "value" and "price" indicates. In fact, the relation of value and price seems quite arbitrary: by sheer assertion London quantitatively fixes value, drawing on a theory of value as located in the worker's labor, as William Dean Howells had also insisted in "The Man of Letters as a Man of Business." Assuming some absolute division between those "who live by doing or making a thing" and those who live "by marketing a thing after some other man has done it or made it" (33), Howells, as the established dean of American letters, could insist that this labor carried a dignity—a moral worth—apart from the amount it might fetch.

But in the absence of any institutional access to publishing—cultural seed money, so to speak—London the proletariat autodidact literally cannot afford to accept such a clear demarcation between making and marketing. More than Howells ever imagined, London appreciated how the price of literary work fluctuated wildly in this mass market, not depending on the kind of product itself or its demand—or even on the author's originality or ambition—but simply on whether the author was known. Yet how was the unknown to become known when the main thing that counted in this business was recognition itself? Verging on an "impossible" Catch-22 scenario, London quickly reaffirms his faith in the power of the individual literary worker to blaze a trail, to make his own name. He concludes his article with two detailed blueprints for success— book publishing and magazine work (his own main choices)—that treat such writing as akin to, respectively, methodical bricklaying and a training school (with the magazine editor playing the role of teacher).

London's rather predictable advice about diligence is less interesting than the problem it is designed to address: how to break into a preexisting circuit of exchange that has no way of independently valuing value. London's vision characteristically settles on "the editorial horizon," Jerome McGann's useful term for the material and institutional production and reproduction of texts. Although editors remain the ultimate "arbiters of success" for London, by what principles do these commercial middlemen themselves operate? Lumping together "the advertisers and the reading public" as a single force driving editorial decisions, London offers a striking observation: "The 'star' system of the American stage is equally in vogue with the American editors."[26]

The great American writer as star actor: although a few conservative critics began drawing on this resonant analogy at precisely the same time as did London, they used it primarily to deplore the promotional practices of publishers looking for a quick profit by puffing a single best-seller or two. London, by contrast, seized on the concept of stardom as an opportunity, anticipating (and subsequently participating in) the twentieth century's emerging "culture industry," as Frankfurt School critical theorists called this historical process of reification.[27] Unlike the 1900 condemnatory essay "The Star System in Literature," for instance, London pursues a far more provocative line of thinking by accepting the fact that "a certain intrinsic value attaches to a name."[28] He goes on to suggest that publishers may be justified in printing familiar authors over newcomers simply by virtue of their renown.[29] As opposed to both orthodox Marxism and bourgeois romanticism, value is located in neither the writer's material labor nor disembodied genius but adheres "intrinsically" to the author's charged sign of prestige. Disseminated within an institutionalized system, the individual name itself generates symbolic capital. Bridging the apparent gap between primary making and secondary selling, the writer's unique trademark remains part of the market but carries a status that cannot be reduced to it.

Turning from these essays to the author's acts of self-construction, it is instructive to see how Jack London helped to put his own advice into material practice. By early 1902 the literary aspirant had made something of a name for himself, a reputation outstripping his actual literary production (two books of short stories plus a few dozen magazine tales and essays) and also surpassing his local public lecturing on socialism. In addition to running for mayor of Oakland in 1901 on the Social Democratic ticket, London was written about and thus entered another crucial sort of textual circuit—newspapers—simply for being "himself." In summer 1901 London agreed to write a series of articles and interviews commissioned by the *San Francisco Examiner* on a variety of topics of local interest, such as a shooting festival or a girl defeating a burglar through her athletic prowess. While this "yellow" (as London called such journalism) might have been beneath him at this point in his career, the headline of one such article—"Governor Taft Tells Jack London about Filipinos and Philippines"—suggests the value of such writing. The implication is that Jack London conducting an interview is a newsworthy event in itself, regardless of whom he was interviewing.[30] In this article and others in the series, the *Examiner* reinforced such an effect by following each headline with a framed oval photograph of London's face—a head shot—to serve as his dramatic byline.

Akin to the American theater's star system, the sort of yellow journalism that began to privilege the figure of the reporter over the events reported could thus be applied to literature across the board. In this context London's willingness to write for the *Examiner* in 1901, just *after* his second book appeared in print, was a brilliant tactical stroke, allowing his name to circulate for prospective readers as yet unfamiliar with his fiction. Such a tactic may appear counterintuitive, reversing the normal hierarchical career ladder of newspaper-magazine-book publishing—a path followed by virtually all American professional writers around 1900. After all, as one contemporary reviewer remarked in a 30 June 1901 article that London pasted into his scrapbook, "How ephemeral is a reputation built upon magazine and newspaper work."[31] But London saw precisely how such ephemera could be used to his advantage. Long after the contents of his yellow writing had faded away, his name and handsome face, shown over and over again in the series, would remain to remind newspaper readers of his books.

In some cases during this crucial period of his literary career, Jack London's getting into print began to take on a life of its own, as his carefully maintained scrapbook of clippings from this time makes apparent. Later I will show how London's close monitoring of his reception helps account for the very genesis of *The Call of the Wild*. But here I simply want to outline some features of this turn-of-the-century publicity apparatus. In May 1902 a local Bay Area newspaper reprinted a sarcastic letter that London sent a grocer who was demanding payment. Demonstrating an interest in the figure of the writer that far outweighed the ostensible subject of his writing, no less than four other newspapers picked up the story, one headline reading "Literary Compositions to Tradespeople." One journalist was led to muse that because the letter made such a "hit" and "was not copyrighted," it should be published despite being "a private communication" or else sold by the disgruntled grocer "as an autograph letter from a great writer" to make up for London's unpaid thirty-five-dollar bill. Just as Andy Warhol remarked that anything he did was art since he was an Artist (more recently revised to be a collector of valuable Art), here anything London wrote had merit since he was a Writer. Similarly, we discover that by August 1902, London's style is already being parodied—a published burlesque (again pasted in London's scrapbook), written by one "John Liverpool" (the name that London would later borrow for one of his many planned autobiographies), mock author of "The Daughter of the Dog," "The Law of His Wife," and "The God of His Mothers."[32] Along these same lines we can also find in the scrapbooks a comic description of London's activity made up entirely from the titles of his early Northland stories that manages to recount the deeds of "The Man on Trail" for two entire paragraphs.

Such instances conflating the figure of the writer with his writing were local in nature, signs of London's growing celebrity in the San Francisco Bay Area. Another extended example lets us see how London contributed to the circulation of his name on a national level. London's breakthrough began with the 10 June 1899 submission of his story "An Odyssey of the North" to the Boston-based *Atlantic Monthly* rather than the local California magazine the *Overland Monthly*, to which he had been submitting most of his Klondike tales. At the same time he also wrote to Houghton Mifflin, the *Atlantic*'s parent company, enquiring about the possibility of their publishing a book collecting those Northland stories he had previously placed in the *Overland Monthly*. London was shrewdly guessing how magazine and book publication might work together to move him beyond a small circle to reach a wider audience.

William Belmont Parker, the Houghton Mifflin assistant editor, responded on 18 July 1899 by cautioning London about the "great difficulty in marketing volumes of short stories" whose "function" is already fulfilled by their individual magazine appearances. He then mentioned "An Odyssey of the North" as still awaiting assessment by *Atlantic Monthly*'s editors. When that story's acceptance finally came a week later (contingent on London's trimming the tale's opening pages), the letter was signed by Parker himself (from Houghton Mifflin). His personal response thus indicated the intimate editorial connection between the publisher's book interests and the operations of its magazine. Acting as an editor for both the magazine and its parent company, Parker was apparently convinced that the story was strong enough to take a gamble on the entire collection—an opportunity that would have been lost had London not simultaneously submitted the story and his idea for a collection to the same editorial outfit.[33]

After the collection (entitled *The Son of the Wolf*) was accepted a few months later, London received a flurry of questions and suggestions from Houghton Mifflin's production/marketing office in anticipation of the book's release the following spring (7 April 1900). These requests crucially allowed London to participate in the material making of his first book and, with it, the making of himself as a national author. On 3 January 1900, for instance, his publishers requested an (auto)biographical sketch, along with a subtitle for the book, suggesting that something like "white silence" would be "a distinct help to the book in the commercial sense." Whether this suggestion about "white silence" inspired London's own subsequent account (to Johns) about the resonant phrase's promotional potential or whether London seized its commercial potential during the very moment of composition, as he claimed, is less important than the curious way the author's fictional plotting and his publisher's advertising strategies both amount to the same thing—making copy. In the next chapter I will be examining how and why this phrase—"the white silence," repeated throughout *The Son of the Wolf*—gives a certain thematic unity to London's first collection of Northland stories.

But the more general point here is that such formal, seemingly aesthetic considerations cannot be divorced from market motives. A book ostensibly written by the individual Jack London and then sold by the publishing house Houghton Mifflin in fact materialized as an object by way of a complex complicity between "creative" author and "commercial" publisher. Sending London twenty more letters in six months, the editors at Houghton Mifflin prompted London about illustrations, as well as the order of the stories (a crucial matter, as we shall see), in addition to soliciting more extensive biographical information, photographs, and, most interesting, "hints for special" reviewers at journals where the young author might have made personal connections.[34]

Beyond simply complying with these requests, London quickly became engaged in more actively prompting his publisher in return once he learned how promotion worked. He suggested additional places for review, distributed some review copies personally, and helped to orchestrate (again, at precisely the right moment) the publication of a flattering interview conducted by Ninetta Eames in the *Overland Monthly* (May 1900) that was used in Houghton Mifflin's advertising for the collection and discussed in the local newspapers. In early February 1900, London also began subscribing to an author's clipping bureau, the kind of newly established service that Twain had begun using only five years earlier.[35] As usual, London's timing was perfect, for this service would enable him to monitor national reception of his forthcoming first book. During the same month, he or one of his friends fed a story to the *Oakland Enquirer*. Announced with the headline "Jack London Gaining Recognition from Leading Eastern Publishers," the article described how "the young author of this city" had received "a personal letter" from S. S. McClure offering to publish his future work. As London clearly understood, it was precisely the "personal" nature of this letter that made it worthy of publicity. After decrying the delay in London's long-deserved recognition, the newspaper account concluded by announcing that a volume of London's stories "is shortly to be issued"—a bit of prepublication advertising offered as a newsworthy event.[36]

Perhaps the most significant single piece of promotion that London, along with his publishers, fashioned for *The Son of the Wolf* was the extended autobiography he sent Houghton Mifflin on 31 January 1900 at their (additional) request.[37] It is a fascinating document. London realized that he was not writing autobiography to express himself—or even to inform his publishers—but to give them something they could use for advertising purposes. We therefore get a string of self-contained phrases and whole sentences written as promotional blurbs: "Folks say I simply insisted upon being taught," or "Always a book, and always reading when the rest were asleep." London knew at this point that John London was not his biological father, but he still claimed his descent from this "soldier, scout, backwoodsman, trapper, and wanderer" in tropes replaying the mythos of James Fenimore Cooper. Thus although he is certainly not the first writer to so shamelessly promote himself (one might think of Whitman's notorious efforts in this regard), for London the apparatus of publicity itself drives his self-conception as a man of letters.

It is no wonder, then, that books figure so prominently in London's folksy presentation, designed to project him as a born author, an "omniverous [*sic*] reader" who "always could read and write." In more intimate personal correspondence describing his early years, London confessed—with a complex mixture of shame, pride, self-pity, and burning anger—his poverty and brutalization as a manual laborer, but here he deems it "worthless to give the long sordid list of occupations," concentrating instead on his toil as a student, both of letters and of life. Not surprisingly, London focuses on his adventurous experience at sea, "tramping and Klondiking" (also prominent in the first version he sent Houghton Mifflin)—his life as "a man amongst men" as he puts it in yet another resonant phrase that turns his literary ambitions into an affirmation of his manhood.

When it comes to connecting such direct manly experience to his bookish nature, London is put in something of a bind. Torn between insisting on his passion for letters and his passion for adventure, London understands that the two fields can converge only in the figure of the self-taught writer, whose will and energy unite disparate spheres, converting an adventurous career into a "literary life." Openly dismissing his early writing as "hackwork for dollars," London thus calls on his impoverished circumstances (justifiably so) to dramatize a potential not yet realized— the familiar and very powerful American story of individual, self-made ambition striving for fulfillment. London needs to insist so clearly that "I have had no literary help or advice of any kind" (ignoring his reading and writing of those professional advice essays) because he wants to cast himself as the Lone Reader. Although he knows he cannot make himself into a man of letters by himself, he can suspend such knowledge by imagining how others would want to read him precisely as such a self-begotten individual. In this way he can appear outside all publishing institutions yet still manage to reconstitute literary history strictly by the strength of his self-directed education. Professing to be "sick" of auto-biography (so that he can get on with his life), London nevertheless concludes his letter to his publisher by carefully reserving the right to look over "the biographical note before it is printed."

In emphasizing the care and control with which London crafted this piece of promotional autobiography, I do not mean to suggest that London falsified or even magnified himself in a show of bad faith. More simply (and more complexly), this is how London saw himself when he began imagining a public for his work, the trademark self that would vindicate him in the eyes of others. Writing himself to be read, Jack London becomes the thing he has written. Although it would be a bit rash to claim that by such promotional writing London could dictate his own reception, a glance at the initial reviews of his first two books does reveal a curious congruence, if not a seamless identity, between his crafted self-image and his public perception. Picking up where the auto-biographical sketch left off, reviewers frequently linked the freshness and virility of his Northland stories directly to his "self-made" stature—more particularly, to his status as "a man of many-sided experience," a phrase that echoes his own self-description.

But as London's scrapbook of press clippings helps us see, this phrase, as well as others, is repeated verbatim in dozens of reviews published throughout the country, with local newspapers each appearing to evalu-ate independently *The God of His Fathers*, his second volume of tales, published by *McClure's* in May 1901. Before syndication of literary reviews, which began later in the decade, how could London's reputation from the start be so standardized and nationalized? The verbatim repetition of entire phrases renders such autonomous reviewing apparitional; as a subsequent explanatory letter to London from Macmillan suggests, understaffed newspapers were in the habit of directly lifting promotional sketches accompanying publishers' review copies and passing off such advertising copy as a literary evaluation. It would be especially tempting to rely on this sort of borrowing for a young writer such as London, who was important enough to merit some attention from the press but not yet big enough to warrant a staffer's own reading and writing time. In so deliberately phrasing his autobiography for his first publisher, London grasped how his printed "stamp of personality" could flow, virtually unmediated and unaltered, from author through publishers and newspapers to the public. Via such an unbroken circuit of letters, the author's message or, more accurate, the author *as* his own message gets transmitted without even requiring that his books actually be read.[38]

Responding (perhaps with some envy) to London's published how-to essays and his friend's growing reputation, as well as to London's many personal letters of advice, encouragement, and criticism, Cloudesley Johns struck a raw nerve in London by astutely suggesting to him in spring 1901 that his "incentive" in writing was simply the "assurance of being able some day to sell any sort of work on the strength of a name." Stung by the accusation, London replied by insisting that "the struggle for a man with a name to maintain the standard by which he gained that name, is as severe as the struggle for the unknown to make a name."[39] Here, the emerging celebrity would seem to be echoing Hank Morgan's meditation in *A Connecticut Yankee* on the difficulty of sustaining a reputation, although by insisting on some external "standard" by which a name is maintained, London conservatively still clings to vestiges of belles lettres idealism, unlike his more cynical Yankee counterpart. London would continue to register this ostensible tension between commerce and art in his next published piece of advice, "Again the Literary Aspirant," which came out in yet another professional trade journal, aptly named *The Critic*, in September 1902. Exploring the "paradox" that "singing

Male Call

into a typewriter and singing out of a magazine are quite unrelated performances" (note the new theatrical metaphors), London poses his familiar question: "The advertisements bring the cash; the circulation brings the advertisements; the magazine brings the circulation; problem: what must be printed in the magazine so that it may bring the circulation that brings the advertisements that bring the cash?"[40]

Refusing to follow up on his previous emphasis on the marketing of authorial name as a kind of capital in itself, London retreats to a far more conventional position that now sees critics, not editors, as "final arbiters," the small number of "discerning" readers who hold out for higher standards, those immortal "masterpieces" that prove that "truth alone endures." Yet despite his best efforts to affirm such ideals, by the end of the essay London begins to make fun of them, returning to the editors, not the critics, who advertise their celebrated authors as the "GREAT JONES" and the "IMMORTAL JENKINS" (52). Observing that "whoever feeds a man is that man's master" (a line that will bear reexamination when we consider *The Call of the Wild*), London turns his attention again to the question of marketing. He perversely imagines a scenario that he would later fictionalize in his novel *Martin Eden*: an editor who agrees "to publish some of the very things I am now refusing" (53) as long as the artist-aspirant first gets a reputation. London's paradox remains unresolved, to be magically "compassed" by the writer's name alone.

Two essays published the following year (1903) represent London's last direct comments on the paradox before he became a full-blown celebrity in his own right. The four bits of advice offered in "Getting into Print" (*The Editor*, March 1903) are strictly pedestrian—work hard, watch your health, develop your philosophy of life, and, added as an afterthought, be sincere. But what remains crucial here is how London prefaces this commonplace advice with a long, first-person retrospective account of his attempts to break into print, presumably of great interest to magazine readers already familiar with his name. London's earlier prescient analysis of the contemporary American editorial horizon thus has given way to energetic self-narration, beginning with his frustrations as a wholly ignorant newcomer negotiating the material conditions of the market:

All my manuscripts came back. They continued to come back. The process seemed like the working of a soulless machine. I dropped the manuscript into the mail box. After the lapse of a certain approximate length of time, the manuscript was brought back to me by the postman. Accompanying it was a stereotyped rejection slip. A part of the machine, some cunning arrangement of cogs and cranks at the other end (it could not have been a living breathing man with blood in his veins) had transferred the manuscript to another envelope, taken the stamps from the inside and pasted them outside, and added the rejection slip.[41]

An episode of enormous import to London, this quest for recognition was subsequently fictionalized in *Martin Eden*, a novel that in turn became a further source of allusion for London in his 1913 autobiography about his alcoholism, *John Barleycorn*. Over and over again London would return to this moment in his literary life. In his essay this memorable passage about the struggle to get into print prepares the way for what amounts to a professional primal scene—London's first letter of acceptance from a reputable magazine for the paltry sum of five dollars, quickly followed by the unexpected and saving offer of forty dollars from the pulp magazine *The Black Cat*, provided he cut his science fiction potboiler by half (which he immediately agreed to do). This legend has become a representative anecdote for virtually all subsequent commentators on London. It is not simply that London is self-mythologizing here. Like many authors, he does so from the very start of his career, confessing in a 30 November 1898 letter to his sweetheart Mabel Applegarth, for instance, that his boyhood theft of a piece of meat amounted to "an epitome of my whole life." More to the point, the author's literary life, turned into legend, stamps the seal of approval on the writing itself; narrating the personal story of getting into print validates that print. No wonder London added "sincerity" to his article's concluding recipe for success.

The key passage of "Getting into Print" pits the "soulless machine" of publishing, imagined as an impersonal system of mail, against the personal integrity of the struggling author, embodied (by implied contrast) as "a living breathing man with blood in his veins." Such a stark opposition between an alienating process of "stereotyped rejection"—

Male Call

made human strictly via the crucial mediating figure of the "postman"—and a heroic individual struggling to remain true to himself serves to redefine authorship in terms of a distinctly masculine writer, now autobiographically and corporeally rendered. Seeking to dramatize his retention of some autonomy despite or within this publishing machine, London transforms the circulation of mail into male experience.

After achieving international fame with the concurrent magazine and book publication of *The Call of the Wild* in summer 1903, London was able to codify this approach in "Stranger Than Fiction" (*The Critic*, August 1903), which eschews advice altogether to narrate a series of typical "Jack London" yarns—hiking in the Klondike, cliff climbing, tramping—activities all designed to illustrate the cliché that truth is stranger than fiction. London's thinking escapes mere banality because he deploys the cliché to comment on thick magazine editors who forced him to tone down his actual experiences—the vital movements of men in a particular time and space—to fit the demands of magazine print. Poking fun at "the editorial mind" (75), London manages to suggest an alternative source for all his writing, the author's personally brand-named true "self."

When that trademark writing occasionally seemed to infringe on or was infringed on by other similar literary representations, London was obliged to ponder the meaning of plagiarism, which became more pressing an issue once he became famous. As we might have anticipated, London tended to treat plagiarism as a question of personal authenticity, not texts. Remarking in a letter on the curious coincidence that both he and Frank Norris each published a story (about a dog wired with explosives) based on the same newspaper article, itself derived from other written accounts, London puts a halt to a potentially infinite regressive intertextuality by claiming how most fictions are anchored in such "facts of life reported in journalistic style." In a later letter he similarly defended *The Call of the Wild* against plagiarism by again assuming "actual experiences of life to be a lawful field for exploitation." From such a starting point he goes on to suppose first that "I am in the Klondike" directly witnessing the episode in question, and then by a series of logical demonstrations he imagines himself step-by-step removed from the scene—not my dog but someone else's, not actually there but told the story by the dog's owner, not directly listening to the story but browsing it "in a plain narrative of incidents"—all in a perfectly seamless move from sight to speech to print.[42]

In this revealing plagiarism scenario, London gradually transforms his person into the language of another, changing the author's role from actor to reader to protect his own words against the charge of theft. But take away that initial supposition "I am in the Klondike" and London would be nowhere as a writer; he can validate his writing only by affirming his own presence on the scene, the sole "lawful field" he can accept for his textual "exploitation." How London specifically construed himself in relation to this field, how and why he would so link legitimation and exploitation, will be the subject of the next chapter: how the author imaginatively sought to position himself in his early magazine short story submissions while he was also pondering the question of a name.

The (White) Man on Trail:
London's Northland Stories

Five months after returning from the Yukon goldfields, Jack London wrote his friend Mabel Applegarth near the end of 1898 an excited and irritated letter describing how one of his Northland tales ("To the Man on Trail") had just been accepted for publication by the *Overland Monthly*. Formerly edited by Bret Harte, the San Francisco–based magazine proposed by letter to pay five dollars for London's work, the first money ever offered for his writing. Complaining that his story was "worth far more" than such a paltry sum by virtue of its length of three to four thousand words (calculated "at the ordinary reportorial rate"), London mused how such a "first class magazine" (or so he thought) could be so stingy, concluding, "Well, a newcomer must excell [*sic*] them [other writers] in their own fields before he is accepted, or else he must create a new field."[1] Ten months later, in August 1899, with some dozen additional acceptances to his name, London sent Cloudesley Johns a letter claiming, "Yet I think I have for some time had an entirely original field in view," an insight challenging his earlier admission to Johns that "almost every field under the sun, and over it too, has been thoroughly exploited by others."[2]

Just three years later, London's published field had expanded considerably, consisting of three volumes of Northland short stories, virtually all of which first appeared individually in magazines. On the appearance of this third volume in late 1902, London wrote his new publisher George Brett at Macmillan and Company: "I want to get away from the Klondike. I have served my apprenticeship at writing in that field, and I feel that I am better fitted now to attempt a larger and more generally interesting field," by which he meant longer novels on a variety of subjects.[3] Although some of London's early work was set elsewhere, the bulk of his writing from 1898 through 1902 took place in the Yukon, the scene of his initial fame as a writer.

London's complex understanding of his Northland writing as a "field" and, more particularly, a field for his apprenticeship will be the focus of this chapter. I shall argue that London's professional ambition to open up, blaze, and inhabit a "new field" corresponds closely to the ambitions of his characters within these short stories to explore, negotiate, and colonize or "exploit" (to borrow London's word) the Yukon territory. As critics such as Earle Labor have noted, Jack London's Northland is less an accurate transcription of his brief experience in the Klondike than a symbolic terrain whose strenuous conditions serve to define and test the author's manhood.[4] Unlike these other critics, however, I do not assume that manhood for London is constituted by a set of universal virtues such as courage, honor, and fidelity. Rather, manliness comes to depend on two related issues with specific historical implications— the question of authorial integrity, which London understands in light of turn-of-the-century publishing institutions, especially conventions of literary regionalism; and the question of positionality within this cultural landscape, a problem that London pointedly construes in terms of Anglo-Saxon supremacy. Linking manhood to theories of race, London constructs a complex fictional system of totemic kinship in these early stories—a patriarchal order that must be defined, invented, and revised progressively in relation to imaginary American Indian wives, white mothers, and American Indian fathers. These three overlapping stages correspond roughly to London's first three Northland collections: *The Son of the Wolf* (1900), *The God of His Fathers* (1901), and *Children of the Frost* (1902).

As London's letters suggest, the imaginary "field" of Northland writing is defined neither by subject matter nor genre but is constituted by the complex *relationship* between genre and subject matter—a relationship mediated in turn by publishing practice. When the editor of the *San Francisco Bulletin* rejected London's early sketch of his return from the Yukon ("From Dawson to the Sea") with the comment, "Interest in Alaska has subsided in an amazing degree," London's response was not to stop writing about the Northland but to write about it in a different way—to fictionalize the landscape in a way that would appeal not to newspapers but to popular short story magazines such as *Munsey's, Frank Leslie's,* and *McClure's.*[5] By such an early miscalculation, London thus learned that the "intrinsic value" of his writing by which he hoped to persuade the local newspaper editor to accept his sketch in fact did not exist in any pure form but depended instead on who would consume it and how it would be consumed: its finding a proper niche in the market.

Before leaving for the Klondike in summer 1897, as an alternative to manual labor London tried his hand at different sorts of writing to make money, composing jokes, poems, political doggerel (for both mainstream parties), horror stories, and essays for submission to all sorts of publications. But after his first Northland tale appeared in the *Overland Monthly* in January 1899, he soon began generic streamlining, producing a series of Northland tales at the encouragement of *Overland*'s canny editor James Howard Bridge. Although he continued to submit previously rejected material, London essentially stopped writing across the board to concentrate on what would quickly become his trademark "new field" of production: a group of short stories loosely united by characters, theme, and atmosphere as well as their common Yukon setting. By February 1899 London was so confident about the importance of situating himself within an increasingly stratified publishing industry that he chided Cloudesley Johns for writing a short story with a didactic purpose, insisting that such purposes do not conform to "the legitimate field of such literary productions." Didacticism belonged instead to journalistic pieces or novels. "You know there is an eternal fitness of things," London playfully remarked, naturalizing the mass market's generic distinctions in the belief that certain higher laws dictated the rules of publishing.[6]

For London those laws extended beyond narrow generic considerations to embrace a wider sense of "field" as offering a particular ideological location *for* legitimation itself. As James Bridge surely understood, London's short stories could easily be marketed to accommodate magazine readers' thirst for local color, so that the young writer's own sense of his "new field" as a spatial metaphor for a certain kind of writing here closely followed the concept of region so influential for late-nineteenth-century American letters. In this sense the remote location of the Yukon would serve as a logical extension, expanding the concept of "frontier" literature, itself a subspecies of regionalism that tended to conceive of its bounded space in relation to a more comprehensive national map. Ostensibly opposing concepts, regionalism and nationalism in fact worked to reinforce each other, as a late 1900 review of London's first book makes clear: "As every section of our country has its annalist in our national fiction, it is meet and proper that the Yukon district . . . should find a writer."[7] As Lauren Berlant has suggested, at the turn of the century the marketing of individual commodities in relation to corporate brand names helped consumer-citizens, via a series of synecdochical expansions, to imagine a national public sphere.[8] So too could individual magazine stories set in an identifiable locale (a matter of market segmentation, if you will) similarly participate in the country's singular "national fiction."

Magazine pieces that were published separately could thus be gathered together as a single book unified by a particular but expansive sense of place—a field of writing internally consistent (region) yet linked to a greater whole (America). Owen Wister's preface to his frontier short story collection *Red Man and White* (1896, illustrated by Frederic Remington) offers one sort of model for such synecdochical logic: "These eight stories are made from our Western Frontier as it was in a past as near as yesterday and almost as by-gone as the revolution; so swiftly do we proceed. They belong to each other in a kinship of life and manners, and a little through the nearer tie of having here and there a character in common. Thus they resemble faintly the separate parts of a whole, and gain, perhaps, something of the invaluable weight of length."[9] The idea of "kinship" allows the stories to cohere internally and suggests as well an ideological connection between Wister's West and the revolutionary principles of American history more generally. As a conceptual space more substantial and permanent than individual magazine stories (which tended to be ephemeral and fragmentary, like much of modern American culture itself), the published book as a material object could thus become the very "field" or "region" of writing to be preserved and cherished: a collection between hard covers made even more respectable by the illustrated art of a Remington.

In his suggestive 1993 analysis of American literary regionalism, Richard Brodhead has shown how the mode operated as a kind of surrogate tourism for upper- and middle-class genteel readers, offering nostalgic glimpses of a way of life apart from culturally dominant practices.[10] Enjoying a series of adventure tales set in the far North, *Overland Monthly*'s (mostly Western) readers could experience vicarious contact with a "new" past, as it were, at once immediate and distant, to borrow Wister's terms. Publishing one London tale virtually each month beginning January 1899, the magazine offered its readers a continuing fictional tour of yet another exotic frontier guided by an expert with firsthand knowledge.[11] From the regional writer's point of view, this emphasis on expertise was crucial for establishing the integrity of his discrete magazine productions. When London was initially hunting for a publisher to bring out his first collection of stories, for example, he adamantly stressed his role as an actor in the landscape, not a spectator, in a letter of inquiry he sent to Macmillan: "The scenes are laid in the Klondike Country. Needless to state, I have been there, and not as a summer tourist, either."[12] Here, London's characteristic emphasis on authentic personal experience as authorizing his fiction reinforces his insistence on the writer as a special kind of insider.

Simultaneously the object of production and an imagined "field" where production takes place, the collected book of Northland short stories afforded London tangible advantages over his piecemeal publication of individual stories in magazines. First, it allowed him to double the value of his work, since he would get paid a second time for the book rights to stories he had previously sold to magazines. Second, it gave him the opportunity to restore cuts in his stories that he had been forced to make by space-conscious magazine editors. Returning to his original typescripts rather than magazine tearsheets, London in effect restored his own authorial integrity, producing a whole—a distinctive unified and ordered corpus of writing—greater than its mutilated parts (to draw again on Wister's 1896 preface). As early as December 1898, after his initial acceptance by the *Overland Monthly* but before meeting with the editor Bridge the following February to arrange for a package deal, London refers in his letters to his stories as part of a "series," with the implication that from the start his early Northland tales were shrewdly designed in relation to one another to form a single body of work.[13]

We therefore need to attend carefully to how London conceived his first collection of stories as a unified book—*The Son of the Wolf: Tales of the*

Far North (Houghton Mifflin, April 1900). As Wister's preface suggests, in addition to region, short story cycles at the time also depended on recurring characters to help establish "kinship of life and manners" between separate tales. Of the nine tales in *The Son of the Wolf*, seven make use of the Malemute Kid, a manly, disciplined, and wise Northland bachelor and veteran (neither old-timer nor young neophyte) who functions variously in the tales as the central participant, a more passive auditor, and/or a moral commentator. James Bridge certainly recognized the unifying value of the Kid for his magazine series; the second story he published ("The White Silence") was already subtitled "Another Story of the 'Malemute Kid,'" a practice he continued by numbering each story as it came out ("Third of the 'Malemute Kid' Stories," and so on)—a marketing ploy from which London took some pains to distance himself.[14] Following Bridge's lead, most critics discussing London's first book of Yukon tales continue to focus on the character of the Kid as a stand-in for the author himself, giving the collection its unifying central intelligence by virtue of the Kid's moral judgments on events and on other characters.[15]

London's own references to the Kid in his letters, however, reveal a certain impatience with his creation. In response to criticism about the character made independently by his friends Mabel Applegarth and Cloudesley Johns, London admitted to an "insincerity of vision" in representing this frontier stereotype, a weakness compounded by the threat of overkill in relying too heavily and too often on a single character to sustain the weight of London's new field. For one thing, the emphasis on character as a unifying principle too closely resembled earlier dime novel, mass-market methods of production that allowed the author to be subsumed and rendered anonymous by standardized, generic fictional protagonists copyrighted and owned by publishing houses, not individual writers.[16] While London understood, as did Bridge, that the continuing but partial representation of the figure of the Kid was the "raison de etra [*sic*]" for an unfolding series, he clearly conceived of these stories as a unified whole that did not depend on the presence of the Kid but rather came together by virtue of London's representations of the Northland landscape, a far broader and more cohesive cultural space than stock individual figures such as the Kid could themselves comprehend.[17] Ambitiously working to evoke an abstract sense of place and theme beyond plot or character, London's collections of Northland tales thus look forward to modernist short story cycles, or rovelles, such as Joyce's *Dubliners* (1914) or Hemingway's *In Our Time* (1925).[18]

In this chapter I examine this figurative regionalism by interpreting the Northland tales as an evolving structure, dwelling less on individual tales than on complex relations or networks among stories. I will look at how London initially built his unifying principle or conceptual "field" by literalizing the atmosphere of the Yukon in two related ways—as the "white silence" and as the "trail." These two recurring Northland tropes combine to generate an opposition throughout these tales between "Inside" and "Outside," with "Inside" standing for an entire set of thematic and ideological concerns, most notably a preoccupation with white manhood. London seeks to locate himself and his protagonists within this ideological space, we shall see, specifically by way of interracial marriage—miscegenation conceived as the grounds to legitimize and renew a lost patriarchal order. Following the trajectory of his first three collections of stories, we will move roughly from white men taking Indian women, to white men honoring their white mothers, and to white men searching for Indian fathers. Such a trajectory demands that we take seriously London's investment in theories of totemism, kinship of life and manners as viewed from the perspective of turn-of-the-century ethnography.

In deciding which Northland stories to examine, we must keep in mind that there are essentially three different sequences to consider once we take into account London's detailed records of his work: (1) the chronological dates of his submission to magazines, presumably very close to the dates of composition, given what we know of London's writing practice; (2) the dates of short story publication in magazines, sometimes years (and multiple rejections) after the tales were written; and (3) the order of stories as they appear in London's books. "The Son of the Wolf," for example, is the second story in the collection of the same name but appeared as the third story in the *Overland* series and was the fifth submission to the magazine, as if London's overt thematizing of race in this title story (to be discussed shortly) occurred to him only after he had already written a number of other Yukon tales. Since the book restored to London the sort of editorial control that he had to relinquish when he submitted piecemeal to magazines, we need to honor his sense of order, aesthetic and conceptual, to appreciate the sort of "field" he sees and makes for himself in these collections.[19]

The Son of the Wolf opens with the tale "The White Silence." Vaguely titled "Northland Episode" (as in a journalist's sketch) when he initially submitted it in October 1898 to *Godey's* and *Lippincott's* (rejected by both), the story was suggestively renamed by London before he sent it to the *Overland*—a crucial sign that he was beginning to understand the deeper implications of his own "regional" fiction as it first started appearing in print (see figure 1). More expansive than the character of Malemute Kid, the trope of "the white silence" presides over this volume and the subsequent two collections of stories, haunting the Yukon landscape until it comes to stand for the Northland itself. The story's plot is simple enough. The Malemute Kid is desperately racing through the fierce, frozen wilderness with his Yukon partner Mason, Mason's pregnant Indian wife Ruth, and a ravenous pack of sled dogs. When a falling tree gravely injures Mason, the starving Kid is forced to abandon his dying, delirious friend and move on to save himself and Mason's wife. Here's how London closes the tale:

> An hour passed,—two hours,—but the man would not die. . . . Malemute Kid roused and dragged himself to his comrade's side. He cast one glance about him. The White Silence seemed to sneer, and a great fear came upon him. There was a sharp report; Mason swung into his aerial sepulchre; and Malemute Kid lashed the dogs into a wild gallop as he fled across the snow.[20]

The clause "the White Silence seemed to sneer," as I have briefly observed in my introduction, was singled out for praise in a letter from Cloudesley Johns, who asked London if he were aware of the great commercial value of the boldly capitalized phrase when he first thought of it. Besides deftly capturing the tale's overriding feeling of menace, "the White Silence" could function, Johns's astute comment suggests, as a more general (trade)marker defining London's Northland as well as the writer's own distinct presence, his personal stamp of self laying claim to this original field—a kind of signature (or rather printed) flourish to help announce his magazine debut. No other writer could use the phrase once

London took possession of it. London himself grasped as much by sprinkling the phrase throughout the collection at key moments in various stories (four times in this opening story alone) to unify the atmosphere of the series and thereby reinforce his own authorial integrity.[21]

That the white silence belongs to a collective state of mind rather than a specific geographical territory London makes clear in the tale by Mason's repeated (and capitalized) references to "the Outside" (3, 5, 13). As a dislocated Southerner who replays childhood scenes from Tennessee while deliriously dying (anticipating Hemingway's "The Snows of Kilimanjaro"), Mason sees the Northland in terms of a strict binary opposition between inside and outside, where "Inside" stands against home and civilization—familiar, white, Anglo-Saxon domestic ideals. Returning to Mason's distinction throughout the collection and in his letters, London reinforces the otherness of his new field, a space requiring specialized, technical expertise for its mastery. London reminds his friend Edward Applegarth (Mabel's father), for example, that "Malemute Kid was no artisan when he lived on the Outside," thereby associating his own craft with the "insider" perspective of the Yukon: a region with its distinct customs and manners.[22] Although London's very first Yukon stories such as "The Test: A Clondyke Wooing" (unpublished during his lifetime) treat the Northland's social manners along the familiar generic conventions of frontier local color, beginning with "The White Silence" the tourist mentality of the reader quickly gives way to a more abstract, less conventional cluster of concerns centering on a search for a single law governing race, writing, and masculinity.

Evoking visual and auditory absence simultaneously, "the white silence" powerfully summons a sense of place by way of negation. London's Yukon is a region curiously devoid of recognizable features, a frozen Northland emptied of meaning beyond London's deliberately half-hearted effort at personification ("seemed to sneer"). Against such sinister blankness, this story, along with many others in the collection, opens and closes with frantic movement on the trail. Being pursued and/or pursuing others in lines across the snow remains the only possible response to "the white silence," that which cannot be directly said or seen. Throughout these Northland stories, trailing serves as the manly counteraction to nature's white silence, the severe activity by which "aliens from a dozen lands" (105), including Native Americans, are molded into a single sort of man.

Like the silence itself, the trail is less a particular location than an imagined condition of being, as London made clear when he angrily complained that the *Overland* botched the title (and significance) of the first story published in the magazine series, turning "To the Man on Trail" into "To the Man on the Trail."[23] When London gave this story the central (fifth) position in *The Son of the Wolf*, he restored his original title, removing the article *the* which the meddling editor had inserted to provide a road map for a field that wanted none.

On trail in the white silence: here is the central drama of the Northland stories, enacted over and over again with various modifications, elaborations, and implications for questions of race, social order, and mastery. These specific cultural implications thus emerge out of the more abstract field of naturalist writing, which London figures repeatedly in his apprenticeship fiction as trailing through whiteness.[24] The motives for such trailing (hardly ever discussed in the stories) are less important than the sheer discipline and exertion of will required to keep going. To stop moving or to deviate from the trail is to die. By imagining the scene of writing as a blank waiting to be marked, London analogizes his own efforts to make a name for himself in print (to work inside the silence) with the strenuous efforts of protagonists such as Mason and the Kid to make something of themselves inside the Northland. Just as London's characters most fear being wiped off the landscape, obliterated or obscured by blankness (as Mason's body is catapulted into emptiness), so too does their author most fear obscurity—the failing to stay on track and get published.[25]

But what, exactly, do these men make of themselves in the white silence? The answer depends on understanding how throughout these early tales London has ideologically inflected the contrast between "Inside" and "Outside": while the "Outside" stands for civilized America, you become a (white) man only once you leave such civilization behind and enter "Inside" the more primitive Northland. More specific, entering the white silence makes Americans into "Wolves," of which Mason is said (in the collection's next story, "The Son of the Wolf") to be "the first" (31). For London, as I suggested in the introduction, "wolf" is a crucial term signifying dominance, a sign of power that manifested itself throughout his writing in a variety of cultural formations—commercial, political, and sexual. But here in its initial incarnation, "Wolf" carries enormous import as a specific kind of racial marker.

Thus the concept of Wolf not only helped afford London the means to unify and establish kinship among his early Northland short stories but also helped supply an analogous sense of kinship for the author himself. Even before we reach the book's table of contents, *The Son of the Wolf* opens with a dedication that sheds light on the volume's striking title: "To the sons of the wolf who sought their heritage and left their bones among the shadows of the circle."[26] Wolf here stands for the white race, an equation London makes abundantly clear in the book's eponymous second story, which describes a white man's victorious theft of an American Indian bride from her tribe, members of which are responsible for naming him as a member of the "Wolf" clan. On trail in the blank Northland, London from the start thus relied on red men to consecrate and socially define the white man, imagined in terms of a totemic designation. Without anchoring his masculinity in such a system of *beliefs*, Jack London would have remained just another ambitious but rootless young American struggling to make a place for himself in a volatile social order.

The dedication's reference to the "sons of the wolf" is a bit more complicated. By making his protagonists (and dedicated readers) members of a second younger generation, London implies existence of a prior original tribe of fathers with which and against which the primal horde of sons must define themselves. Who these mythic patriarchs are and how to find them remains London's central concern throughout the Northland tales. While it might be tempting to launch into psychobiography by examining London's preoccupation with patriarchy in the light of his own illegitimacy (revealed to him just as he was beginning to write professionally), I am less interested here in exploring the missing father in London's life than in understanding the missing father in American culture at this time. As many historians have noted, the turn of the century registers a growing crisis in American masculinity, as increasingly rationalized forces of economic incorporation made the market a less and less viable place for men to test their manhood.[27] London's response to this crisis, we shall see, is to look elsewhere, to reinscribe communal (white) manhood in relation to the Northland's tribal fathers, who come to represent a solidarity or sense of belonging set against the capitalist marketplace.

The third and perhaps most interesting aspect of the book's dedication follows from my previous two observations—that the "heritage" of the sons cannot be taken for granted but must be "sought" among the shadows of the Arctic Circle. Conflating bloodlines with patriarchy by way of that ambiguous word *heritage*, London implies that in the Yukon, white men *become* white men—that they must acquire and earn their racial/gender designations. In the White Silence men are made into members of the Wolf. More pointedly, the title story "The Son of the Wolf" suggests how London's protagonists become more white not simply by virtue of their contact with Indians but especially by virtue of their intimate contact with native women. For London's protagonists this contact is less an expediency than a necessity, the primary path toward racial self-realization and solidarity. Only by seriously entertaining miscegenation can London imagine himself belonging to a social group—a clan—in which white unity need not depend on a fixed habitat, lines of descent, or common blood.[28] Because his own white blood, viewed in terms of social caste, was so marginal, London transforms Anglo-Saxon "heritage" into an end (not a given) that must be earned by hard work, fought for, and won. A writer more confident in his status as a white man would not have been driven to search for it so incessantly.

The idea of a totemic clan as a racial grouping was so appealing to London because it allowed him imaginatively to secure a place in the social order that was not strictly determined by class or birth. In a brilliant if idiosyncratic revision of critical commonplaces about turn-of-the-century American notions of race, Walter Benn Michaels has shown how white supremacists discovered how to reinvent themselves by moving away from markers of color to more invisible, more abstract signs of white empire (becoming Clansmen of another sort in the process). In this view the white man's imperialist aspirations become something of a problem, insofar as contact with nonwhites brings with it the threat of contamination.[29] However useful in highlighting the constructedness of Progressive Era racial categories, Michaels's rigorous analysis, based as it is on Southern anti-imperialists' views of African Americans, fails to account for the paradox London encounters in his Northland: how whiteness abroad cannot be constructed from itself, as it were, but depends on being affirmed by nonwhites, the Native Americans who originally bestow the sacred "Wolf" name. The irony here is that fearing polluted blood, London's Indians (the "Raven" clan) endorse the logic of racial purity by refusing to allow interracial marriage, whereas the "Wolf" himself, affirming his natural superiority, unsuccessfully pleads his case for such mingling as inevitable before he is compelled to take his bride by force.

But by so questioning Michaels's provocative attempt to uncouple racism from the ideology of American expansionism at the turn of the century, I do not mean to endorse the far more familiar position that assumes white imperialism must define itself *against* its passive, subaltern "other." It makes little sense to accuse London of being a racist or to defend him against such charges without first appreciating how London is seeking in his Northland field to reinvent the concept of race itself.[30] In this respect the red men of this fictive region, however romantically stereotyped, are granted a certain power over their Anglo-Saxon brethren, since the Wolf must depend on the Raven to name them as such, to introduce them to native ways, and ultimately to help them rediscover their true fathers. London's search for some collective social formation to embody manhood outside the capitalist market leads him to conceive of a totemic system by which identity is conferred through kinship that establishes fundamental laws of conduct via the exchange of women.

Following the strict logic of totemism, London's thinking on race dictates that members must mate outside their own clan. London's brand of naturalism thus extends beyond juvenile playacting (the ersatz primitivism of the Boy Scouts or Teddy Roosevelt's hunting parties) to accept the prohibitory force of the taboo (specifically, exogamy) as governing all social order. Theories of totemism were so vigorously debated among ethnographers at the turn of the century because such explanations carried important implications for understanding the bewildering cultural dislocations brought on by modernity. Whether the slant of these theories was psychological (Freud) or sociological (Durkheim), writers sought in primitive totemism a crucial way to analogize their contemporary situation.[31] In *Totem and Taboo*, for example, Freud compared the thinking of savages to childhood neurosis, whereas from a different vantage point, Durkheim located in the elemental forms of religious life the foundations for complex modern society. To trace just one key thinker on the issue, James Frazer began in 1890 by assuming that totems represented invulnerable places to guard the souls of individuals, then shifted some years later to a sociological theory that took totemism to be a system of cooperative magic (a "magical producers' and consumers' union," to borrow Freud's memorable summary), only to return in 1910 to a psychological theory whereby the origins of totemism can be found in "the sick fancies of pregnant women" whose awareness of impending birth compels them simultaneously to conceive the totem for the clan.[32]

Despite the striking resemblance between this last account and the rendering of pregnant Ruth in "The White Silence" that opens *The Son of the Wolf*, no evidence suggests that Jack London was directly affected by such scholarly debates among ethnographers. More likely he initially drew his inspiration from Herbert Spencer's popular *Principles of Sociology* (1885), which treats totemism primarily as a primitive form of nicknaming that became literalized and collectivized by subsequent generations.[33] Building on this notion of totemism as linguistically garbled ancestor worship (by way of a kind of misidentified trademarking), London imaginatively connects the totemic "Wolf" clan with the white race by assuming some abstract law by which men could find their place in society—a patriarchal order to be discovered (or rediscovered) only on the Inside. Freud relied on an oedipal model to account for his primal horde rising against the father and then instituting communal laws among themselves. But London (akin to Durkheim and structuralist anthropologists such as Lévi-Strauss following in his wake) is more interested in the totem as a fundamental form of social organization that depends initially on the "traffic in women" in his stories.[34] From this starting point, we shall see, London's Northland tales will begin to register the "Wolf" clan's transformation into the (white) capitalist state, whose goods have replaced brides as objects of commercial exchange.

What London refers to as "the ethics of the Northland" (117) in his early story "To the Man on Trail" thus carries far wider significance when viewed in the context of totemism. London clarifies the precise nature of this code in a remarkable letter sent (to Johns) four days after he had submitted his final Malemute Kid story:

Remember, there is even a higher logic than moral or formal logic. Moral and formal logic demonstrate thoroughly that women should vote; but the higher logic says she shall not. Why? Because she is woman; because she carries within her that which will prevent, that which will no more permit her economic and suffragal independence, than it will permit her to refrain from sacrificing herself to the uttermost to man. I speak of woman in general. So, with the race problem. The different families of man must yield to law—to LAW, inexorable, blind, unreasoning law, which has no knowledge of good or ill, right or wrong.[35]

London's perfectly conventional adaptation of Darwinian rhetoric to contemporary social problems is less interesting here than the way that such discourse enables him to establish some sort of abstract relation between women and races he perceived as inferior. In a subsequent letter to Johns (5 July 1899), London associates the law's marking of difference with his own by way of a striking metaphor: "Where am I to draw the line?—At the white." Repeated as a kind of refrain in other letters to Johns, "drawing the line" serves as yet another version of the author's professional "trailing" in and of his Northland tales, an attempt to demarcate a new field governed by its own higher law. As I have insisted, this field does not encode nature or the primitive as much as express a set of cultural anxieties about masculinity and race manifested as questions of social hierarchy. Invoking some transcendental law, at once external ("higher") and internal ("carrie[d] within her"), which operates to dictate relations between races and between men and women, London thus struggles to fix his own problematic social status, which he imagines, incessantly working on trail, in terms of rules regulating kinship. Such a law conflates the distinction between mastery and submission, allowing London to imagine himself in a position of dominance (as a white man) and simultaneously obedient to a code entirely outside his control, subject to a higher authority that serves to legitimize his exploitation of the Northland and its natives.

In the stories themselves the transcending of civil manners by the seemingly unsentimental law means that the calculating Malemute Kid must shoot Mason to save himself and Mason's pregnant wife Ruth—three lives versus one. Similarly, in "To the Man on Trail" the Kid is justified in helping the man on trail to escape from pursuing police because this desperate criminal (named Jack) is guilty only of stealing the exact money that had in effect been unfairly taken from him in the first place, squandered by an unscrupulous partner. Under the guise of hard-boiled Darwinism, London's twist on nature's ruthless struggle for survival lets him smuggle into the Northland his own sort of romanticized morality. But although this code of honor superficially resembles the standard frontier justice meted out in so many turn-of-the-century magazine tales of the West, London's ambition is more complex: when the Kid's mates complain about the man on trail's thievery and lying ("Worse than an Indian!"), the Kid's response is to declare majestically that "a whiter man than Jack Westondale never ate from the same pot nor stretched blanket with you or me" (117–18).

Inscribed by the law, London's "man on trail" Jack thus also becomes inscribed by "whiteness," a racial marker linked in turn to the problem of marriage in the Northland, as the Kid's comment about sharing blankets suggests. With two interesting exceptions, no white women figure in the collection *The Son of the Wolf.* To simulate civil society in the Northland, London's male Wolves face three alternatives. First, they can imagine marriage in its absence: stealing the money to return home to the Outside, the rugged but tender Westondale, with a "hint of womanliness" (108), carries a picture of wife and child near his breast. Second, they can "marry" each other, as in the chilling tale "In a Far Country," which depicts a relationship gone sour: the story of two white men separated by class (rather than sex or race) stuck in a cabin (a surrogate domestic space as opposed to being on trail) who end up killing each other in a fatal mutual embrace. Not until *The Sea-Wolf* (1904) would London again try to represent such intimate violence between men. Third and most crucial for his Northland field, London's Wolves take Indian brides.

While I have already discussed how miscegenation centrally informs the first two tales of the collection ("The White Silence" and "The Son of the Wolf"), interracial marriage runs throughout the book, offering a unifying thematic thread to accompany the atmospheric unity generated by "the white silence." For example, in "The Men of Forty-Mile" (the first story composed in the series, positioned third in the collection), Malemute Kid, intervening where there is "no law in the land" (57), cleverly resolves a frontier dispute that is triggered by a racial slur, one man calling another's half-breed wife by the lower-caste term "Siwash." The story also invokes as key actors in this spectacle of justice the very same white man–Indian squaw couple violently wedded in "The Son of the Wolf," just as that story in turn explicitly refers back to the Mason–Ruth pair in "The White Silence" as a precedent for Northland miscegenation. The final three stories in the collection continue with variations on this theme, respectively introducing an American Indian man (Sitka Charley) together on trail with a married white woman ("The Wisdom of the Trail"); Malemute Kid's tricking a straying Wolf into reuniting with his abandoned Indian wife ("The Wife of a King"); and the desperate search of an Indian prince for his Indian bride, taken away by a white man ("An Odyssey of the North")—the complex concluding tale of the collection that enacts London's most obsessive and intense rendition of trailing.

As his biblical naming of the squaw "Ruth" in the opening story makes all too apparent, London sees these various marital relationships in terms of a complicated theology of race in which the tangible fruits of union are less important than the idea of union itself. While the widow Ruth's pregnancy in "The White Silence" looms large over the entire collection—like the silence itself—for the most part London backs away from the impending birth of the half-breed, preferring a more abstract drawing of (race) lines that rehearses in various forms the first commerce between Wolf and Raven clans represented by the original couple, Mason and Ruth.[36]

Over and over again in these tales, native women are referred to as daughters of "the soil" (for example, in *The God of His Fathers*, 56, 196)—inevitably and directly connected to the landscape. Serving as the counterpart to the sons of the Wolf, London's daughters of the soil thus enable a genealogy joining together law and nature, the merger of two ostensibly competing sources of authority. At this early stage in London's thinking, the fact that these women are a part of nature means that their status as nonwhite is fixed, unlike an American Indian man such as Sitka

Charley, who can negotiate whiteness, as I will argue, by obeying and enforcing the law of the trail.

London's traffic in native wives serves to naturalize three related Northland ideologies—the dominance of the white man, the importance of work, and the affirmation of patriarchy. Conceiving of these women as forces of nature allows London to make their deification of their white husbands seem equally natural. Not only does London repeatedly stress that these women prefer the Wolf to their own kind because white men treat them better, but he also implies, following the "higher logic" of his letter to Johns, that such worshipful obedience of woman to man is somehow natural in and of itself. Presumed alone to be untouched by civilization, Indian women in these stories approximate a pure state of womanly servitude and strength. In the story "The Son of the Wolf," the ravished daughter of the soil turns out to be no less than the literal sister of Ruth in "The White Silence," thus establishing close links between stories by way of blood ties between American Indian women. Gazing "reverently" at the white man's "great hunting-knife" (*The Son of the Wolf*, 28), the squaw Zarinska participates willfully in her own abduction, heroically warning her new "husband" against the arrows shot by prospective mates from her own tribe and thereby confirming "the Law of the Wolf" (50).

That these Northland squaws actively help their white "lords of creation" (18) points to subtleties in London's rendering of race that go beyond puerile male fantasies. He is less interested in them as sexual objects than as coworkers who unlike their "idle . . . white sisters" (10) are not confined to a separate domestic sphere. Mason's dying praise of Ruth, for example, centers on her capacity as trader, hunter, and speedy carrier of news. While these wives are never seen laboring on trail apart from men (Ruth remains silent throughout the story), they are economically valuable as producers rather than consumers. They are so valuable, in fact, that the bachelor Malemute Kid, otherwise "shy" (13) of native women, registers Ruth's worth by regarding her with "vague jealousy" (16) as a kind of rival for his comrade Mason's manly affection—an affection earned and displayed at work in camps and mines and on the trail.[37]

The higher logic of the Law that turns woman's submission to man into instinct thus also makes the squaw's work natural. Our childhood memories of reading Jack London play tricks with us if we seem to recall these stories filled with adventure, gold prospecting, and striking it rich. The dominant activity running throughout the tales is work, not play—material toil on trail, valued in and of itself, since London rarely stops to indicate or consider the reason for such toil. This toil is ennobled by London's figurative daughters of the soil, who are not common native women but literally and invariably stolen daughters of chiefs and kings. The royal heritage of these women workers is in fact crucial—a designation that will eventually lead London to understand that the common father of his sons and daughters—the tribal patriarch uniting law with nature, Wolf with nature—must be red. The question then becomes: in the absence of white fathers, where is the ancestral father who sets the law for his royal sons and daughters to follow? London begins to seek an answer in the trio of stories closing the collection, which significantly were also the final three he composed for the book: "The Wisdom of the Trail," "The Wife of a King," and "An Odyssey of the North."

Although all three stories were written within a few months of one another, it makes sense to discuss them in the order of their submission to magazines to appreciate how London's thinking on race was developing. London first sent out "An Odyssey of the North" to *McClure's* in May 1899 and then the next month to *Atlantic Monthly*, where it was accepted, becoming the first of his Northland tales to appear in a prestigious national publication. Whereas the *Overland Monthly* had paid him $5 or $7.50 per story in the series, the *Atlantic* offered London $120, thus confirming for good his calling as a professional magazine writer. With the publication of this single story, London hit the jackpot financially as well as culturally, for the *Atlantic Monthly* clearly represented access to the dominant genteel centers of publishing on the East Coast; on the strength of this story, as I have shown in the previous chapter, London was able to land his first book contract with *Atlantic*'s Boston-based parent company, Houghton Mifflin, to publish *The Son of the Wolf*, even though eight of its nine tales had first appeared in the California-based *Overland Monthly*.[38]

London had unsuccessfully submitted (non-Yukon) material to the *Atlantic* before. The key to his success this time was to imagine a tale told by an Indian, to give voice to one of the victims of "the law of the Wolf," rather than to continue to focus on the Wolf himself, as in his previous *Overland* stories. As Brodhead has suggested, genteel regionalism at the turn of the century wanted the voices of the dispossessed to be heard.[39] In the very next issue of the *Atlantic* (February 1900) following the appearance of "An Odyssey" (January 1900), we find the serialized version of Zitkala-Sa's "The School Days of an Indian Girl." Authenticity thus shifts ground from the expert charting foreign territory to the native witness already on the Inside. According to London's logic throughout the collection, this insider must be an Indian prince, a chief and son of a chief who stands at the center of the Northland's patriarchal order. In this story, the native prince is frantically trying to take back his intended Indian bride stolen on his wedding night by a white Wolf. In "An Odyssey of the North," being on trail no longer leads to miscegenation but now means desperately and tragically trying to undo it.

Both formally and thematically the story marks a significant breakthrough. London frames the tale with his standard local color scenario of Malemute Kid and his mates, formed from "many breeds" by the "common life" of the North into a "certain type" (192). An Indian returns half-dead to camp to discharge a debt of money he owed the Kid. Dubbed "Ulysses" by these men, the silent, strange Indian "Naass" begins to narrate his story of wandering and pursuit, leaving Malemute Kid and the others to recede into the background as passive listeners who are drawn further and further into the interior of the Indian's experience. The narrative thus closely resembles the structure of Conrad's *Heart of Darkness*, which had just begun to be serialized in *Blackwood's Magazine* a few months before (February 1899).

More important, London uses the tale to complicate racial categories. Unlike his previous protagonists, the story's Wolf is not Anglo-Saxon but Scandinavian (Axel Gunderson), so that the clan of the white man is repositioned at a slight remove. Second, and most crucial, London gives mixed blood to the Indian Naass and his lost princess Unga, imagining a mythic ur-contact between Indians and two white men emerging from the sea who would each father "the father of my father's father" (217). These strange white men, according to the myth of origins related by Naass, establish the law of primogeniture against the native's matriarchal lineage and thereby in effect create patriarchal order. According to London's thinking here, the patriarchal law of the fathers can be restored and sustained only through continual acts of transgression that function to replay that original mythic encounter: Axel takes Unga from Naass, just as the two white fathers had first taken Native American women. With the introduction of this myth, the Northland's interracial commerce suddenly resembles a return to the scene of a prior crime.

At this point we must admit a certain degree of inconsistency or contradiction on Jack London's part. Substituting totemic categories for social class by way of presumed laws of exogamy, London reconfigures the oedipal triangle in racial terms, with white fathers triumphing over their red sons. Unlike the prospect of the half-breed that London has steered clear of since "The White Silence," London's myth curiously works to reinforce a kind of racial purity, now reconceived in terms of the patriarchal structure emerging from that initial miscegenation. As direct descendants of these two fathers, Naass and Unga recognize their difference from other Indians in their respective tribes, a difference that compels Naass initially to heed "the call of kind to kind" (219–20) by wooing her. Only by uniting the two halves, London suggests, can wholeness be restored to the race.

Here, just as London's Wolves become more white by virtue of marrying Raven wives, so too do his Indians become more red by virtue of their mythic white fathers. Outside this myth, however, these white fathers have become increasingly difficult for London to locate in his new field, for once the phallus is given to the tribe through its women, then patriarchy no longer resides solely with the clan of the Wolf, who become governed by an increasingly abstract and remote set of laws. Despite London's best efforts, these laws oppose, rather than complement, tribal patriarchy, for as London himself gradually comes to recognize, one key source for that abstraction turns out to be his own naturalist writing—the instrument of power by which he has imaginatively been appropriating or "exploiting" (to reinvoke his term) Northland territory.

As in his previous Northland tales, the abducted bride Unga participates in her own stealing, grows to love her Wolf, so that the son Naass is left alone to fight for and against his white father, displaced and only partially demystified as the superhuman Axel Gunderson, "a king of Eldorado" (204). As we might expect, the tale concludes with a moral dilemma—Naass lets Gunderson die of starvation and abandons Unga after she refuses to go with him—that enables Malemute Kid to allude to things "beyond our justice" (251). But such a concluding platitude is finally less interesting than the means by which London makes his trio come to terms with one another. After working in a long succession of jobs, mastering a series of civilized skills, Naass obsessively trails the couple, eventually meets them (unrecognized), and then leads them, all three starving, through "the White Silence of the North" (239), down a hellish abyss hiding a lost cabin filled with "worthless gold" (241), to "the white forest" filled with "the ghosts of the past" (244), where all three finally confront "the White Silence" (246). Imagining such an end, London uncannily replays the opening story of the collection ("The White Silence"): two men and an Indian bride, starving, on desperate trail, dying. In the white silence Unga dies, but Ruth survives, while Naass has come to assume the narrative function that Malemute Kid had played in the opening tale, so that the Indian man effectively now takes the place of the white man.

By choosing to conclude *The Son of the Wolf* with this powerful story, London clearly recognized the symmetry of his book, a new field that amounted to a well-defined set of concerns. London's decision to conclude with "An Odyssey" makes sense aesthetically, but the two stories he wrote soon afterward help to trace a new direction in his thinking for his subsequent two collections of Northland stories. Compared with "An Odyssey," "The Wife of a King" is a rather slight tale that eschews mythic trailing to return to the stilted sort of frontier comedy of manners that marked London's earliest unpublished Klondike efforts. Malemute Kid helps an Indian wife get her white master back by tricking the irresponsible husband during a costume ball into thinking that she is a mysterious Russian princess. As James McClintock has pointed out, the story works at cross-purposes, since the abandoned Siwash bride can be restored to her status only as long as she passes for white.[40] Labeled "Last of the Series" in London's publication records, "The Wife of a King" is illuminating in its very incoherence, for by dramatizing such passing, London allows that Indian women may not necessarily be so tied to nature: that a few dancing lessons, speech lessons, and new clothes (Malemute Kid's parting gifts of civilization for the entire series) can convert red into white. This Siwash wife is the first of a number of "white" squaws to show up in London's Northland, culminating in the second and final Yukon tale to appear in the *Atlantic Monthly*, "Li Wan, the Fair."

No longer rooted in nature, London's Indian wives threaten to destabilize his racial categories. Such destabilization is already a threat for his men, whose gendered position on trail—pursued and pursuing (like Gunderson and Naass)—tends to blur the difference between red and white. The first paragraph of "The Wisdom of the Trail," the last story London wrote for the collection, reaffirms the centrality of patriarchal order at some expense to race, which calls for fundamental redefinition, as London's opening suggests:

> Sitka Charley had achieved the impossible. Other Indians might have known as much of the wisdom of the trail as did he; but he alone knew the white man's wisdom, the honor of the trail, and the law. . . . Sitka Charley, from boyhood, had been thrown continually with white men, and as a man he had elected to cast fortunes with them, expatriating himself, once and for all, from his own people. Even then, respecting, almost venerating their power, and pondering over it, he had yet to divine its secret essence—the honor and the law. . . . Being an alien, when he did know he knew it better than the white man himself; being an Indian, he had achieved the impossible. (144)

By such explicit commentary London introduces his most interesting Yukon protagonist, first mentioned briefly in "The Men of Forty-Mile" (53–54; see also 113, 133). This Indian man remains an "alien" in his own land because the terrain London is negotiating clearly does not correspond to geography but rather has become a highly complex and conflicted ideological ground. As a hired guide and official letter carrier, in essence a *professional* man on trail, Sitka Charley is crucial for London's Northland mapping, appearing at key junctures in his subsequent collections, which can no longer rely on the simpler character of Malemute Kid to enforce "the law."

What makes Sitka Charley's first appearance as protagonist so fascinating here is that he is introduced in conjunction with a white woman, Mrs. Eppingwell, suggesting some structural connection in London's scheme of things between Indian men and white women. Only one other white woman plays a central role in the collection, but that tale, "The Priestly Prerogative," concerns itself with marital infidelity by way of a rather conventional love triangle that steers clear of race altogether. In "The Wisdom of the Trail" London must vigorously and immediately insist on the white woman's status as "Mrs.," married, significantly enough, to an (absent) captain—a sign that his once lawless Northland is at this point in effect under (invisible) white military occupation. Making his heroine already a wife, he thereby quickly rules out the taboo of reverse miscegenation. London is either incapable or uninterested in imagining such a sexual union, preferring instead to develop a more abstract relationship between red man and white woman. What they share in common is a mutual admiration and respect for the higher logic of the law itself, as inscribed by the trail. Unlike the other, weak white women he had met, for Charley Mrs. Eppingwell represents "a new breed of woman; and ere they had been trail-mates for many days, he knew why the sons of such women mastered the land and the sea, and why the sons of his own womankind could not prevail against them" (150).

Such allegiance to his new masters (male and female) means that Sitka Charley must be willing to execute two fellow Indians in cold blood for disobeying his order to save food, an ending London ironizes by making the shootings take place at the very end of the trail, in reach of civilization (unbeknownst to Charley). Much more extraordinary than the ironic killings, however, is the peculiar logic that backs them up— Sitka Charley's understanding of Mrs. Eppingwell as mother of the master race that gives the law and thereby acts to "nourish his manhood" (152). Whereas in his earlier stories Indian women serve as sites of conflict between white and red races, here London imagines only one race, like Abraham's one God, which "white" Indians like Sitka Charley had better join if they want to be saved. Briefly celebrated in the abstract as early as "The Son of the Wolf," white mothers such as Mrs. Eppingwell are tangibly introduced because such a new religion of race requires new myths of origins to bolster the two-white-men-from-the-sea ancestry narrated by Naass (another Indian man on trail) in his story.

London clarifies the connection between white women and this new kind of racism in an interesting passage near the beginning of "The Wife of a King" that in its Old Testament intonations prepares the way for his second collection of Klondike stories: "Then another exodus came over the mountains from the prolific Southland. This time it was of women that became mighty in the land. Their word was law; their law was steel. They frowned upon the Indian wives, while the other women became mild and walked humbly. There were cowards who became ashamed of their ancient covenants with the daughters of the soil, who looked with a new distaste upon their dark-skinned children" (164). Lest we think London is simply indulging in poetic fancy, this account of the consequences of white women entering the Northland corresponds quite closely to historical accounts of women in fur-trade society during the eighteenth and nineteenth centuries. In *Many Tender Ties*, for example, historian Sylvia Van Kirk essentially confirm's London's explanation by showing how the appearance of white women in Western Canada heightened racist thinking and practice.[41] But London swerves from history into racial myth by making these white women serve as mothers more than wives, so that they do not rival squaws (still fondly embraced by London as workers), as much as suggest the preconditions that have engendered white mastery in the Northland in the first place.

Although London moves forward chronologically in his second collection, focusing on white women in the Yukon to offer a historically accurate second stage of colonization, he thus moves *backward* in mythological time by treating these women as symbolic mothers who are presumed to give birth to the law. London's dedication to his second volume of stories, aptly titled *The God of His Fathers and Other Stories* (published in May 1901 by McClure, Phillips), signals his shift from the daughters of the soil to white women: "To the daughters of the wolf who have bred and suckled a race of men." Ostensibly a counterpart to the dedication of his first volume, this one actually works quite differently. For one thing, although the opening reference to "daughters" is meant to correspond with the "sons" in the first dedication, London abruptly jumps two generations to their role as breeders, leaving the question of the totemic origins of "the Wolf" still unresolved. Second, although the sons of Wolves must find and make their own heritage in the Northland, heritage is here reduced to biology in a last-ditch effort to anchor "a race of men" to (mythic and collective) blood, blood that must be female because under patriarchy mothers can be known when fathers remain invisible or missing.[42]

London can renaturalize race only by theologizing it, as the title story of the volume (directly following the dedication) makes clear. A missionary readily renounces his Christian God when threatened with death by a savage half-breed, whereas another, stronger white man is sacrificed for refusing to renounce "the God of my fathers," which stands for his own divine whiteness, not his Christianity. Yet London's white supremacist stance in this story lacks conviction not only because of the triumph of the bitter half-breed Baptiste the Red—"in whose country there was no god" (33), the tale concludes—but, more significant, also because London has much difficulty throughout the rest of the collection imagining a "country" where the God of his fathers can in fact dwell.

London's problems are threefold. First, turning race into an institutionalized religion goes against his faith in the sacred power of individual will. London's totemic logic insists that the white Wolf is not to be subserviently worshipped as a god but rather joined as a living force.[43] Second, his continuing appreciation for the work of Indian women makes it hard for him to imagine white women on trail (beyond Mrs. Eppingwell, who will turn up again in "The Scorn of Women"). Third, while white mothers offer some abstract genealogy, the Northland remains too barren a location to sustain patriarchal law in the absence of tangible fathers.

London renders this emptiness literal in a minor comic story entitled "Jan, the Unrepentant." Facing the insane and apparently deadly "Berserker rage" of a wild Scandinavian (perhaps patterned after the Swede in Stephen Crane's "The Blue Hotel" [1898]), a group of Northland types seek to dispense frontier justice by lynching the offender, just as Malemute Kid had threatened to do in "The Men of Forty-Mile." But when they search the landscape for places to tie the rope, they encounter a "dreary, desolate, and monotonous" field devoid of features: " 'No trees, no bluffs, no cabins, no telegraph poles, nothin',' moaned Red Bill; 'nothin' respectable enough nor big enough to swing the toes of a five-foot man clear o' the ground' " (151). Although London resolves this dilemma of absent things by conveniently restoring the presumed murder victim to life (making lynching unnecessary), the tale's epigram points to a larger problem: "For there's never a law of God or man / Runs north of Fifty-three" (140).

Despite London's desire for a maternal lineage, white women have trouble filling this blank lawless space, for native women cannot be replaced on the trail so easily. For example, in "The Great Interrogation," a recently widowed Mrs. Sayther comes to the North and tries to reclaim her former love by appealing to racial theory, asserting intimate bonds of "race affinity" between them, the "dominant, evolved race" (56). But insofar as he has already become acclimated to the Yukon, the Wolf Dave more vividly appreciates his Indian wife Winapie, who has saved his life (by killing a grizzly bear!) and who has the last word in the story by telling the " 'Merican woman" to go back home. Similarly, in "Where the Trail Forks" another white Wolf risks his life to save a chief's daughter from tribal sacrifice, even though it is she who reasons that their crossing of trails, "one white and the other red" (191), has resulted in evil.

White women pale in comparison to their native sisters. London spells this fact out most dramatically in "Siwash," a story he had high aspirations for, sending it out (as previously mentioned) to *Harper's Monthly*, *McClure's*, *Scribner's*, *Atlantic*, *Cosmopolitan*, and *Outing* before settling for *Ainslee's*. That so many genteel, high-circulation national magazines rejected the story may have had more to do with ideology than aesthetics, as we can begin to surmise from the tale's opening line: " 'If I was a man—' " (86). Spoken by a young white woman (Molly) with "the cumulative grit of five American-born generations" (87), this initial complaint challenges each of the two British men in the tale to "show his manhood" (89). Holed up in a tent during a raging storm, they respond not with action but with a story—by now the very familiar account of the forceful abduction of an Indian chief's daughter, who boldly stands by her man, only to die seven years later in childbirth amid "the Silence" (111). Although Molly is praised for her "spirit" by the Britons, who understand that it "takes a woman to breed a man. . . . Takes a she-cat, not a cow, to mother a tiger" (94), the American woman's value lies only in her potential motherhood, not as a mate. The Siwash, on the other hand, so loyally serves as wife and helper that her husband finally accords her the status of "white, clear through" (111), while Molly, the "little woman" (113), is left to crawl back into the tent after failing to brave the storm. In the white silence, "Yankee blood" (112) counts but little.

Laboring to derive some insight into national character, London draws a distinction between British and American, only to have such a difference overshadowed by that between the two "white" women, one defined by blood, the other by her work. In another male-bonding ritual of storytelling, "Grit of Women," native woman's work is again praised, this time by Sitka Charley, who begins his long account by declaring: "Brothers, my blood is red with Siwash, but my heart is white. To the faults of my fathers I owe the one, to the virtues of my friends the other" (163). Starving, half-dead on trail, Charley's Indian wife Passuk sees him through "the Silence" until she reaches "the end of the trail for Passuk" (182) and dies. With his simultaneously bringing an end to Passuk's life and to the narrative, London's obsessive trailing has come to stand for the very process of tale-telling itself.

These stories put London in something of a holding pattern, as if all he could do is retell the same sort of tales he invented in his first volume, this time focusing on the act of storytelling as a means to collective manhood, with women functioning as the objects of narration. But whether in terms of American mothers or native workers, such accounts cannot adequately take up the crucial question of patriarchy raised by *The Son of the Wolf*—on trail, how can white sons without fathers continue to reproduce themselves, to reproduce race ideology? To answer this question, London is compelled to give up blood mothers in search of some prior source for the "Law of the Wolf."

Just as he has moved backward in mythic time by moving forward to a second stage of colonization that emphasizes the role of women in the Yukon, so must London move backward further still by tracing the third and final stage of white conquest: the destruction of the Northland's indigenous peoples, the sons and daughters of the soil. Only by acknowledging and admitting this historical destruction can London imagine ancestral fathers, the tribal patriarchs who alone can fill the void left by missing white fathers.

Without a doubt, American anxiety about masculinity at the turn of the century is intimately engaged with the practice of imperialism, but in ways far more complex than has been generally allowed, at least in the case of Jack London.[44] Calling his third collection of Northland stories *Children of the Frost*, London wrote to George Brett at Macmillan's in early 1902—just as his literary career was beginning to take off—that the "idea" of the volume was to write "a series of tales in which the reader will always look at things from the Indian's point of view, through the Indian's eyes as it were. Heretofore the viewpoint in my Northland stories has been that of the white man's [*sic*]."[45] Perhaps more telling, his assumed Indian perspective compelled him to confront the consequences of his previous efforts to define manhood along redrawn racial boundaries—lines which he had scrupulously tried to preserve but which were now becoming crossed.

London tries one more time to maintain (but also bridge) the differences between these two clans in "Li Wan, the Fair," a curious, disturbing story he first submitted to *McClure's* in August 1901, which was also rejected by *Harper's*, *Century*, and *Scribner's* until it eventually ended up in *Atlantic Monthly* a year later. The penultimate tale in *Children of the Frost*, "Li Wan, the Fair" not only closes the sequence of narratives in which native women are rendered "white" but also suggests why in many of his subsequent tales London shifts from daughters of the soil to concentrate on their kingly fathers.[46]

Preparing to sell furs to whites, "Canim, the Canoe" brags to his Indian wife about his superior cosmopolitanism: "My trail is like the world; it never ends. My trail *is* the world. . . . You, Li Wan, are my wife, and the wife travels the husband's trail wheresoever it goes. It is the law" (206). Canim is so enamored of what he has seen on his trading journeys that he goes so far as to wish, "The next time I am born, I would be born a white man" (212). Yet as their trail approaches civilization, it is the native woman, not the man, who is given to strange "dreams," "fantasies," and "visions" of the white world. It gradually dawns on us (if not on Li Wan herself) that she was born white. A defamiliarized captivity narrative brilliantly played backward as an atavistic return to a prior racial state, the story of Li Wan reaches its haunting climax when she suddenly is seized with a vision of her true ancestry and screams out: "*Daddy! Daddy!*" (216).

A "daddy's girl" through and through, Li Wan can but dream of the missing white father, who otherwise remains absent from the tale—and from London's Northland in general. As the Indian pair travel through "the chaos of greed" (218) and devastation brought on by the whites' gold mining, Li Wan's childhood memories turn to more feminine domestic scenes—memories that she seeks to confirm by stealing away from her husband to approach the cabin of two white women, a young woman and a widow, Mrs. Van Wyck, who "played at living close to the soil" (223). While Li Wan desperately begins to express in her native dialect that "my mother was like you" (225), then trying to speak in her dimly recalled (literal) mother tongue, the two white women treat their "blood sister" strictly in terms of commodity exchange, offering in pidgin English to buy or trade for her authentic Indian jacket ("Changee for changee? How much?" [228]).

One side desiring family, and the other, material goods, their miscommunication culminates in an astonishing display: Mrs. Van Wyck's own gown suddenly flies open, "exposing a firm white breast, which had never known the lip-clasp of a child." London continues with an even more astonishing passage: "Mrs. Van Wyck coolly repaired the mischief; but Li Wan uttered a loud cry, and ripped and tore at her skin-shirt till her own breast showed firm and white as Evelyn Van Wyck's. Murmuring inarticulately and making swift signs, she strove to establish the kinship" (228). But labeling Li Wan a "half-breed," the two white women still refuse to accept their blood sister, who is then violently taken back by her angry, uncomprehending, brutish husband at the narrative's end.

So the white father turns out to be only a dream, and the white mother, no mother at all, while Li Wan's own synecdoche for whiteness— the firm bare breast ready to suckle a race of men—fails to convince her sisters of kinship. In the figure of the bartering Mrs. Van Wyck, London has explicitly associated this failure to find kinship with the devastation of natives and nature brought on by the imperialist expansion of capital into foreign markets. Given such wholesale destruction, London must turn elsewhere to reestablish his Wolf clan, must look to the people who bestowed the totem in the first place. While not every story in *Children of the Frost* focuses on red fathers (and some, like the opening story "In the Forests of the North" about a white man going native, reiterate the same set of concerns raised in the first two collections), there is a decided new emphasis in this third volume on reconfiguring patriarchy itself, a subject that London explores in a cluster of tales about old and dying Indian men.

Whereas the conflict in the first two Northland volumes centers on the clash between the red and white races and between men and women, in this group of tales London's attention turns to two conflicting versions of the law. For example, in "The Law of Life," one of London's finest and best-known stories, a stark contrast is set up between an Indian tribe's familial obligations and the larger "law of life" that dictates the survival of the species at the expense of its individual members. Yet by rendering the cruel abandonment of the tribal chief Koskoosh at the hands of his grandchildren from the subjective point of view of the reminiscing elder facing death, London undermines the very Darwinian rhetoric that is supposed to serve as the patriarch's abstract consolation. The story makes a fleeting but crucial reference to the poisonous influence of the white man: a missionary whose introduction of "talk-books" and "painkiller[s]" is associated in Koskoosh's memory—linked together in a single sentence, significantly enough—with his abandonment of his own father the winter before the white man arrived (42–43). In the context of the volume's cluster of tales detailing the destruction of Indian culture, we should read London's resigned acquiescence to the Darwinian law of nature as itself a displaced misrecognition of the white man's law of domination.

Other stories in the volume reinforce this reading. In "Keesh, the Son of Keesh," a young Indian prince who has "left the Raven to worship the Wolf" (166) is torn between the missionary Mr. Brown's "higher morality" and the demands for blood made by his native bride-to-be. Keesh can resolve the crisis and desperately maintain his beleaguered manhood only by perversely killing his own people—the council of defiant elders who had mocked his religious conversion—a bitter ending that suggests how racial suicide, literally the bloody beheading of red patriarchs, may be a preferable alternative to racial domination. In a similar linking of manhood with genocide (this time, intertribal), "The Sickness of Lone Chief" retells the story of two old men, "withered repositories of tradition and ancient happening . . . the last of their generation and without honor among the younger set" (145), while "The Death of Ligoun" recounts the bloody enforcing of "the Law" among a "circle of chiefs"

(194)—a tale told by an aging, lesser warrior ("Palitlum, the Drinker") reduced to reciting such legendary feats in exchange for alcohol. The drinker's performance over, London closes this tale in a haunting fashion that repeats its opening: "I saw the shadow of a man's torso, monstrous beneath a huge inverted bottle" (183, 198).

As the ending of "The Death of Ligoun" suggests, London recasts his own (white) role in these stories, sometimes explicitly, sometimes by implication, as a first-person auditor who functions as a cultural witness to the destruction of Indian patriarchy. The Ligoun and Lone Chief stories are especially poignant in showing the debilitating effects of drink, anticipating Jack London's autobiographical account of his lifelong bouts with alcohol (*John Barleycorn* [1913]). Mentioned as a token of commerce as early as "The Son of the Wolf," the bottle in "The Death of Ligoun" more pointedly serves to commodify native patriarchy itself. While Palitlum is able to preserve a shred of dignity by refusing to accept ten bottles of "Three Star" for the sacred knife of Ligoun used during the mythic potlatch, he is willing instead to offer his tale to the narrating "I" in return for drink. Ostensively paying "honor" to "the great man" Palitlum, the narrator participates in his emasculation by converting one kind of ancient totemic law governing the (recited) potlatch into the economic law of the marketplace.[47] His body a mere "shadow," the professional storyteller Palitlum becomes the very thing that has purchased his tale. Equating man with bottle, London frightfully discharges his own growing anxieties about the cost he must pay to make a living in the publishing business.

Having ranged over more than a dozen stories culled from three volumes in making a case for London's complex, developing, and systematic representation of white manhood in the Northland, I want to conclude by looking closely at a single tale that sums up many of the crucial issues raised in this chapter—"The League of the Old Men." Positioned (and written) as the final story in *Children of the Frost*, "The League of the Old Men" was regarded by London as his best short story.[48] It is a tremendously resonant narrative that also anticipates London's subsequent work in fields other than the Klondike, particularly his political writing. The tale consists of three parts: an introductory frame that depicts Imber, an old Indian housed in military barracks who has voluntarily left trail to give himself up for arrest to white authorities in the town of Dawson; his courtroom trial for the (literally) countless murders of white people; and his own extended, first-person confession, followed by a brief return to the scene of the court. While such a formal structure offers a shifting set of perspectives on red patriarchy, London makes clear from the opening paragraph that in moving from trail to trial, the story, like others in *Children of the Frost*, will concern itself with conflicting versions of the law. Here's how London bluntly introduces white rule: "It has been the custom of the land-robbing and sea-robbing Anglo-Saxon to give the law to conquered peoples, and ofttimes this law is harsh" (233).

Given the enormity of Imber's crimes (which defy all rational calculation), however, in this case the law doesn't seem harsh enough, as the white citizens and judge—obvious surrogates for the reader—struggle in the rest of the story to come to terms with an alien, red version of justice. The opening frame bitterly ironizes their opacity, describing the patriarch's first encounter with a quartet of civilized townsfolk: the office clerk "Little Dickensen," who becomes the "hero of the occasion" by confronting the old man; Dickensen's friend Emily Travis, whose dainty white womanhood provokes "disgust and wonder" in the old man; the Anglicized Indian Jimmy, "clad in approved white-man style," who translates into pidgin English Imber's demand to see "chief white man"; and, finally, a boyish policeman whose "splendid masculinity" is admired by the old man, who wonders (to Jimmy) as he is being led away how such a scrawny specimen as Emily Travis could be "mother of men so big, so strong."

London's somewhat heavy-handed mockery of white manners bespeaks another sort of deeper anxiety. In his Northland now, masculinity and authority are no longer so intimately or directly linked, since the "stalwart" policeman here serves merely as a minor functionary of the state. The precise location of "chief white man" remains something of a puzzle for Dawson's citizens too, as Jimmy and Dickensen debate whether Imber means the "Governor" or the "Captain." But both civil and military rule depend on a higher abstract authority, as London makes clear when he turns to the drama of the courtroom. Moving from an external account of Imber's actions into, via free indirect discourse, the old man's thoughts, London lets him muse "on their Law that never slept, but went on unceasing" (242). By so rendering the dry courtroom proceedings from Imber's dreamy perspective, London increasingly defamiliarizes the law itself, until we reach a stunning moment in the narrative.

In the courtroom the Indian Jimmy has been replaced as a poor and informal interpreter by Imber's own nephew Howkan, who (like the Anglicized Keesh, son of Keesh) "had fallen among the mission folk and been taught by them to read and write" (243). When Imber hears his long-absent family member read back his confessions of murder as part of a legal deposition, he is staggered by an overwhelming mystery: "But how dost thou know, Howkan? The chief man of the white men told thee, mayhap? No one beheld me, and him alone have I told" (244). When Howkan impatiently replies that "it be there in the paper, O fool," Imber "stare[s] hard at the ink-scrawled surface" and finally understands: "As the hunter looks upon the markings of the snow [animal tracks] and says thus and so and here, dost thou, too, look upon the paper and say thus and so and here be the things old Imber hath done?" (245).

Reinvoking the white silence/man on trail dynamic of literary naturalism running throughout London's Northland tales, the old patriarch's analogy seeks to return writing to nature. But more crucially in the particular context of the courtroom, Imber's insight reinscribes writing as nothing less than the law itself—a technology of power and the central instrument of the state's surveillance, how the "chief white man" comes to know what can be known. Dismissing his uncle's own speech as "woman's tongue," Howkan further suggests how in enforcing the law against a dying patriarchy, writing operates as a specifically masculine form of domination. Although London insists directly after this scene that Imber's newly spoken confessions were "reduced to writing" by a clerk, such a reduction is the necessary price that London knows he must pay as a professional man on trail trying to make a name for himself in a new publishing field.

In the third and final section of "The League of the Old Men," London tries to work against the tightening association between writing (*his* writing) and "chief white man" by allowing Imber to speak freely and directly in his own voice, with the pretense that the nephew Howkan is transparently translating the "deep tones" of the old man "word for word." While turn-of-the-century theories of totemism such as Spencer's centered on the designation's relation to language as a kind of inscription, verbal or visual sign, magical emblem, or even tattoo, London would disengage such sacred naming from writing altogether by insisting on the Indian's status as illiterate. Only insofar as tribal patriarchy is imagined to be immune to writing can it be preserved.[49] Like other stories in *Children of the Frost*, the narrative gives way to extended uninterrupted quotation, as London attempts to conceive of some alternative to the law—a communal location for masculinity that he can imagine only by rendering, via a kind of spoken elegy, its death.

Although the epic story that this "bronze patriot" (247) tells is a familiar one, its details carry interesting political implications that extend beyond the Northland. Instead of the myth of white ancestry that Naass offers in "An Odyssey of the North," Imber recounts a myth of white conquest, in which a single, solitary, and starving white man, with a "strange" short-haired dog, enters Indian territory, and then another, also with short-haired dogs and guns for trade to make Indians feel "big" compared with "woman[ly]" bows and arrows, and then a third white man, bringing "all manner" of "presents and great promises" (249–51).

Recounting how the first white man repays the tribe's hospitality by stealing the chief's daughter (only to discard her when she grows older), Imber in effect retells the opening story of *The Son of the Wolf*'s Ruth and Mason from the other side. Yet while London's first volume of stories concentrates on miscegenation as a way to establish the son of the Wolf in the Northland, the red father's interest lies elsewhere, for he sees (and London along with him here) that such traffic in women is in fact merely a symptom of a larger problem, the black mark of commerce that stains all Indian culture, conceived by London purely as lost patriarchy.

What rendered Indian men impotent, according to Imber, is neither white ravishers per se nor even white weapons (akin to the technology of writing) but commodity exchange itself: "Trade! trade! all the time was it trade! One winter we sold our meat for clocks that would not go, and watches with broken guts, and files worn smooth, and pistols without cartridges and worthless" (252). While Imber insists by these particulars that white men took unfair advantage of the Indians, his repetition of "trade" also suggests how such commercial relations by their very nature poison manhood itself. In this regard racial purity becomes less an issue for Indian men than for their "wolf" dogs, as the tribe desperately tries to preserve something of value, now defined strictly in terms of the white man's market. In a striking phrase that we will shortly have occasion to reconsider in the context of London's most famous dog story, Imber insists that it is the lure of capital that compels the young to leave the tribe, heeding "the call of the white men" (like "the call of kind to kind" that Naass obeys in "An Odyssey of the North"), until only the aging fathers linger, surrounded by "the ghosts of old shamans" (256).

Accustomed to viewing Indians as vanishing Americans since the mid–nineteenth century, London's readers might still have found such an account of ongoing white imperialism troubling, if not entirely novel.[50] But it is the second half of Imber's story that remains far more shocking. Instead of allowing the white man to "grow fat" and "prosper" by laying "a heavy hand over all the world and tread[ing] mightily upon its peoples" (254–55), the elders of all the tribes band together in a single secret organization. The aim of these realigned patriarchs is to fight to assert themselves against the law (of the market) by killing whites whenever and wherever they can. In rousing his fellow elders to such action, Imber recalls his reasoning: " 'This be a tribe, these white men,' I said. 'A very large tribe, and doubtless there is no longer meat in their land, and they are come among us to make a new land for themselves' " (256).

Having rhetorically reconfigured the Wolf clan as a tribe of "fat" capitalists, London, implicitly punning on "red," can thus reconfigure Indian patriarchy as a dying breed of precapitalist revolutionaries intent on restoring "the good young days, and the free land" (257). Imber's explanation of the white man's search for foreign "meat" squares neatly with the standard Marxist account of the inevitable predatory expansion of capital into markets abroad—an analysis of imperialism that London himself had articulated as early as 1898, just as he was composing his first Northland stories, in a lecture which he delivered on numerous occasions to Bay Area audiences and which was entitled "The Question of the Maximum."[51]

As the last of these elders, Imber must ultimately yield to the "mail-clad race, the lawgiver and world-maker among the families of men": "I am very old, and very tired, and it being vain fighting the Law, as thou

Male Call

sayest, Howkan, I am come seeking the Law" (260). Leaving red for white means abandoning the unwritten code of the fathers for the inscribed rules of the capitalist state. Given his grasp of the inexorable repressive authority of this law, London concludes his tale a bit romantically by imagining the court's "square-browed judge" to feel "softness" in his heart. In the wake of cultural patricide, the listener's remorse fills in for guilt that cannot be more fully acknowledged.

But in so vividly replaying patriarchy's destruction by commerce, London has allowed for a less sentimental, if only partial, resolution to his quest for manhood, one that demands he bring his own literary naturalism to account: that field of writing he has been exploiting (legitimately) all along. For the final myth recounted by Imber concerns the first pair of white men he slays to inspire his compatriots: not just any two sons of the Wolf but men with "pouches" containing "many papers" with marvelous "markings on them"—mailmen.

"Congested Mails":
Buck and Jack's "Call"

In the story of the first white man recounted by Imber in "The League of the Old Men," dogs figure prominently. Before the mythic moment of encounter, the old man insists, "Our Dogs were wolves." But the strange, weak white man brings with him an equally weak, short-haired dog, which, like his white master, mates with a native bitch to produce a strange new breed of dog—"big-headed, thick-jawed, and short-haired, and helpless," with more dogs and white men to follow. From wolf to big-headed dog by way of white incursion: such an evolutionary scenario culminates a fascination with hybrid "wolf-dogs" that runs throughout London's first three collections of Northland stories and prepares the way for his most famous dog of all, "Buck" in *The Call of the Wild.* That London's most enduring and popular creation should be an animal can perhaps be explained as simply a curiosity of literary naturalism. But far more telling is the fact that London should imagine himself as a dog, an autobiographical projection, as I shall argue, in many ways more profound and revealing than the explicit versions of himself he would offer subsequently in *The Road, Martin Eden,* or *John Barleycorn.*

Neither purely savage nor civilized and an illiterate mail carrier like Sitka Charley, Buck remains London's most intimate alter ego. What was the dog's genesis? As we might expect, when asked this question London alluded to his personal authenticating experience in the Yukon. "Yes," he wrote to Marshall Bond, an old acquaintance from the Klondike, "Buck was based upon your dog at Dawson" (named "Jack"), just as London's depiction of the Judge Miller ranch in the novel was based on the ranch of Bond's father. When asked a few months earlier specifically about the name "Buck" (Why not leave it "Jack," after all?), London shifted from factual experience to offer a more text-based explanation for his hero's identity—that he pulled "Buck" from a list of dog names he had filed away, one of many such name lists he kept as part of his discipline of professional writing.[1]

But beyond a mere list of names, "Buck" followed logically from London's previous Northland writing, his inclination to use dogs to dramatize and gloss white/red human relations, especially the consequences of miscegenation. To offer yet another seminal account for London's famous hero along these lines, we can turn to a series of early notebook jottings entitled "Alaska Short Story Stuff," where we find this interesting series of ideas for plots: "A white woman marries Indian buck—a dashing Indian buck, and her disillusionment. I must write a powerful tale of a man and a wolf-dog. Also a wolf-dog (sort of biographical, like a man), indomitable, fearless, ferocious, and unscrupulous."[2]

One sort of Northland romance has quickly given way in London's mind to another sort of story, curiously related to the first plot idea. But the conceiving of the "wolf-dog" for London in his early tales may have less to do with race per se than with a peculiar kind of cross-fertilization between the natural world and the world of words, as the inadvertent pun on "buck" above implies. Like the Northland's native patriarchs, Buck is a primitive inscribed by a law that he cannot read. In "A Relic of the Pliocene" (*Collier's Weekly*, January 1901), one of London's infrequent attempts at a tongue-in-cheek tall tale, to look at one more instance, the fearsome mammoth encountered in the tale is overshadowed by the "new breed of dog" created by a pet animal's mating with a wolf and soon after destroyed by the beastly mammoth in question. Bemoaning the loss of "the mother of a new race," the storyteller and his audience in the narrative seem less astonished at the mammoth and more fascinated with this destroyed "brand-new, unclassified, uncopyrighted breed."[3] The discovery of a living, long-lost relic is one thing, but the loss of a possible copyright for a new wolf-dog is really a cause for concern. The destruction of the new (copyright) rather than the resurrection of the old (natural history) galvanizes London's energy in this story.

One final source for Buck makes the most compelling case for the dog's proximity to print rather than to the Klondike. As I briefly discussed in my first chapter, London was accused of plagiarizing from another (nonfictional) account of dogs, Egerton Young's *My Dogs in the Northland* (1902)—a textual circuit that he took some pains to break by referring to his own direct experience in the Yukon. Franklin Walker and other scholars have acknowledged London's debt to Young, but the precise way in which Young's text came to London's attention is worth considering. As part of his clipping service, London was sent and pasted into his scrapbook a review of Young's book by the *New York Times Saturday Review* dated 6 December 1902—the precise moment, give a few days as far as we can tell, when he actually began writing *The Call of the Wild*. The review was sent to him because it opens with a reference to his own work: how Jack London's tales give but "a slight idea" of how dogs act in the Northland, whereas Young's new book offers a fuller account. Finding himself reviewed in comparison with another writer, London takes up the challenge to write a better, stronger dog story; hence *The Call of the Wild*'s likely origins in London's newspaper reading of himself: how the story itself begins, as we shall see.[4]

I have taken such pains to establish Buck's link with letters because from the novel's initial reception until today, its readers have tended to take the dog's status as an animal for granted. At most, critics debate some minor bones of contention about how animals do or do not behave in the wild, but they accept as given the essential animal nature of Buck. In keeping with London's own insistence on authentic factual experience against the charge of plagiarism, readers of *The Call* have assumed nature as the story's true ground. But to dispute this ground is inadvertently to raise larger questions about the status of the novel's hybrid dog-hero, as a brief look at a contemporary controversy surrounding London's animal stories will make clear. As an added bonus, we get to see London square off against the president of the United States.

Frustrated by a recalcitrant Congress, Theodore Roosevelt in 1907 sought to divert himself by playing the role of literary critic. He took as his texts—no surprise—animal tales, among them London's dog stories. Lumping London together with popular boys' naturalists such as W. J. Long, Roosevelt dismissed these authors as mystifying "nature-fakers." If London and these other writers really understood nature, Roosevelt charged, they wouldn't go about humanizing animals in such preposterous and unbelievable ways. Taking on Roosevelt in an essay published

Male Call

the next year, London countered by accusing the president of being "homocentric," a rank "amateur" unschooled in the principles of evolution that insist on an intimate "kinship" or strict unbroken continuity between animals and humans. Early in the article London does admit some crucial difference—that his "dog-heroes" were "not directed by abstract reasoning." But he points out that he "clogged his narrative" and violated his "artistic canons" with such phrases as "he did not think these things; he merely did them" in order to emphasize this difference rather than cover it up, as Roosevelt implied.[5]

Teddy and Jack challenging each other's authority about (and over) nature: My aim here is not to settle this rivalry between one of America's most flamboyant and virile presidents and one of its most flamboyant and virile writers, a dispute that is still being waged today in more sophisticated ways among sociobiologists, cultural constructivists, animal rights activists, and others.[6] Although it is difficult to imagine what sort of representation of nature could avoid being "homocentric," it seems equally naïve to attempt to measure London's "dog-heroes" against some absolute standard of verisimilitude, as Roosevelt would have it. A more central issue is the peculiar narrative self-consciousness alluded to by London that attends the directing of his animal protagonists. Reviving the dispute the following year (1909), the critic Frederic Taber Cooper makes the point nicely:

There is a vast difference between thinking of man as a healthy human animal and thinking of him as an unhealthy human beast—and the Call-of-the-Wild school of fiction is tending toward precisely this exaggerated and mistaken point of view. The chief trouble with all the so-called Back-to-Nature books is that they suggest an abnormal self-consciousness, a constant preoccupation regarding the measure of our animalism. Now, it is a sort of axiom that so long as we are healthy and normal, we do not give much thought to our physical machinery. . . . But this, in a certain way, is precisely what the characters in the average Call-of-the-Wild novel seem to be doing, or at least what the authors are constantly doing for them. They seem, so to speak, to keep their fingers insistently upon the pulse of their baser animal emotions—and this is precisely what the primitive, healthy savage is furtherest removed from doing.[7]

Deftly conventionalizing London's narratives as already part of a literary "school" by means of those three small hyphens, Cooper raises the key issue of self-consciousness but mistakes a cause for an effect. Introspection in London is not simply some abnormal, degenerate end-stage alternative to "healthy savage" human animalism but rather a logical prerequisite for such natural primitivism, manifesting itself most starkly (as Cooper's wording suggests) in the confusion between what his characters seem to be doing and what London as narrator does *for* them. In this sense the entire concept of nature that underwrites the literary naturalism of London is fundamentally "faked," to borrow Roosevelt's memorable phrase.

Tracing the reversion of a domesticated dog to a savage wolf-beast in the primitive Yukon, London in fact manages to address a set of "unnatural" cultural issues in *The Call of the Wild* (1903): vocational training, the quest for social approval via diligent work, the material conditions of literary production, the meaning of manhood, and the price of fame. These complex concerns all center on the practice of writing, I will argue, following the lead of a number of more recent studies that seek in various ways to revise the still-prevailing understanding of American literary naturalism as a mode grounded in deterministic laws of environment and biology. Christopher Wilson, for example, makes a compelling case for Progressive Era writers, including London, as participating in an emerging culture of professionalism that treated writing as a discipline and business. However valuable, Wilson's excellent study does not discuss in any detail how such vocational concerns are enacted in the fiction itself—my emphasis throughout this book.[8]

Written at a crucial juncture in London's career, just as his apprenticeship work in magazines was beginning to attract a wider national audience that was anticipating longer, more substantial fiction from him, *The Call of the Wild* dramatizes London's own struggle to gain recognition as a writer. Reading the dog Buck's "calling" as a mail carrier in the light of his author's aspirations, I further hope to show how London's narrative is important insofar as it renders literal, even more so than do the Northland stories, what Walter Benn Michaels and Mark Seltzer have identified as a particular characteristic of naturalist writing—texts that tend to draw attention to their own peculiar status as material marks.[9] As my introduction indicates, these critics take a somewhat narrow view of such writing, assuming its production as self-generated or generated with the help of machines. But as we have seen, naturalist production for London automatically entails publication: how writing gets into public print, how the artist/dog (in the case of this novel) becomes known once letters are circulated and delivered in the wild.

To analyze London's constructing of nature in *The Call of the Wild*, we need to begin by examining more closely Buck's double status as "dog-hero," as well as the related, vexed doubling between character and narrator. Most critics rely on terms such as "anthropomorphism," "beast fable," and/or "allegory" to explain Buck, but the technical representation of an animal center of consciousness and the rhetorical *effects* of such a center are more complicated (and interesting) than these terms generally allow. Look at London's verbs for instance. It is easy enough to compile a list of mental actions attributed to Buck that would seem problematic, to say the least: at various points in the narrative, Buck "imagine[s]" (20), "decide[s]" (24), "realize[s]" (24), "kn[ows]" (25), "divine[s]" (26), "wonder[s]" (33), and so on, over and against London's catchall convenient verb phrases "dimly aware" (21) and "feel[s] vaguely" (138).[10] These relatively innocent epistemological quirks centering on matters of cognition are presumably inevitable, to invoke London's own accusation about Theodore Roosevelt's "homocentrism." But very early on in the narrative these verbs are crucial for giving the reader a basis for identifying with Buck as a thinking presence who is on occasion disturbed by dreams and memories, as when the "scene" of Curly's death returns to trouble his sleep (45) or when he stared into a fire and "thought of Judge Miller's big house" (112), then reviewing other scenes of his recent past.

To be fair, London usually takes scrupulous pains to avoid such unmediated access to Buck, achieving in the process a far more ambiguous and complex representation of his dog-hero. When Buck is initially caged, for instance, London writes, "He could not understand what it all meant" (23), followed by two interrogatives. As in the case of Frank Norris's *McTeague*, it is uncertain whether these free-floating questions belong to the character or to the narrator thinking for him; the result is a mental state that exclusively belongs neither to Buck nor to Jack but seems shared somewhere between them. London's use of the modal "could" in the sentence above reinforces this ambiguity: is Buck's lack of understanding a structural incapacity stemming from his nature as dog or only a temporary limitation to be overcome by greater force of insight or knowledge when the "meaning" of his experience would now become available to him? As we shall see shortly, this sort of question is crucial once we move from the static representation of Buck to consider how he is directed as "hero," how he and his mind grow and change as London plots for him.

Before looking at *The Call of the Wild*'s plotting, it will be useful to consider briefly some precursor texts, the better to zero in on the peculiarities of London's animal tale. Two extremely popular immediate precursors are most pertinent here: Kipling's *Jungle Book* (1893) and Ernest Thompson Seton's *Wild Animals I Have Known* (1898).[11] Drawing on a literary tradition that extends back to Chaucer and beyond, Kipling's Mowgli stories are beast fables, filled with "Mother Wolves and Father Wolves" commenting wisely about quite complex social rules and regulations—"the Law of the Jungle." Clearly the effect of having animals speak in their own (human) voices is quite different from London's narrating for his mute hero. Like most beast fables, Kipling's talking animals serve to defamiliarize the human world (babies are "naked cubs"). When London on occasion tries such an effect—for example, referring to gold in his opening paragraph as "yellow metal" (15)—the results are feeble, for he's clearly not really interested in using his dog to make humans seem strange; if anything, it is the natural realm, not the cultural, that gets progressively defamiliarized during the narration.

Seton writes beast fables for children as well, often substituting a Native American mythos for Kipling's Orientalism. Seton also writes about animals in a naturalist vein, a vein to which London was closer than he perhaps cared to admit in his 1908 defense against Roosevelt's accusations. Like Buck and his sled mates, Seton's "wild animals I have known" are heavily invested with various traits of character such as sullenness, courage, fidelity, and pride. A fierce wolf dies of a broken heart at the loss of his freedom and the loss of a beloved mate, an abandoned sheepdog spends years waiting patiently for his undeserving master, and so on. But since Seton's narration depends simply on stringing together anecdotes, we never really see the origins or development of these humanized personalities, nor do we see how these animals socially interact with one another (a strong feature of Kipling's tales). And because he sees himself as a naturalist rather than a novelist, Seton tells his shaggy dog stories by attributing personality from the outside without presuming to register any internal mental states within the animals.

Neither exactly beast fable nor sentimentalized anthropomorphism, London's careful plotting of and for the mute Buck might suggest that allegory would be a more accurate critical category. Mark Seltzer has recently made a case for such allegorizing by wittily dubbing London and his animals "men in furs."[12] But it is *The Call of the Wild's* very resistance to transparent allegory that is remarkable insofar as we continue to imagine London's hero as a dog despite all his complex mental attributes. London's surprise at his contemporaries' assessment of his tale as an allegorical treatment of the human jungle may very well have been feigned.[13] Yet the fact remains that he does manage to make Buck look and act like a dog-hero until the very end of his narrative, even if at times Buck's nature as a beast needs to be reinforced by simile. When we read at one point that Buck enters camp so exhausted that he "lay down like a dead dog" (77), we are forced to make a dizzying series of negotiations that prevent us from resting easily in either human or animal realms.

How does London manage this effect? First, Buck is powerfully gendered in ways that cut across species lines, so that his maleness allows London to hold onto the animal as a "he." Second—and more complex— is the pattern London sets up in the first half of the narrative whereby Buck is put into a situation not under his control and invested with a human mentality and morality to evaluate the situation, to give it *values* that coincide with London's own as narrator; he is then represented as reacting to that situation by way of "instinct." This black-box biological explanation enables London to maintain the doctrinaire survival-of-the-fittest logic that ostensibly drives his plot.

I say "ostensibly" because there are really *two* plots driving London and Buck, and the far more important one (neglected by most critics who have been blinded by the text's dog-matic Darwinism) has more to do with values than with instincts. The central paradox informing the narrative is that Buck must learn to be wild. Wildness in this book is not simply a state of nature to be gained or regained by a reversion to type, as the naturalist plot of primordial atavism would have it. Instead, attaining wildness entails disciplined education—technical and moral—a distinction collapsed by the representation of work/writing. The famous "call" that Buck heeds thus has more to do with a vocation or professional calling than some mysterious instinctual pull toward nature. *White Fang*, the companion piece to *The Call of the Wild* that seems to reverse direction by tracing the progressive taming of a wild wolf, is in this sense less a sequel to Buck's experience than a simple replaying, making explicit what is only more covert in the earlier tale. To name Buck's training a "paradox" may be a bit generous, however; more accurate, a massive set of contradictions about Buck is at the heart of the narrative, which moves in two seemingly opposite directions at once: toward nature from culture (the standard naturalist plot of decivilization), and, in a more troubled but also more passionate manner, toward self-transcendence that cannot be fully contained by the conventional naturalist model.[14]

For one thing, the naturalist plot of decline depends on some clear demarcation between nature and culture, however much a continuum exists between the two poles (as London argued in his reply to Roosevelt). Without some such clear distinction, no linear plotting can make much sense.[15] London seeks to keep the two distinct yet linked by three sorts of mediations, all centering on the vague notion of "primitive law" (32): the "law of club and fang" (43); the representations of Buck's inherited racial memory, during which the dog reverts back to a prior savage state of attendance on now "hairy" (113) masters (examples of London's "men in furs"); and the curious introduction at a key juncture late in the narrative of a tribe of Indians, the Yeehats, who presumably operate somewhere in between Buck's world and Jack's world. In the case of all three mediations, London draws attention to the very "faking" of nature that he would gloss over. By eliding club and fang under a single savage "law," for example, London confuses the means of human instrumentality with its ends, in this case training via conditioning, as a behaviorist might say. While it might be argued that both club and fang seek to establish dominance, London carefully insists that the man in the red sweater beats Buck to gain obedience, not conciliation. Similarly, why in the world should masters, hairy or otherwise, be dwelling in Buck's racial unconscious, as if human mastery over nature were somehow natural in itself?[16] Such questions point to the cross-purposes at work throughout the novel as London tries to negotiate—or navigate—his dog-hero between the animal world and the human world.

Taking stock of his hero at one point during his narration, London himself captures this doubleness quite nicely: "His development (or retrogression) was rapid" (61). Trying to have it both ways and still avoid commitment (by using *or* rather than *and*), this assertion follows close on the heels of a more extended bit of commentary, a good example of London's self-conscious protesting—or narrative clogging—that he himself pointed out in his own defense:

> This first theft [of a slice of bacon] marked Buck as fit to survive in the hostile Northland environment. It marked his adaptability, his capacity to adjust himself to changing conditions. . . . It marked, further, the decay or going to pieces of his moral nature, a vain thing and a handicap in the ruthless struggle for existence. It was all well enough in the Southland, under the law of love and fellowship, to respect private property and personal feelings; but in the Northland, under the law of club and fang, whoso took such things into account was a fool. . . .
>
> Not that Buck reasoned it out. He was fit, that was all, and unconsciously he accommodated himself to the new mode of life. (59–60)

Unlike a typical character in a realist novel who possesses a highly developed moral nature subject to decay, Buck is a dog from the start; London's fixation on morality immediately triggers his anxiety about Buck's reasoning, or lack thereof. Precisely when moral considerations are introduced—considerations well beyond the issue of Buck's adaptation to his environment—London thus feels compelled to register some sharp distinction between beasts and men at the same time as he goes on to insist that "civilized" Buck "could have died for a moral consideration, say the defence of Judge Miller's riding-whip" (60). That Buck "civilized" begins life under a judge is no coincidence, especially since it would presumably be the judge's "moral consideration" and not the dog's own that would motivate the animal's defense of the whip, which serves to redefine questions of "private property" and "personal feelings" in terms of the "law of love and fellowship." A resonant symbol for Southland mastery, the riding whip functions simply as a sleeker version of the club that disciplined Buck in the wild.

Focusing on the programmatic aspects of the story's naturalism, Charles Walcutt surmises that London makes his hero a dog because "if Buck were a man there would have to be some kind of ethical responsibility."[17] The decay of his "moral nature" can thus be tossed aside without the reader losing respect for Buck. But London is *obsessed* with his dog-hero's moral nature and the question of "justice" (37); it is precisely Buck's sense of value, especially his own worth in the eyes of others, that wins our respect, as a quick glance at the early chapters demonstrates. The clear succession of emotions that Buck experiences in the opening scenes, cast as a captivity narrative, is quite striking: "a fine pride in himself" in ruling over the Judge's ranch as a "sated aristocrat" (18); "rage" when his "quiet dignity" (20) is repeatedly affronted by his captors; obedience (33) to the law of the club (obedience explicitly distinguished from "conciliat[ion]"); shame (anger turned inward by others' disapproval) when laughed at by "onlookers" (39); hatred (45) of his immediately recognized rival Spitz.

Pride, dignity, anger, obedience, shame, and hatred, all culminating in "imagination," a "quality that made for greatness" (97), which finally allows Buck, perversely enough, to kill his dreaded rival. Animals may have a "logic of feelings,"[18] but these emotions are not necessarily structured by a coherent narrative leading to self-fulfillment. Buck's character develops along the lines of a traditional nineteenth-century bildungs-roman, in which identity is a process of becoming via moral education: a portrait of the dog as a young artist, if you will. Compared with the figures inhabiting, say, Stephen Crane's *Maggie* or Norris's *McTeague*, Buck is not only smarter but also has a clearer sense of right and wrong—is *more* human.

Such acquired humanity casts doubt on a key argument underpinning June Howard's valuable ideological analysis of naturalism. Demonstrating how the genre's preoccupations with force and fate serve to express middle-class Americans' fear of proletarianization, Howard insists that turn-of-the-century naturalist texts starkly polarize the categories of helpless brute (character) and privileged spectator (narrator). But Buck's education, via work, suggests that for London these class-based antinomies are not as rigid and absolute as Howard suggests, that an upwardly mobile working dog (and his narrator double) can be a humanized beast without necessarily becoming a brute.[19]

Learning his many "lessons" (see, for example, pages 32, 44, 51), knowing his proper place, disciplining his body, and struggling for approval, Buck fulfills a higher calling. This calling has less to do with the wild than with the dignity of labor. *The Call of the Wild* thus strictly follows the dictates of the bildungsroman plot in that transforming nature by work leads to self-transformation—leads up from slavery to freedom. For Buck and Jack, work initially becomes the source for identity, the means to make a name for themselves. Functioning as a path to self-transcendence, labor in London's narrative thus carries enormous philosophical import—Hegelian import, to be more specific.

Hegel, not Darwin, offers the common ground for the often-noted split in London between his Marxist socialist side and his preoccupation with Nietzschean supermen. Marking a division between nature and culture, Hegel posits self-consciousness as separating humans from animals—the same sort of crucial distinction that London evoked in his response to Roosevelt's "nature-faking" charge. Self-consciousness can be gained, according to Hegel, only when animal desire negates itself, that is, moves outside itself to desire something beyond self-preservation. Beyond the instinct to survive is the desire for desire itself, manifested as a quest for recognition. This struggle to be valued, to be found worthy by others, demands the dominance of one man over another; hence the origins of a master/slave dialectic whereby the conquered slave ("having subordinated his human desire for recognition to the biological desire to preserve his life"), by working, becomes master over nature and in doing so frees himself from nature as well as from himself, from his nature as a slave. Quite simply, work humanizes, freeing the slave from the master, whose idleness fixes his identity as static.[20]

This may be a fairy tale, as Marx's historical-materialist explanation for subjugation makes clear, but it is Buck and Jack's fairy tale, nonetheless. Dog recognition, not dog cognition, becomes the central issue in the narrative, first in terms of how Buck is evaluated by humans, then by his fellow dogs, and finally and most problematically by his lover and master John Thornton. Initially valued strictly for his potential for work (size, strength, and ferocity), Buck's "worth" is measured in human terms by money in the marketplace (as in many slave narratives) and by other means of rational calculation: " 'One in ten t'ousand' " his new owner Perrault "comment[s] mentally" (34) during the moment of exchange, to be quickly followed by a reference to the "justice" (37) displayed by these new masters.

Once Buck enters into social relations with his fellow sled mates—also the precise moment he enters into work—then his "worth" takes on a new meaning. As London introduces his crew of dogs, one by one he gives them each a distinct personality—introspective, appeasing, fair, wise, lazy, and so on—largely with respect to how Buck values them and to how they value Buck. More to the point, perhaps, is how intimately these evaluations become linked to Buck's "calling," his learning to pull the sled with his mates. The ability of Sol-leks, for example, to "command respect" is limited by his lack of "apparent ambition," until Buck later sees him at work with his partner Dave and "learns" to value their "even more vital ambition" (49). Like the two "new kind of men" (37) driving them, on the job Dave and Sol-leks suddenly become "new dogs, utterly transformed by the harness. All passiveness and unconcern had dropped from them. . . . The toil of the traces seemed the supreme expression of their being, and all that they lived for and the only thing in which they took delight" (55).

When London tries to give this Hegelian self-transcendence via labor a Darwinian slant, the results are quite peculiar, as in the famous "ecstasy" passage that London inserts right before he has Buck kill Spitz:

There is an ecstasy that marks the summit of life, and beyond which life cannot rise. And such is the paradox of living, this ecstasy comes when one is most alive, and it comes as a complete forgetfulness that one is alive. This ecstasy, this forgetfulness of living, comes to the artist, caught up and out of himself in a sheet of flame; it comes to the soldier, war-mad on a stricken field and refusing quarter; and it came to Buck, leading the pack, sounding the old wolf-cry, straining after the food [a rabbit] that was alive and that fled swiftly before him through the moonlight. He was sounding the deeps of his nature, and the parts of his nature that were deeper than he, going back into the Womb of Time. (91)

Buck's ambition to lead the pack, otherwise always expressed in terms of work, suddenly is manifested as hunting a wild rabbit in the heat of the kill. London matches this primal thirst for blood by moving spatially inward ("deeps") and temporally backward ("Womb of Time"), so that transcendence can be converted into, or *repressed*, as instinct—"the deeps of his nature." But the first half of the passage undermines the latter half, insofar as London needs to keep on reminding us of our forgetfulness, illustrated by examples of an artist and soldier at work producing, or at least willfully acting, not unconsciously tearing into raw flesh.

In an interesting footnote to his influential reading of Hegel, Alexandre Kojève remarks that animals do have "techniques" (a spider's web), but that for the world to change "essentially" and become "human," work must realize a "project" or, as he says a bit later, be activated by an "idea."[21] Through a regimen of service and self-discipline, Buck's "idea" embodied in work is to become the leader of the pack by conquering "the disciplining" (48) Spitz, his rival for mastery. Once he defeats Spitz in this "war" (79) and gains from both dogs and humans the recognition and respect for which he has struggled, then what is there left for him to do? Since Buck is part of Jack's plot, since London in the act of narrating is himself working *for* Buck, we are able to see glimpses of a larger project informing the labor of narration. That idea or ambition is writing itself.

Buck has been associated with writing from the very first sentence of the story: "Buck did not read the newspapers, or he would have known that trouble was brewing" (15). This is certainly a strange way to introduce a dog-hero, making Buck's (not) reading at first seem a matter of mere preference rather than possibility (using *did* versus *could*) and thereby establishing a kind of subjectivity, via a reference to the materiality of writing, that fades away by the end of this opening paragraph. Before it is clearly fixed that his protagonist is an animal, London's little joke here is to make us imagine the act of reading and then immediately negate that reading by embodying the reader as a dog. The result is a trace or residue leaving the possibility of Buck's comprehension of print, as if the news of the Klondike gold strike that occasions his subsequent captivity is somehow available to him, verging on knowing what he cannot know. In this way literalizing the operations of the unconscious, London positions Buck midway between a passive sign to be read and a reader of signs himself.[22]

The relation between dog and letters persists far beyond this opening joke. Just after the man in the red sweater disciplines Buck, for instance, London carefully preserves the animal's proper name—and hence the essential continuity of his identity—by having the man read out loud the notice describing the contents of the crate: " 'Answers to the name of Buck,' the man soliloquized" (31). Addressing only himself, the man by contrast requires no proper name because his identity is already fixed as a master, so that the red sweater, sheer external covering, can stand throughout the narrative for a self (or rather a law) that has no interior, for us as well as for the dog.

The most important link between Buck and writing concerns his very work itself, his toiling in the traces to deliver letters. It is quite extraordinary, though hardly ever noticed by critics, that in a tale ostensibly devoted to representing the howling, blank, and frozen white wilderness of the Yukon, both men and dogs serve a noble civilizing function, bringing mail to the most remote outposts of progress, "carrying word from the world" (110). Even more pointed, these "new men" François and Perrault act as official agents of the state, "couriers" carrying various "government" (Canadian) "despatches" (47, 52). It is the very "important" (52) and "urgent" (87) nature of these dispatches, moreover, that accounts for the urgency of London's own labor as writer—the need to get his message out, to be recognized by others for his work and make a name for himself. As in the case of Poe's purloined letter, we never see the contents of these important dispatches, for London's emphasis falls on the delivery of mail, how writing gets circulated, distributed, and published after it is initially composed. But toiling in the traces that leave their own marks on the white landscape, both Buck and Jack fulfill their calling.

In his discussion of London, Mark Seltzer anticipates my claim about the inscription of writing on landscape, only to reject such an interpretation by insisting that a mechanics of literary production under what he calls naturalism's "body-machine complex" forecloses such a "traditional" notion of writing as a means to self-identity. Here Seltzer is implicitly interrogating the work of Walter Benn Michaels, who has pro-vocatively argued that for the naturalist writer, self-possession via the work of writing entails a self-consumption, leading to a particular sort of representation—writing that is neither identical to its material marks nor independent of its materiality.[23] Seeking to challenge Michaels's positing of self (and totalized market) as a closed circuit of exchange, Seltzer tends to overemphasize the role of technology in literary production, at least in the instance of London, whose understanding of writing is less mechanistic than organic, drawn from the animal realm, as Seltzer's own powerful reading of "men in furs" shows. As my reliance on Hegel indi-cates, I would argue that London holds very traditional assumptions about work and writing; in response to Michaels's thesis, however, I will make a case for London's modernity by suggesting how he understands that an author's circulated name—in effect a commercial totem or magic trademark—can ultimately carry more weight than the making of marks themselves.

Working like a dog finally is not enough, then, and by implication, neither is writing like one. Once Buck vanquishes Spitz to achieve his highest ambition as top dog, "giving the law" (107) to his mates, he is soon after sold off (by "official orders" [110]) to a new (nameless) mas-ter, also a mailman but not ostensibly a government courier. London's plotting here becomes less urgent. The disenchanting of work actually begins shortly before Buck becomes leader of the pack. In a long, self-conscious, and overheated passage celebrating "that nameless, incom-prehensible pride of the trail and trace" (80), London conflates Buck's desire for mastery over Spitz with the pride that all these dogs take "in the toil to the last gasp," the "ordained order of things that dogs should work" (83). But for Buck to gain supremacy over the pack, he must *disrupt* work, must break down "discipline" to "destroy the solidarity of the team." Describing this "challenging [of Spitz's] authority" (88) in terms of an "open mutiny" (82) or "revolt" (88), London points to a gratification beyond work: "He [Buck] worked faithfully in the harness, for the toil had become a delight to him; yet it was a greater delight slyly to precipitate a fight amongst his mates and tangle the traces" (89). It is surely no coincidence that in the very next paragraph London allows Buck and his fellows to go off chasing that wild rabbit. Working gives way to hunting, an activity more akin to play or sport that celebrates blood lust (desire) more than eating for survival (need).

Although London does his best to offer the spirit of defiance as a means of transcendence that surpasses discipline and servitude, Buck is finally no demonically driven Ahab, for the problem instead seems to be more mundane: sheer disgust and exhaustion with work itself. With Buck now at the lead, London suddenly remarks that "it was a monotonous life, operating with machine-like regularity. One day was very like another" (111). A few pages later, his last desperate effort to restore the nobility of work has precisely the opposite effect. In London's most extended treatment of another dog, something goes "wrong" with that wonderful worker Dave, who becomes "sick unto death" (117), suffering from a mysterious "inward hurt" (119) that would not go away despite his overwhelming "pride of trace and trail" (117). London settles this existential crisis the best he can, consecrating in reverent tones the fact that "a dog could break its heart through being denied the work that killed it" (118) and then finally putting Dave out of his misery with a pistol shot whose meaning Buck "knew" (120). So much for Hegel.

Speaking for Buck, why should Jack in the end also find that "his heart was not in the work" (138), even as this "heart" can still remain "unbreakable" (146)? A significant clue can be found in a curious little essay entitled "How I Became a Socialist," which London first published in March 1903, just as he was negotiating the book publication rights to *The Call of the Wild*.[24] The most productive and important year of his life, the year 1903 also saw, among other personal matters, the publication of London's book *The People of the Abyss*, an account of his journalistic foray the previous summer into the East End of London, where he poignantly charted the conditions of the British underclass.[25] In both essay and book London's central metaphor for this underclass is an abyss or bottomless pit; what he makes clear in his essay is that "socialism" primarily serves simply to keep him from falling into such a pit. London begins autobiographically by remarking that as a young "MAN" he used to be "one of Nietzsche's *blond beasts*" (270), "one of Nature's strong-armed noblemen" who proudly believed that "the dignity of labor was to me the most impressive thing in the world" (271). Associating such "orthodox bourgeois ethics" (272) with "rampant individualism," (277) he claims that this "joyous individualism" (272) was "hammered out of me" (277) as soon as he began to come in close contact with "what sociologists love to call the 'submerged tenth' " (273)—the underclass that industrial capitalism uses up and discards. Conveniently forgetting his own (illegitimate) birth *in* the pit of the working class, London ends his little story with an italicized vow strange enough to quote in full: "*All my days I have worked hard with my body, and according to the number of days I have worked, by just that much am I nearer the bottom of the Pit. I shall climb out of the Pit, but not by the muscles of my body shall I climb out. I shall do no more hard work, and may God strike me dead if I do another day's hard work with my body more than I absolutely have to do*" (275). This oath is remarkable for at least three reasons. First, in disavowing his own beginnings in the pit, London "confesses" that he is primarily motivated by the "terror" of joining the underclass. He expresses absolutely no solidarity, the working-class consciousness that Marx and Engels saw as necessary for revolution. Second, given his terror of the pit, work itself becomes terrifying; the object is not to struggle to make work less alienating and thereby to rehumanize it but merely to "run away" and escape it altogether. Third, and perhaps most remarkable, London simply equates manual labor with "hard work." I take "hard" here also to mean "difficult," so that he is by implication suggesting that brain work would somehow necessarily be easy. But then trying actually to imagine his "reborn" life without such deadening hard work, London is forced to admit, "I was running around to find out what manner of thing I was," a state of being that he rather optimistically labels "Socialist" (277–78).

London's essay might more accurately have been titled "How I Became a Successful Author," for it carries enormous implications for my previous discussion about the presence of writing throughout *The Call of the Wild*. Earlier I emphasized the physicality of writing for both Buck and Jack: hauling the heavy letters inch by inch through a blank white wilderness. Writing's materiality thus renders nature immaterial. But London's distinction between hard work and easy work suggests a second, more abstract notion of writing whereby the author controls and manages the deployment of letters but does not actually carry them. In the scene of writing that informs the narration up to this point, London is slave, figured as Buck toiling in the traces, and *simultaneously* figured as master, the plotter who directs the course of the sled and the beasts he uses (buys and sells) to pull it. The writing master thus hopes to exempt himself from the degradations and destruction of the capitalist market. But once hard work is fundamentally called into question, starting with the death of the dog Dave, how can letters be moved at all? That is, how can writing be strictly easy? Commenting on Hegel, Kojève notes that the bourgeois worker under capitalism has no master but nonetheless freely accepts enslavement by the idea of private property, of capital itself.[26] London turns this fear on its head by imagining "socialism" as a state of mastery without slavery, without any hard work, so that the writer is now free to roam in search of "what manner of thing" he has suddenly become. In the end London is left looking for a kind of easy work to replace the hard work that he has given up.

Given this disenchanting of hard work and hard writing, London would seem to be abandoning his dog-hero's project for self-transcendence as well, so that it is difficult to imagine how Buck's education can proceed. With the sacrifice of Dave, the plot threatens to stop dead in its tracks. One clear possibility is to fall back on the Darwinian model of instinctual regression, which, we have seen, has so far consisted mainly in Buck and the other dogs chasing rabbits. I am perhaps being flippant here, for at key moments in the narrative, London powerfully evokes a sense of a "dominant primordial" (67)—manifested as "ancient song" (63), "wild fathers" (87), "blood-longing" (207), and so on—pulling the beast Buck back into his primitive past. But these passages are quite literally *lyric* in that they are almost always detachable from the plot, neither closely following from prior events nor leading to others. The relationship between chasing rabbits and the "ecstasy of living," for example, is tenuous at best. Such ecstasy is powerful, in fact, precisely insofar as it can effectively escape London's plotting.

Powerful and dazzling, such intermittent evocations of nature keep Buck an animal and are therefore exactly the points of resistance that prevent the type of transparent allegorizing which I earlier rejected but on which I might again seem to be bordering: Hegel in furs. Insofar as London depends on his role as plotter, deploying and delivering letters to give him his status as writing/publishing master, such ecstatic moments effectively threaten to sever the ties between Jack and Buck. At the risk of slighting the dog's ostensible return to the wild, I want to pursue for the remainder of this chapter the problem of authorial mastery—a growing concern for London that manifests itself in his partial disengagement from Buck the dog as a primary source of identity in the later stages of the novel and his increasing identification instead with human characters.

What remains for London then, before letting go of his plot—letting humans "pass out of Buck's life for good" (110)—is to comment on the writing of the story itself, via a series of cautionary tales with interesting consequences. Instead of development or reversion we get a kind of stasis or holding pattern as London presents a pair of moral lessons about bad masters and good masters. This structure of alternating bad and good masters bears a close resemblance to many animal tales for children (such as *Black Beauty*), as well as to episodic slave narratives.[27] More important, from this point on in London's narrative, morality will no longer be rooted in Buck's nature, or even in his masters', with the plot beginning to take on decidedly theologic overtones.

First we have the bad masters, an unlikely trio of husband, wife, and wife's brother. They appear on the scene immediately after London alludes to "congested mail"—a striking homonym punning on the impasse in his plot and along with it the thwarting of Buck's manhood. New "official orders," from nowhere, suddenly demand the sale of the dogs, who are now said to "count for little against dollars" (125). Up to this juncture in the narrative, Buck's continuity of identity depends on carrying letters, but Charles, Mercedes, and Hal are not couriers with urgent dispatches. What they are doing venturing through the North, in fact, remains to the end a "mystery of things that passes understanding" (126): a faint New Testament echo (Philippians 4:7) that would seem to refer to London's own uncertainty about their motives as much as to Buck's uncertainty, just as the subsequent paragraph's narrative commentary—"a nice family party" (129)—would seem to capture Buck's own ironic disgust as well as London's.

Here, then, is Buck and Jack's worst "nightmare" (145)—toil without writing, toil without project, toil without meaning. Not only are their motives uncertain, but these new masters are technically incompetent to boot: "They were slack in all things, without order or discipline" (138). In the most prolonged departure from Buck as a center of consciousness for the narrative, London gives us an unsubtle satire about the dangers of domesticated, irrational, and feminine disorganization (the sin of "dishes unwashed" mentioned twice). Confronted with an alien environment, the overcivilized family registers chaos, whereas the state of wildness clearly depends on strict regimentation, again possible only through regulated work. Given the absence of such service, at once ennobling and enabling, nature can only now be represented by negation: what it is not. The two men unwisely overburden the dogs, the family quarrels, Mercedes gives in to "the chaotic abandonment of hysteria" (154), and they finally and foolishly fall through thin ice, taking with them all their dogs, except for the presciently stubborn Buck. A kind of providential punishment for their poor mastery, the "yawning hole" (157) that they leave in their downward wake serves brilliantly to literalize London's little fable of negative transcendence. Hal and Charles and Mercedes have truly become the people of the abyss.[28]

Once the bad masters drop out of the picture, we might expect Buck to attend immediately to the beckoning call of the wild. But before he can be free of all encumbrance, he owes a debt of gratitude to his savior, John Thornton, a debt he will pay back in spectacular fashion. Entitled "For the Love of a Man," the John Thornton chapter seems totally out of place, contributing neither to Buck's working education nor to his instinctual regression. The episode instead functions as a religious parable of sorts in which "love" as a single, unifying transcendental signifier is meant to subsume—in effect, cancel out—both the dignity of labor and the law of club and fang. And what a love it is—"feverish and burning, that was adoration, that was madness" (163)—that emerges intense and full-blown, out of nowhere, and strains, if not absolutely bursts, the boundaries of London's plot.

As the repetition of "adoration" makes clear, Buck's passion is religious and therefore not ostensibly a form of slavery: perhaps the dog-hero will find his true "calling" as a disciple. London seems to be working on the analogy that Buck is to other dogs as Thornton is to other men. Unlike the "law of love and fellowship" that operated on Judge Miller's ranch in the Southland, Thornton's love in the Northland is driven by more transcendental principles. Thus Buck can meet his match only by worshiping a god, an "ideal master" (163). As perfect master, however, Thornton grants Buck an all too perfect freedom, letting him do nothing and consequently, in Hegelian terms, forcing him to be nothing. Even though Buck cannot overcome bad masters without some necessary providential aid, at least his passive resistance to the family trio allows London to maintain his dignity. But dignity becomes a problem for both Jack and Buck once love dissolves all such resistance, freeing them *from* work instead of freeing them *to* work. Trying to sustain an impossible oxymoron (ideal mastery) by an imposed religious analogy (Christ incarnate), London ends up by constantly operating at cross-purposes, oscillating wildly, as Buck does, between elevating Thornton and ignoring him so that he can then heed his call.

Thornton's progressive diminishment manifests itself in two connected ways: his odd assumptions of various gender roles, and equally strange simulations of work. In keeping with his status as ideal master, he is initially figured as a benevolent father, seeing to "the welfare of his [dogs] as if they were his own children" (163). The problem is that Buck is no ordinary pet but a special being—closer to his master, closer to humans (if other dogs are dogs), closer to a god (if other dogs are just human). Portraying the intense intimacy between Buck and Thornton, London is compelled to level the difference between man and beast, to make them share the same ontology. First London equalizes their respective powers of verbalization: the moment he rescues Buck, Thornton is said to utter "a cry that was inarticulate and more like the cry of an animal" (153), whereas a few pages later Thornton sees Buck's "throat vibrant with unuttered sound" and gushes, "God, you can all but speak!" (164). When letters disappear, "with the mail behind them" (114), then sounds will have to do.[29] The communion between the two grows more problematic once London gives their mutual love a physical basis; in addition to Buck's religious "adoration" by way of his respectfully distant "gaze" (165), we are privy to a more corporeal sort of love play where the two males "embrace" and "caress" each other until Buck's "heart would be shaken out of his body so great was its ecstasy" (164).

From god the father to male lover, Thornton more and more plays the part of wife—and a badly treated one at that. London first introduces Thornton in this chapter as "limping" (161) and homebound, a condition that reinforces Buck's growing sense that his love for John "seemed to bespeak the soft civilizing influence." In the wake of the bad masters satirized in the previous chapter, this influence is clearly feminine and domestic, "born of fire and roof" (166), and therefore to be avoided at all costs. Lest I seem unduly harsh about London's opinion of the feminine here, a brief review of the four "shes" in the novel should set things straight: they are (1) Curly, who is savagely ripped to shreds by the other dogs and thereby conveniently becomes the source for Buck's hatred of his (male) rival Spitz; (2) Dolly, "who had never been conspicuous for anything" (78) but suddenly goes "mad" (dog hysteria?); (3) Mercedes, who "nurse[s] the grievance of sex" (143); and, finally, (4) Skeet, Thornton's "little Irish setter," who "as a mother cat" nurtures the wounded Buck, whose "dying condition" prevents him from "resent[ing] her first advances" (162). He is mercifully saved from the threat of a same species, heterosexual relationship only by finding a higher love in John. Once Buck starts to feel the pull of the primitive, then Thornton's own feminine domesticity decidedly becomes a nuisance, as the dog more and more takes to hanging out with his wolf companions, "sleep[ing] out at night, staying away from camp for days at a time" (206). Prone to sentiment and tears (see, for example, pages 151, 189, and so forth), the wronged Thornton can only wait at home for the straying, unfaithful lover now "seized" by "irresistible impulses" (200) and "wild yearnings." A vulnerable victim finally unable to defend himself in the wilderness, Thornton is anything but lord and master by the time he meets his fate.

Thornton's "calling" as a worker follows a similar trajectory. Like the previous bad masters, this good one also does not deliver letters. Nor does he do much of anything. A wounded god, he lazily waits, as Buck does, to heal himself. Love, of course, is the means of healing for both, but this mutual passion soon begins suspiciously to resemble a curious kind of work whereby Buck must prove himself all over again. Their love turns into a series of perverse tests (edited from the story's first serialized version); while defending his master against a legendary desperado and then saving his life (tests two and three) can be explained in terms of Buck's gratitude, a payback, how do we explain Thornton's command that Buck jump off a cliff (test one)? Fortunately unconsummated, this "experiment" that Thornton calls "splendid" and "terrible" (173) may strike the reader as not simply "thoughtless" but downright sadistic, especially once we imagine for a moment (as we have been invited to do) that Thornton and Buck are human lovers.

Perhaps even stranger is Buck's final (fourth) test, yet another "heroic" "exploit" (179) that explicitly takes the place of work. Boasting like a proud lover about the prowess of a mate, Thornton borrows money to bet heavily against a famous "Bonanza King" (180) on Buck's ability to haul a heavy sled. Here the hard work of Buck as a sled dog delivering letters is mocked as a kind of "free play" (185), especially when Thornton actually wins the bet, which is made for cold hard cash (sixteen hundred dollars)—rationally calculated—not for honor or dignity. By means of an empty gesture (the sled goes nowhere and is filled with dummy weight), Buck's worth thus gets converted into market speculation. We have come full circle, since London's plot is initially triggered by betting as well: recall that Buck is sold in the first place to pay off the lottery debts of the Mexican gardener whose "faith in a [gambling] system . . . made his damnation certain" (19). For both Manuel and Thornton, Buck equals bucks.

"When Buck earned sixteen hundred dollars in five minutes for John Thornton, he made it possible for his master to pay off certain debts and to journey with his partners into the East after a fabled lost mine, the history of which was as old as the history of the country" (193). So begins the final chapter of the novel. Given the narrative's earlier emphasis on work, the devastating irony of that term "earned" is a bit troubling, as is the perfunctory nature of the rest of the rambling sentence, as if Jack simply wants to get his story over and done with, swiftly make his *own* Big Buck, and go home to enjoy the fruits of his labor, now that those "certain debts" have been discharged, thanks to Buck's five minutes of love.

Here the autobiographical and vocational dimensions of the narrative become most apparent, for John Thornton clearly doubles for John "Jack/Buck" London, as the excellent 1988 edition of London's letters helps us see. Linked by London's obsessive concern with the material conditions of his craft, the writer's life and fiction tend to merge. The sixteen hundred dollars that Thornton wins by gambling on Buck, for example, virtually matches the eighteen hundred dollars that London sought (and got) as an advance from Macmillan, his book publisher. In an extraordinary pair of letters written near the end of 1902 to his editor George Brett, London lays out an absurdly ambitious scheme to write six books in *one* year, plans preoccupied with word counts, dollar amounts, debts, profits, market values, financial risk, and production timetables— the stuff of rationalized capitalism. At this time London (like Thornton) also enjoyed "doing credit on a larger and Napoleonic scale," in effect trading on the promise of his name.[30]

Yet despite London's heavy investment in the writer's market, the heroic deeds that Buck has performed for his master suggest another sort of economy operating in the end, one that depends less on Buck's work as a mail carrier and more on the spreading of his "reputation" and "name . . . through every camp in Alaska" (174). That is, the sign that Buck finally produces for himself is not confined to letter delivery but emerges from the marked consequences of his exploits, which "put his name many notches higher on the totem-pole of Alaskan fame" (179). The shift from written marks to notched totems entails a shift in the narration from work to adventure. In contrast to London's previous Northland short stories, here the totem is not a racial marker but functions instead as a token of prestige. Heroism now suddenly leads to a "wandering" (195) search for that "fabled lost mine"; although the Lost Cabin remains a mystery, Thornton's fabulous get-rich-quick scheme of course succeeds, London curtly narrating how "like giants they toiled, days flashing on the heels of days like dreams as they heaped the treasure up" (197), while "there was nothing for the dogs to do" (198). This self-conscious modulation into legendary fame and fortune looks forward to Buck's eventual apotheosis as immortal Ghost Dog, a kind of concluding emblem for London's career aspirations as a writer.

If this novel is an allegory at all, it should be read as an uncanny anticipation of the course of London's professional "calling," his great popularity—starting with the very publication of *The Call of the Wild*—as well as his subsequent struggles to maintain and manage his own success in the literary marketplace. Striking it rich, London's revenge on his public is not to stop writing, as Buck stops working; instead, London becomes driven, drives himself, to write more, to write about himself, about his own fame, over and over again until he eventually breaks down. In this respect his fate as a writer closely resembles the fate of the workaholic dog Dave, whose chronic "inward hurt"—"something . . . wrong inside" (116) that cannot be fixed—ultimately kills him. Imagining the career of Buck, London traces a more satisfying path, since dogs have to work but wolves do not. As totemic leader of the pack, Buck is obliged only to "muse" (228) dutifully at the final resting place of his beloved master, nature's own altar of the dead, sometimes bringing his wolf companions along with him. In this way we are reminded that from start to finish, Buck has never lost touch with civilization.

London's delivered letter, the letter that is Buck, thus arrives safely at its destination, called by the wild. From Judge Miller's ranch to John Thornton's grave, we have followed a single unbroken circuit compelling Buck to heed the law of the (human) master—mastery internalized as self-control during his middle passage working on trail. Justice means love, which in turn exacts obedience. Yet from this Lacanian set of trials— the judge's riding whip, the man in the red sweater, the pride of toiling in the traces, and, finally, Thornton's histrionic tests of affection—there emerges some sort of recompense, the dog-hero's payback in the currency of fame. How such a mark fits into the novel's stricter disciplining logic remains to be seen.

During the novel's concluding wish fulfillment of permanent celebrity, London makes one final effort to sustain some moral tension in his narration by representing Buck as torn between his allegiance to his adored human master and his increasing kinship for his wild wolf "brother." But this growing dilemma within Buck between devoted domesticity and wild "restlessness" (206) is conveniently cut short by the sudden introduction of a band of Indians—the Yeehats—who render the question of the dog-hero's moral choice rather moot. Without a "trace" (222), Thornton's exit in the narrative as sacrificial victim (courtesy of the Yeehats) is as surprising as his entrance as perfect master and lover. Unlike the natives who people London's Northland short stories, here the Yeehats do not serve primarily to represent lost patriarchal order but function more conventionally, as surrogate assassins, to mediate between savagery and civilization. While Thornton's abrupt departure allows London and his readers to return in the end to Buck as a primary source of identification, such a reaffirmation of the wild exacts its own price.

A kind of parody of the primal horde of sons whom Freud imagines as slaying the father in *Totem and Taboo*, the Yeehats kill Thornton and his mining partners while Buck is off fulfilling his nature as primordial beast by tenaciously stalking an old "great" (217) bull moose. London thus offers an astonishing series of displaced murders: while Buck is killing moose, mediatory primitive Indians kill his white master; said Indians are in turn killed in a rage by Buck, who must revenge the master's murder, London explains, "because of his great love for John Thornton"—a love, London adds, by which Buck "lost his head." With "reason" now firmly entrenched as instinct and "passion" (220) conversely located in civilization, London's booby-trapped naturalism finally explodes, forcing us to scramble for other sorts of supernatural explanations. Having tasted men's blood, "the noblest game of all" (223), the dog-hero is finally free to become Top Wolf, leaving both the human world *and* nature behind for good (or at least until he reappears as White Fang). Buck's toil carrying mail has gained him respect and recognition, but his passionate killing ultimately grants him the magical power of "Ghost Dog," a fearsome totem more lasting than civilized man's paler version, fame.

The difficulty is that in Freud's version of this sacred myth, Buck (the son) must kill Thornton (the father) directly so as to resolve the crisis in authority by and for himself. Nietzsche's retelling similarly demands that Buck (the human) directly kill Thornton (the god). But by introducing middlemen, London chooses *for* his animal-hero a weaker resolution that begs the fundamental question of Buck's moral self-transcendence. Slaying for Buck, the savage Yeehats in effect allow the dog to remain civilized but thereby drain Thornton's sacrificial murder of its sacred force. Although he may be a "Fiend incarnate" (221; see also 27, 103, 157, and so forth) when it comes to killing the Indians, Buck simply isn't man enough to do the job himself.

Buck's masculinity has been a central issue throughout the entire narrative—on Judge Miller's ranch, in captivity, at work transmitting messages, and finally as a "killer" in the wild (207). In the end, then, perhaps Buck's true calling depends less on whom he murders than on the spectacular way he does it, given the crucial transformation in the novel from toiling in the traces to instant success during the staged sled pull. London's progressive disenchantment in the story with work registers the growing fear felt by many turn-of-the-century American men that the market, increasingly abstract and rationalized, could no longer offer the grounds to define manhood, particularly in terms of those ideals of self-reliance, diligence, and mastery at the heart of nineteenth-century liberal individualism. Once the workplace diminishes in significance in the new century, then masculinity threatens to become primarily a performance or pose displayed for its own sake, like the theatrical shows of passion that characterize the Thornton-Buck relation ("as you love me, Buck") and the dog-hero's equally melodramatic conquests of bull moose, Yeehats, and wolf pack—just before which Buck is said to stand "motionless as a statue" (224).

Such emblematic representations are designed to give Buck mythic stature, so that naturalist reversion to the wild and mythopoetic quest can converge in the end. Following London's lead, readers of *The Call of the Wild* have continued to treat turn-of-the-century dislocated manhood as universal myth. A Jungian approach to the novel, for instance, gives the narrative greater coherence by interpreting it as a series of initiation rites that begin with the mythic hero's clubbing and culminate in the ritual slaying of moose and Indians that releases the archetypal Ghost Dog and his progeny (a slew of motherless small Bucks).[31] Aside from the fact that Buck kills the wrong men, my problem with such a reading is that London wears the unconscious, collective or otherwise, on his sleeve, so to speak; like the nameless man in the red sweater who shows his true (and only) colors all too clearly, London's unconscious is similarly exhibited as external.

Applied to London's famous dog-wolf story, a psychoanalytic reading would represent one more attempt to find the true "nature" in literary naturalism, a human "nature" now located in the author's (Jungian) unconscious. I would be more inclined to read Buck's ritualistic slayings in the light of a political unconscious, noting the great proliferation of animal metaphors running through political rhetoric and cartoons during the Progressive Era. As early as 1900, for example, Teddy Roosevelt, for one, was likening himself to a strong "bull moose" to be used on the Republican campaign trail.[32] Roosevelt, of course, is key here, given his highly public, dual roles of naturalist and politician—a duality he himself underscored when he refused to take seriously London's socialist views as well as his animal fiction. Roosevelt's refusal signals that he recognized some implicit link between these two seemingly separate bodies of London's writing.

In this regard the turn-of-the-century political iconography of the wolf is especially pertinent, above and beyond the animal's more intimate appropriation by London as his personal trademark or totem starting with *The Son of the Wolf*. Musing on a symbolist poem entitled "The Red Wolf" (1893) by Bliss Carman, London in an early letter to Cloudesley Johns speaks at some length about his views in comparison with the Applegarths and Anna Strunsky on the meaning of the poem's "wolf"— whether the animal (and accompanying Yellow Dwarf) stand for despair ("subjective, the internal") or the "fear of want" ("objective, the external").[33] That the "wolf" would be subject to an economic interpretation suggests the figure's allegorical currency in politics at the time. For instance, in a cartoon entitled "Roosevelt's Biggest Game" published in the *New York Herald* in November 1902, a few weeks before London began writing *The Call of the Wild*, the president is depicted as having just shot and killed a colossal wolf, on its back with open mouth, the label "The Coal Strike" spread across its chest. By peacefully resolving the 1902 anthracite coal strike through arbitration, Roosevelt is imagined as being able to kill the "wolf" without having to choose directly between capital and labor. Identified simply as "The Strike" itself, the dead wolf represents the violence felt on both sides. But, more important, the image of wolf can simultaneously stand for each individual side as well: the fear of want, that is, hunger knocking at the workers' doors, as well as the greed and rapacity of the coal barons—a familiar association that London directly makes elsewhere in his polemic political writing.[34]

Just as the wolf in the Roosevelt cartoon functions to collapse the distinction between strikers and owners, so too does Buck's conversion into wolf in London's narration serve to blur the distinction between civilization and savagery, hard work and free play, delivering letters and being a letter oneself, and, most important, (wage) slavery and social mastery, both cast in terms of nature's "law" of the wild. Burying his humanity, like a bone, deep within his animal-hero, London thus manages in his naturalist masterpiece to dramatize vividly his position as a writer laboring in capitalism's mass market without having to recognize himself as such. In his subsequent and earlier works, London would be compelled to explore the relation between mastery and slavery far more overtly, even as he continued to rely on nature to ground his understanding of complex social relations. To borrow yet another memorable phrase coined by Teddy Roosevelt (in 1906), there is thus an intimate link between London's "nature-faking" and his "muckraking"—a set of connections best examined by turning to London's explicitly socialist writing.

4

The Subject of Socialism:
Postcards from London's *Abyss*

I n his final chapter of *The People of the Abyss* (1903), London closes his
account of East End slums by measuring the lot of "civilized" English folk against Native Americans living in Alaska: "In a fair comparison of the average Innuit and the average Englishman, it will be seen
that life is less rigorous for the Innuit; that while the Innuit suffers only
during bad times from starvation, the Englishman suffers good times as
well; that no Innuit lacks fuel, clothing, or housing, while the Englishman is in perpetual lack of these three essentials." London then goes
on to quote the authoritative opinion of the scientist Thomas Huxley:
" 'Were the alternative presented to me I would deliberately prefer the
life of the savage to that of those people of Christian London.' "[1]

The Huxley citation suggests how the ironizing of "civilized" versus
"savage" had already become something of a standard trope for social
reformers by the time Jack London visited the East End in summer 1902.
But such a comparison would carry a special weight for London's readers familiar with his three previous collections of Yukon stories as well as
The Call of the Wild, written soon after *The People of the Abyss* was drafted
but published the summer before London's sociological study appeared
as a book in fall 1903. Trading on his established reputation as a firsthand expert of the Northland, London's allusion to the Innuits is designed to resonate with an authority that could match the science of
Huxley. Throughout *The People of the Abyss* such authority draws on
London's role as a naturalist reporting from the field—a close, sensitive,
yet objective observer committed to documenting (human) nature acting
out its biological imperatives in a fatal (social) environment.

London's apprenticeship writing naturalist fiction encouraged him in

The People of the Abyss to move comfortably back and forth between the human and the nonhuman, treating the citizens of the East End as grotesque, brutalized animals struggling daily to survive.[2] Assuming economic scarcity as a mediating link between nature and culture, London's naturalizing of poverty is thus in perfect keeping with the logic of his Northland stories, which under the presumed operation of higher laws often represent, I have suggested, intense cultural concerns: labor, competition under capitalism, professionalism.[3] These laws allowed London a chance to legitimize himself, turning his marginality into a source of power by making racial kinship take on the function traditionally assumed by class privilege. Reconceiving social hierarchies in terms of manhood and prestige, London could imagine his own uplift while still retaining his affinity for the underdog: a stance of sympathy rather than identification that would all too permanently and hopelessly mark his own status as subjugated. Yet if the rhetorical effect of such naturalizing in the Yukon fiction is to displace cultural anxiety (render it unconscious as it were), for a book ostensively dedicated to social reform, invoking animal nature is potentially counterproductive, shocking middle-class Americans into acknowledging the brutes of the English abyss but fixing their brutishness as inevitable, beyond human intervention.

Buck's successful transformation from dog to wolf by virtue of disciplined work and then sudden fame might nonetheless suggest that if an animal could cross species boundaries, perhaps people too could rise above their circumstances. For London the key to such a possibility resided less in the abject British subjects themselves than in dramatizing his own complex attitudes toward them: how London oriented himself, as author, to the underclass and how he understood the character of his own writing. As he explained to his editor George Brett soon after returning from England, his new book could be read as a kind of foreign correspondence "from the field of industrial war." Trading fields (the Klondike for the East End) would move London's work closer to journalism: sympathetic eyewitness accounts that eschewed coherent plotting in favor of more immediate sensations and impressions. Telling Brett in a subsequent letter that as "correspondent-stuff" the manuscript lent itself to serialization, which would enhance its sales as a book, London also insisted while still in England, "It is not a novel, by the way, but a dive by me into the Under-World." In another, more personal note sent from the East End to Anna Strunsky (which we will have occasion to discuss again in the next chapter), London claimed, "It is not constructed as a book should be constructed, but as a series of letters are written—without regard to form."[4]

Conceiving of his writing explicitly as a journalist's field dispatches may have released London from the burdens of literary form, but such a conception generated its own set of problems. As in the "white silence" of the Northland, the geographical location of the East End carried symbolic value, offering grounds for the writer London to prove himself. But unlike the field of Northland fiction, here the writer is less naturalist storyteller than naturalist reporter wandering through the crowded, haphazard streets of the East End. Because there is no steady and straight trail that helps the toiler in the traces to keep on track and avoid menace, manhood—including London's own—must be maintained by other means. In the absence of any orienting plot to contain or anchor masculinity, the man of letters threatens to revert to bestiality, subject to the same economic forces which have degraded and dehumanized his English counterparts and which have destroyed Native American patriarchs such as Old Imber in "The League of Old Men."

Writing letters home, the reporter approaches perilously close to his subject or else remains too far removed. Borrowing the same trope of primitivism that he had playfully invoked in his first novel, *A Daughter of the Snows*, to refer to the hidden dangers of the Yukon, London in his opening pages enlists (again a bit playfully) the aid of "Thomas Cook & Son, pathfinders and trail-clearers" to help him navigate the East End, figured from the start as a more hazardous place than "Darkest Africa" (3).[5] As London's awkward mocking tone hints, casting himself as an adventurer exploring uncharted, exotic territory runs a risk in the opposite direction—trivializing the abyss precisely to avoid falling into it. In either case, without a map or guiding perspective to frame his "dive" into the underworld, London's letters may then amount to little more than a static heap of details, by turns lurid, exciting, and/or entertaining, one piled on top of the other with no coherent plan or pattern. In his letters to Brett he explicitly rejected the role of muckraker by suggesting that he was not going to assign blame, theorize, or delve into causes.[6] But without some clear agenda going into the abyss, it would be difficult for both London and his readers to understand what sort of plot they were following.

Mixing description, personal narration, and social analysis, *The People of the Abyss* is a hybrid text that can initially be best understood in light of the particular conditions leading to its publication. London traveled from California to New York in July 1902 on commission from the American Press Association (APA) to cover the aftermath of the Boer War in South Africa. While he had covered some local events and had interviewed politicians for San Francisco newspapers, this was London's first stab at international journalism, a chance to emulate adventurous reporters such as Stephen Crane, Frank Norris, and Richard Harding Davis. When the trip fell through because the South African officials he had intended to interview had left the country, London decided to travel to England as planned (using money already advanced by the APA) rather than remain stranded in New York. Left to play the curious role of a commissioned reporter without a story to cover, London cooked up the idea of a study of the East End slums. Yet even less than two weeks before he arrived in England on the eve of Edward VII's coronation (9 August 1902), London wrote to the socialist editor John Spargo that although he might "do some writing on the London slums," his "main idea" in traveling to England was "to get a vacation."[7]

Later in this chapter I will discuss how *The People of the Abyss* compares generically to other previous popular examples of journalistic forays into poverty such as Jacob Riis's *How the Other Half Lives* (1890) and Walter Wyckoff's *The Workers* (1898), both published by Scribner's, Macmillan's rival. But for now my interest is in the strange mixture of commission and improvisation that resulted in *The People of the Abyss*, the fact that London was charged (and paid) to produce writing for a specific occasion, which (when erased) he quickly turned into a vacation (by definition, a break from work), when then led him to invent on the spot another subject for writing. My aim is not to disparage London's motives or to question his commitment to social reform but to suggest how literary improvisation at once energized London and yet underscored his problematic positionality in relation to his subject. Such an improvised quality helps explain the multiple identities London imagined for himself as writer of this study—

African explorer, undercover reporter masquerading as a down-and-out American sailor, roving war correspondent.

These identities are not always mutually compatible, as we shall see, and so the internal coherence of the book remains something of a puzzle. Calling attention to his text's apparent lack of form as its virtue, London nonetheless tries to unify his writing in two related ways. First, he assumes as his single subject the people of the abyss, whom he confines to the sufficiently removed confines of England's East End. London thus takes a global problem—natural selection under capitalism (what he calls "commercial selection")—and turns it into a more local set of circumstances from which he remains exempt by virtue of his American identity.[8] Nationality, rather than social class, becomes the operative concept to define difference. Second, beyond his status as an American he tries to imagine all the various roles he plays in his text as versions of a single crucial activity—the work of a writer—that would in turn give him, as in the case of Buck in *The Call of the Wild*, a transcendent unitary identity.

To arrive at such unity, the location of the abyss and the meaning of work in it need to be brought into relation with each other. Oppressed early on in the book by the claustrophobic atmosphere of the East End, London puns on his own name to suggest a new direction for his writing: "And I thought of my own spacious West, with room under its sky and unlimited air for a thousand Londons" (32). Equating space in the West with opportunity, London thus draws on familiar American myths of success (national and personal) to free himself from the sort of fixed social categories that so limit the brutish British underclass. Part adventurer, part reformer, part investigative journalist, London struggles throughout the *Abyss* to imagine multiple identities ("a thousand Londons") that would help make sense of his experience for an audience accustomed to reading his trademark magazine stories. Taking himself, in all his various roles and guises in the book, as his plot, London affirms his vow in the book's preface to "measure manhood less by political aggregations than by individuals" (viii).

Referring as much to the author as to the city, "London" thus becomes the compelling center from which to attack capitalism—his vivid impressions, his own memories of tramping, his pity, and his outrage, all focused on the subjugated, passive inhabitants of the abyss. But we need not choose between these two meanings of "London," since the author strives to convert the impotence of one into the power of the other—to transform his fellows' misery, by the sheer force of his own indignation and compassion—into a call for social justice aimed at his readers. London's socialist politics become in effect a politics of sincerity, the power by which he both understands the East Enders trapped inside his text and also seeks to move his middle-class reading audience from the outside. Following his own early advice essays to aspiring writers, London assumes sincerity as the true grounds to effect social change—integrity that itself comes to depend on the author's body, the ultimate measure of his manhood in the book, as we shall see.

In 1902, was Jack London yet a large enough figure, did he have a big enough name as a writer, to so dramatize politics in his person? George Brett recognized the need for a more comprehensive perspective when he wrote to London on 17 December 1902, just as London was beginning to compose *The Call of the Wild*. Brett urged him to add a concluding general chapter to soften *The People of the Abyss*—to make it less pessimistic (and more commercially appealing). London responded, in effect, with *The Call of the Wild* itself, which succeeds, I have argued, in representing an intelligent, upwardly mobile, and obsessively driven animal who works to avoid becoming a brute. By imagining himself as Buck on trail, London affirms labor as the means to dissolve master/slave power relations (at least until John Thornton arrives on the scene), thereby affirming his masculinity, understanding what it might mean to be an illiterate mailman: to carry letters without being able to read them. *The Call* thus functions to act out and simultaneously repress London's personal, professional, and political concerns, returning them, for the time being, to a collective cultural unconscious beyond the reach of his dog-hero.

Such a response or solution is not available within the confines of *The People of the Abyss*, given the way London had conceived of the British underclass, even before he landed in England, as little more than brutish victims of industrial capitalism,[9] and given the way London abandoned linear plotting to emphasize his reactive role as a first-person witness and participant. Such an assumed starting point made Brett's request for an upbeat ending impossible. London's much more modest response to his editor's advice was to add that final chapter, which introduces the Innuits in order to question the categories of "savage" and "civilized" and which concludes, a bit feebly, by calling for greater efficiency and less competition in the running of government and economy.

If London sounds indifferent and unconvincing in his conclusion, it is because he clearly has little investment or faith in a rational management approach to social reform along the lines of an Edward Bellamy or an F. W. Taylor. London's brand of socialism in general and his understanding of efficiency in particular are far more idiosyncratic, deriving less from abstract theories of social systems than from his own complex sense of his work as a writer. Even in those essays and fictions where he arrives at a compelling critique of monopoly capitalism that anticipates subsequent Marxist insights into hegemony and reification, such insights are always tied to London's uneasy position within the system he is trying to analyze.

Given the pull toward biography that has dominated London studies from the start, it is certainly tempting to gloss London's politics in terms of his own rise from poverty to middle-class respectability to a would-be country gentleman.[10] But biographical explanations are part of the problem here and not the answer; shaped by those particular discourses available to him as an aspiring popular American writer working within a given set of publishing institutions, London's thinking depended as much on what print made of him as what he made of it. Once again we need to consider the intimate link for London between his various expressions of "self" (customarily defined in terms of one's core desires, beliefs, and values) and his ambition to earn a living as a professional writer. In this case London's public identity as a political thinker actually predates his reputation as a writer, for at least locally in the San Francisco area Jack London was known from the age of nineteen as a soapbox orator, writing letters to newspaper editors and engaging in debates as a member of the Socialist Labor Party.[11] But even here London's identity is framed for him as an object of discourse as much as it is self-generated, as we can see by looking back at a remarkable pair of articles, among the very first published instances of "Jack London" to appear in print.

The first article was published in the *San Francisco Examiner* on Christmas Day 1895, a few weeks shy of London's twentieth birthday. As befitting the new journalism of a Hearst publication, the article opens with a series of bold headlines that tell a little story in themselves: "Jack Loudon [sic], Socialist," "The Adventurous Career of an Oakland Boy Who Traversed the Continent On a Brakebeam and Shipped as a Stowaway," "NOW IN THE OAKLAND HIGH SCHOOL," and "A Youth With Up-to-Date Ideas Who Will Make a Lasting Impression on the Thought of the Twentieth Century." Introduced by way of a misspelling, "Jack Loudon" is first identified as the recognizable if exotic type "Socialist," a label that emphasizes the person and not the content of his thinking. Along the lines of a 1990s *People Magazine* profile, London's person (as personality) continues to be foregrounded with the next pair of headlines, which first highlight the boy's "adventurous career" and then reassure the *Examiner* readers (with capital letters) that London is now respectable, having given up tramping for school. The fourth headline closes this minidrama by drawing glibly on the language of advertising ("Up-to-Date Ideas"; "Lasting Impression") to make a rather hyperbolic prediction about London's impact on the future, again stressing the effect of the boy's ideas without saying anything about what those ideas are.[12]

As a brisk and efficient bit of product packaging, these four headlines do a masterful job of making their subject appealing for newspaper readers, particularly in a Christmas issue devoting space on other pages to the lives of other local Bay Area schoolchildren. Having so dramatically caught the reader's eye, the headlines lead to a three-part scheme: an introductory sketch written from the *Examiner*'s Oakland office (concluding with the reporter A. Walter Tate's byline), followed by "What Socialism Is," a six-paragraph exposition by London, with a boxed cartoon drawing of Jack in three poses that serve to bridge the Tate introduction and London's exposition. Befitting the rhetoric of advertising that drives the entire construction of a public person, the cartoon is entitled "Jack Loudon, the Boy Socialist of Oakland"—the second of many iconographic representations of London's boyish good looks.[13]

Attempting to keep its readers interested, Tate's sketch opens with two short general paragraphs emphasizing the need to attend to socialism but then zeros in on the figure of the "Boy Socialist of Oakland" to disprove the misconception of "the general public" that socialists are "cutthroats, incendiaries, assassins, or thieves." After foregrounding his personal relation with his subject ("I first met him . . ."), Tate goes on to detail the highlights of London's brief "career" as a tramp and stowaway. Leaving aside the article's factual inaccuracies, what is most interesting here is how biography, cast as a series of "adventures," is invoked to draw connections between tramping, socialism, and letters. "It was while tramping over the country that he became interested in socialism," Tate concludes, as if socialism had no independent philosophical or political basis but rather had to be derived strictly from a given set of personal experiences. The *Examiner* thus inaugurates a long tradition (still operating today) of tying London's ideas directly to his life.

It would be one thing if such personal experiences were linked to larger social or economic conditions, but Tate earlier in the article had explained London's motive for tramping in the first place as stemming from his admiration of "Dickens, Cooper, Irving and Hawthorne." According to Tate, London the young lad became "infatuated with the idea that he would have a glorious time riding the brakebeam and seeing the places of which these authors wrote." Conceived as a sort of literary homage, London's journey is made to resemble "My First Visit to New England," the first chapter of William Dean Howells's *Literary Friends and Acquaintances*, serialized in *Harper's Monthly* just the year before. Offering in effect a personal history of American literature, the eminent man of letters presents a nostalgic account of his youthful encounters with antebellum literary giants such as Hawthorne and Emerson.[14] London's own cross-country traveling is similarly imagined to reenact the plots of famous novelists, with "socialism" as an end result, now understood in terms of a "fine fellow's" adventurous career. Politics, cast into the terms of culture, is measured by the person of the aspiring writer.

Given the blurring of first-person quotation and third-person description so common in the interviewing practice of turn-of-the-century American journalists, it is difficult to say if London himself offered such an astonishing explanation for his tramping—whether London chose to omit his participation in the march of Kelly's Army (the western part of Coxey's 1894 Industrial Army of the Unemployed) or whether Tate did the omitting for him. Certainly, as we shall see, London in later essays would cast tramping in an entirely different light as a form of discouraged work. But even as a kind of implied work, the association between tramp-

ing and letters is quite revealing, as if London and/or Tate were compelled to explain an "adventurous career" as the preliminary raw material necessary to build another, more influential professional calling: the
philosophical man of letters.

London's own exposition following Tate's sketch plays up the literary
angle, opening with a grand rhetorical flourish: "Socialism and Christmas. How incongruous this specter, stalking forth when all is joy and
merry-making!" It closes with a similarly florid reference to "cooling
rain" coming to "the dry, parched earth." Although "specter" might in
fact allude to "The Communist Manifesto," London introduces the figure precisely to disavow its threatening (Marxist) nature, emphasizing,
like Tate, how socialism is not to be feared but instead accepted as "an
all-embracing term" to describe anyone "who strives for a better form of
Government." What seems to be simply youthful naïveté on London's
part—mushy liberal pluralism of the weakest sort—more likely attests to a
profound understanding of his audience: a clear appreciation of where
his words were to appear in print and what he could and could not say if
he wanted to continue to attract readers. But perhaps my own emphasis
on London's shrewd reading of his public is equally mislocated, focused
as it is on his individual person. Given the way the *Examiner* has constructed him in appealing headlines and biography, it is difficult to imagine what else he could say as "the Boy Socialist of Oakland." While he
does insert a single sentence about "a more just application of labor,"
such a line is overshadowed by the far more interesting subject of London himself.

The second article on London's politics appeared in the *San Francisco
Chronicle* approximately seven weeks later (16 February 1896). Like the
first article, the aim is to take something deemed exotic or marginal
("socialism") and make a case for its centrality, at the same time ridding
it of menace (a mere "boy" socialist), with the understanding that the
newspaper reader could be made to feel that an issue was important and
inviting, without necessarily giving that reader much clue to the sub-
stance of a given subject. This time the (anonymous) reporter spells
London's name correctly, includes a less cartoonish rendition of his
handsome profile, and does refer to his participation in Kelly's army
of industrials. But he is still labeled "the Boy Socialist" in the head-

lines, which again stress the biographical transformation from "Industrial Tramp" to "High-School Student"—the same implied trajectory of a career anticipated to be influential.

What's most striking about this article, in fact, is its sheer duplication of the first one: the *Chronicle* piece ends with a paragraph that repeats, virtually verbatim, phrases and entire sentences (set off by quotation marks) that appear in London's Christmas Day *Examiner* exposition. Either London offered identical remarks in his public speaking or passed out a sort of press release or position paper for this second interview; most likely, the *Chronicle* reporter simply cribbed from the earlier article without even bothering to seek London out or perhaps was given a copy of the article by London, who developed a lifelong habit, after all, of clipping and saving articles about himself. In any case, we discover, as in so many of his early literary reviews pasted into his scrapbooks, one piece of print echoing another. The *Chronicle* reporter bends over backward to give the impression that London's quoted comments on socialism were spoken directly in his presence in order to stress the boy's personal charisma: "the young man is a pleasant speaker"; "He says on the subject when asked . . ."; "says London to his hearers." But the words themselves simply refer back to other words already existing in print. Fixed in black and white, a person's public construction takes on a life of its own, no longer requiring the immediate intervention of the individual to sustain the effects of an interesting personality.

What distinguishes London from a host of other modern American celebrities objectified by newspaper and magazine print at the turn of the century is that he profoundly realized the special power of the popular media to make him—a process of reification that he understood in turn as a symptom of an emerging postindustrial capitalism. London's awareness of the relation of objectification and capitalism surfaces early on in London's writing, most notably in his extraordinary short story "The Minions of Midas," which was rejected by *The Black Cat* and *McClure's* before it was published a year later in May 1901 by the American edition of the British magazine *Pearson's*. Formally, this tale is one of London's most complex: the narration consists of facsimiles of seven extortion letters from a secret terrorist organization ("The Minions of Midas") delivered to Eben Hale, "Money Baron," whose right-hand assistant,

Wade Atsheler, frames the letters with his own explanatory letter and newspaper clippings sent to the story's first-person narrator, "John." As the story ends, John is implored by the suicidal Atsheler to make this information public in an effort to stop the terrorists, whose actions "mark in red lettering the last days of the nineteenth century," as the Minions themselves dramatically declare.[15]

Although "The Minions of Midas" gains a passing hyperbolic reference in Irving Stone's "biographical novel" *Jack London: Sailor on Horseback* as "the first proletarian story" to reach a national audience in America, Philip Foner reads the story with acute embarrassment and condemnation as revealing London's "limitations as a socialist." Committed to making a case for London as a radical writer in his own image, Foner points to the problematic representation of the self-proclaimed fictional terrorist organization, concluding that "much had he [London] yet to learn as a socialist."[16] Most London commentators have simply ignored "The Minions of Midas" as a contrived potboiler, originating (as London admitted to Johns) from "a chance newspaper clipping" and submitted to the pulp magazine *The Black Cat* with the intention of winning "minor" prize money.[17] But precisely for being so self-consciously disparaging *as* hack, "The Minions of Midas" served to release London from the philosophical pretensions that sometimes plagued his overtly socialist essays, enabling him to give freer reign to sensational fantasy, in this case not so much private daydreaming as a more public nightmare with disturbing political implications for both mainstream bourgeois readers and party-line leftists.[18]

The story bears a striking resemblance to "The League of Old Men" (published a year later and discussed in chapter 2), a tale charting the conspiracy of a secret band of Native American terrorists in the Northland who are bent on stopping the intrusions of white capitalism. "The Minions of Midas" is likewise neither "proletarian" nor exactly a betrayal of the working class. Rather, this earlier urban story suggests how traditional nineteenth-century models of class conflict were no longer making much sense for understanding American monopoly capitalism at the turn of the century. As Wade Atsheler concludes in his letter to John, "Instead of the masses against the classes, it is a class against the classes" (443)—a more abstract kind of power struggle fought on a different sort of battleground, with different weapons: not strikes in the workplace or union organizing but massive accumulations of capital and the control of communications technology.

As Foner clearly saw, the motives and tactics of London's mysterious group of terrorist mailmen are dubious at best when glossed in the terms of orthodox socialist ideology. Demanding in their first letter to Eben Hale twenty million dollars cash, Minions of Midas members explain that "today's struggle for existence" requires a "qualitative" change in fulfilling property's rule of "might," now understood in terms of "brain, and not brawn" (435). Anticipating London's own vow in "How I Became a Socialist" to avoid hard manual labor at all costs, the Minions of Midas identify themselves collectively as "a new force," members of the "intellectual proletariat" as opposed to "wage slaves." This identity requires enormous capital to put into operation, their logic runs, and hence their little "business proposition," with the threat of the murder of "a workingman" if the twenty million is not delivered (436).

Singling out a worker for their first victim, the Minions of Midas do not represent an alternative class in conflict with capital but rather function as a double or shadow emanation of capitalism itself. Acting in effect as its unacknowledged agents, the Minions dramatize how the system will literally kill those who labor for and under it. It is not a question of beating the capitalists at their own game—Foner's uncomfortable explanation, following Anna Strunsky, Joan London, and a host of others trying to explicate London's idiosyncratic politics—for this story vividly shows that no other game is to be played.[19] "We are part and parcel of your possessions," reads their last letter to Hale (who finally chooses suicide out of guilt for their murders rather than give in to their demands), "creatures" like Frankenstein's monster compelled to "turn upon the society that has created us" (442).

The blackmailing Minions of Midas claim in the conclusion to this closing letter that they operate under "the same natural law" (443) as does their ostensible enemy, but their repeated references to "survival," the "fittest," and the "law," as in London's Northland stories, may have less to do with Darwin's biology than with the logic governing postindustrial market relations. We can begin to appreciate London's grasp of these power relations by looking at the terrorists' curious explanation for their choice of a name. In the closing lines of their first letter, the minions allude to the cursed golden touch of the mythic Midas—a catchy name taken as "our official seal" for which they have made big plans: "some day, to protect ourselves against competitors, we shall copyright it" (436). In this way London conceives of the terrorist organization as a corporate entity founded on the very structure it seeks to dismantle.[20]

The detail of copyrighting that at first glance may seem merely odd or frivolous turns out to be quite significant when viewed in the light of London's lifelong preoccupation with authorial naming as a kind of trademark(et)ing. This reference to copyrighting and competition suddenly makes great sense within the terms of this particular story as well, once we shift our attention from how they act and what the Minions of Midas say (their political justifications) to consider the *way* they convey their revolutionary messages. As I have mentioned, the entire tale is constructed as a series of copies of letters and telegrams from the Minions to Hale (the originals are held by the police) and sent by Hale's assistant Wade Atsheler, along with newspaper clippings, to be published by his friend John.

These newspaper clippings are not incidental to the story but central, because the Minions soon begin to use the medium of popular print to communicate their killings. Initially dismissing the extortion as a joke, merely a "literary curiosity," Hale and Atsheler learn of the first death, for example, by reading the morning paper to discover, "as befitted an obscure person of the lower classes, a paltry half-dozen lines tucked away in a corner, next a patent medicine advertisement" (437) detailing the news of the workingman's mysterious murder. Measuring social class by the minimal quantity of print devoted to the story as well as its obscure location within the paper, the newspaper maps or objectifies the victim for Hale and Atsheler, who are compelled to peruse the press with increasing urgency to follow the public affairs of the shadowy organization.

As the sensational killings accelerate (including "babies," "children," and "aged men") and as the victims become selected from an ever ascending social order (from common laborer, to policeman, to police inspector, and to the best friend of Hale's own daughter—a judge's daughter), the Minions themselves must become increasingly bold and inventive messengers to escape detection by the network of secret agents hired to find them: "With its communication the M. of M. continually changed its method of delivery" (note the snazzy, abbreviated "M. of M." trademarking). The Money Baron Hale's forces try to fight back by using modern communications of their own, but a quick telephone call to an intended victim fails when the victim (the police inspector) is strangled in midsentence. Audaciously pinpointing the time and location of planned murders that are then confirmed by media reports, the Minions soon appear to predict events—actively to make the news rather than have the news reflect what has already happened.

Eventually confounding "the United States Government" itself in its disruption of the foundations of state law and order, the organization's "new force" (436) extends beyond "glaring Jack-the-Strangler headlines" to make news in other venues. Having their "hand on the inner pulse of the business and financial world," the Minions give stock tips to Hale and Atsheler, secret "information" that only they possess, with London's emphasis again falling on their method of delivery (439).

London thus imagines a perfectly efficient, instantaneous exchange between capital and its shadow, with no energy loss, because members of the proletariat, as potential surplus workers, exist only to be obliterated by murder. London's terrorist fantasy has developed into a more all-consuming vision of total information access and command—brain technology by which power circulates and is maintained within this more abstract system of capitalism. Unlike the illiterate, precapitalist native patriarchs of "The League of Old Men," these urban terrorists are hyperliterate, relying on print as their prime instrument of control. Letting the letters, telegrams, and newspaper accounts of the M. of M. speak for themselves, Wade Atsheler in the end passes along these documents before taking his own life, with only the slim hope that their publication, thanks to the "electric currents" of the worldwide press, might end the Minions' reign of terror (444).

Where is Jack London, the author, in all this wild strangeness? As with any social fantasy, it is difficult to say. The narrative is clearly driven by the increasingly megalomaniac representation of the worldwide operations of the M. of M., particularly its thirst to dominate the media, in ways that feed London's own desire to control print and not be subject to the control of others (publishers, editors, literary agents, and so on). But London's formal allegiance in the story rests with the capitalists—not the Money Baron Hale himself as much as his sympathetic young assistant Atsheler, whose own suicide note frames the Minions' (black)mail and whose personal anguish over so many innocent deaths counterpoints the cruel indifference of the organization. By giving the capitalist an individual voice and making subversive terrorists act (and communicate) like an impersonal corporate entity, London manages to preserve the shadowy anonymity of the organization, thereby reinforcing its structural links to monopoly capitalism. But the rhetorical effects of such a split are confusing indeed, obscuring any clear sense of London's position within the system he had been so energetically articulating.

When London is able to comprehend clearly his position within the mass market, then his structural grasp of that system's abstractions weakens, whereas when that grasp is strong (as in "The Minions of Midas"), then his sense of his own relation to corporate capitalism begins to lose clarity. Making totemic kinship in his Northland fiction assume the traditional function of class relations helped London construe an alternative basis for power. But more directly imagining the "red lettering" of media terrorists (The Minions of Midas) instead of red patriarchs (The League of Old Men), in effect turning class struggle into a spectacular battle over communications technology, London cannot figure out where he himself stands as a publishing author. Centering on his representations of work in relation to power, this tension between subject and system shows up again and again in his writing. In the nonfiction essays on socialism that London published between 1900 and 1905, for example, such tension manifests itself by way of a set of rhetorical confusions and indecisions.

Take the well-known essay "The Scab." London begins with a well-bounded set of definitions linking the scab to working/hiring conditions under capitalism, bitterly defining the "generous" laborer as one who responds to a surplus army of workers by "giving more of a day's work for less return."[21] But quickly London's irony gets the best of him as he starts to broaden the scope of his definition, which, like the terrorist contagion of the ever-expanding Minions that sweeps through the world, soon threatens to encompass just about anything and everybody as "scab," including the capitalists themselves, the predatory foreign relations of the United States government, and even those authors (like London himself) who jump from one publisher to another to get paid higher royalties.

By the essay's end, "scab" ("universally bad") has come to stand for a kind of innate moral evil by which groups and individuals work to take advantage of other groups and individuals. The question of social class drops out and, with it, capitalism's surplus army of labor, to be replaced with a vague but intense comparison between styles of work in the United States and Britain. This analysis follows up on patriotic comparisons implicit in *The People of the Abyss* by suggesting how the British are less likely to become "scabs" precisely because they don't work as hard as Americans. Conflict between owners and laborers that leads to tensions between legitimate and pretend workers now gets reconfigured as differences between national attitudes toward work, so that London can express what is at stake for him personally in his analysis only by losing sight of the defining difference between capital and labor.

Like "The Minions of Midas," the essay "The Scab" is a source of embarrassment for those critics such as Phillip Foner or Carolyn Johnston who are determined to analyze London's political writing strictly by its content. Johnston attempts to explain the essay away by referring to the conceptual muddles and factionalism plaguing the entire American socialist movement at the turn of the century.[22] But any self-respecting American socialist, whether belonging to the Socialist Labor Party (led by DeLeon) or the Social Democratic Party (led by Debs), would have recognized the patent absurdity of London's analysis, which ends up, despite itself, inadvertently admiring the hardworking laborer and nation (a projection of London himself) struggling fiercely to get ahead at the expense of others. More to the point, perhaps, is that "The Scab" first appeared in the January 1904 issue of the *Atlantic Monthly*, the publishing site of London's breakthrough Northland story "An Odyssey of the North" precisely four years earlier. Whether London wrote "The Scab" specifically with the *Atlantic* in mind or whether the magazine selected the inoffensive essay to represent "socialism" is less important here than the link between the respectable, middle-class periodical and the increasingly broad moral tenor of the essay itself.[23] As in "The Boy Socialist of Oakland" articles appearing years earlier in San Francisco newspapers, London's effort to reach a (national) audience requires that he reconceive—or, rather, internalize—his readers' expectations about the subject of socialism, now imagined directly in relation to his own ambitions to gain success by hard work.

Let me again stress that in so emphasizing London's publication practice I am not suggesting that he compromises himself by selling out his principles for profit. London made little money from his overtly socialist writing, with few exceptions (most notable and most ironic the two-hundred-dollar prize he won in a 1900 competition sponsored by *Cosmopolitan* for his essay "What Communities Lose by the Competitive System"). But from the start his "self" is already always defined by publishing institutions, and even his essays on socialism that appeared in less mainstream magazines suffer from a similar sort of acute rhetorical uncertainty that we find in "The Scab."

For example, in a review of two important books on the labor problem that first appeared in the *International Socialist Review* ("Contradictory Teachers," 1 May 1903), London offers a rather shrewd if disinterested discussion of the two diametrically opposed studies, noting the strengths and weaknesses of each and pointing out assumptions that the two authors share in common. Yet writing for a magazine that would clearly have encouraged one view over the other, London simply summarizes: "Mr. Ghent beholds the capitalist class rising to dominate the state and working class; Mr. Brooks beholds the working class rising to dominate the state and the capitalist class. One fears the paternalism of a class; the other, the tyranny of the mass" (214).

Coming next we might imagine the reviewer's intervention, London's *dialectical* resolution of these contradictory points of view. But instead the essay breaks off, as if he were unable to decide whether Ghent or Brooks were right about where the interests of the Progressive Era "state" were located. Unlike in "The Scab," positions here are not blurred but simply left hanging in the air. Similarly in "The Class Struggle" (*Independent*, November 1903), London's most detailed, wide-ranging, and lucid analysis of class conflict in terms of hegemonic power relations, he finishes with an open-ended query instead of the answer that would inevitably have followed from Marx: "The question now is, what will be the outcome of the class struggle?" (49). Seeking to examine labor under capitalism for a middle-class audience interested more generally in social reform, London downplays customary socialist polemics and prophecy but also dismisses bourgeois solutions—efficiency, ethics, and so on—leaving the readers of the *Independent* with little to choose.

Although I have been emphasizing the original place of publication for these articles, this issue is a bit moot, for by 1903 London had begun to conceive of them as a single body of work suitable for a book. On August 15 he mailed a letter of inquiry to Brett, stressing that his "sociological and economic essays" on "industrial conditions" were "written in a popular style" and were mostly "up to date," uncannily echoing the same headline slogan invoked by the *San Francisco Examiner* eight years earlier. As with his first three collections of Northland stories, London saw this collection of essays, eventually published by Macmillan under the dramatic title *War of the Classes* (April 1905), as an opportunity to generate yet another new "field" of writing, which is what his letter to Brett promised in conclusion. As the earlier "Boy Socialist" articles implied, here London too bills socialism as preparatory to a new kind of literature, "the biggest work I shall ever do," so that (for Brett, at least) London's identity as socialist remains connected but subordinated to his ambitions as a fiction writer. For the publication of *The People of the Abyss* in fall 1903, this not only meant that his established reputation as a "popular" fiction writer would help sell the book (as he wrote to Brett late in 1904, advising a fifty-cent paper cover edition) but also that he assumed more fundamental ties between his political thinking and his novel writing.[24]

That tie, I have already suggested, depended on London's ability to project and sustain a coherent public image of and for himself. Unlike the early Northland collections, however, the *War of the Classes* does not seek to create authorial integrity via a careful ordering of the sequence of essays. Instead, London affixes a preface designed to introduce his socialist ideas by discussing his public role as a socialist. To explain his socialism, London thus resorts once again to autobiography, not so much how he first became such a "weird sort of creature" (the subject of "How I Became a Socialist," which concluded the collection) but rather how such a creature was treated by the press—a kind of retelling of "The Boy

Socialist of Oakland" newspaper articles from his now prominent position as a well-known author.

As in "The Minions of Midas," the press becomes the site of a social power struggle as London seeks to correct the public's false impressions of him. While the written representations of "The Boy Socialist of Oakland" were quite respectful, feeding Horatio Alger myths of success, in the preface to *War of the Classes* London has a vested interest in claiming that a decade earlier he was demonized as "pathological" and "abnormal" by these reporters and patronized by his fellow citizens. London needs to revise personal history in this way because he wants to dramatize how "times have changed," how a few years later "my socialism grew respectable" (as if it were not always so). Following in the wake of his public acclaim as a fiction writer, London's growing respectability in 1905 poses more of a threat than his prior demonizing, so that he must take pains to brand himself as a hard-nosed radical committed to defeating capitalism: "This is the menace of socialism, and in affirming it and in tallying myself an adherent of it, I accept my own consequent unrespectability" (xiv).

London can afford to be more forthright in this preface than in many of the essays themselves because he is not selling ideas here but an attractively tough version of himself, a rebel with a cause akin to his role as virile Yukon naturalist. But by the end of the preface he has considerably softened his rhetoric to admit that his essays are intended to "enlighten a few capitalistic minds," so that the tough self-image can remain while the revolutionary content has moved into the background. Tracing the public's shift from disrespect to respect, London presumes to reclaim his menacing status on his own terms in order to insist on integrity: "It was not I that changed, but the community. In fact, my socialist views grew solider and more pronounced" (vii). Only by consolidating such a unified personal and corporate identity can Jack London as "socialist" make his essays on "socialism" hang together.

In this way London tends to imagine questions of power strictly in relation to himself. If this seems to be an unfairly cynical reading of his politics, let me note again how such an (auto)biographical frame of reference had been provided for him from the time of his initial emergence as a public figure in 1895. His recourse to revisionist personal narrative a decade later not only gives his socialist analysis more weight but also helps smooth the transition from proletariat obscurity to celebrity. Beginning with "The Boy Socialist" articles, that transition came to depend specifically on London's personal experience as "industrial tramp"—a key identity that informs an interesting body of his writing, which we will briefly discuss before returning to *The People of the Abyss*.

London's early "road" writing is important because it so dramatically serves to bridge the difference between politics and literature by way of a biography that in turn carries enormous implications for understanding London's attitude toward work. Cutting across a number of genres, London's essays, poems, and short stories about the lives of tramps are driven less directly by publicity, perhaps, than his other early work.[25] Labeled early on in print as a tramp himself, London represents unemployed workers in ways that suggest an intimate investment. But as in his other social writings, here too London often seems caught between imaginatively reenacting his past and distancing himself from it.

His earliest representation of tramping is an 1894 diary describing his experience crossing the country as part of Kelly's industrial army. Like his 1897 Yukon diary, this journal is rather modest, mostly avoiding social commentary to concentrate on the daily conditions of eating, sleeping, and traveling on trains. In the case of both diaries, the weakness of London's imagination stems from the fact that he is primarily addressing himself and not any specific audience—the concrete, material end of publishing that so energized and spurred his writing.

When he comes to translate his experiences into fiction, the results are curious indeed. Consider, for example, " 'Frisco Kid's' Story," which first appeared in his high school yearbook (February 1895) and which he later submitted to the *Atlantic Monthly* on 11 June 1897 (before he left for the Yukon)—one of his very first attempts to break into a national publication. This important short story begins with a question "Who am I?" and then continues: "Why I'm de 'Frisco Kid.' An' wot do I do? I'm on de 'road,' see! Say, youze ain't got nothin' agin me, have yer, mister? . . . Wot! A quarter? Dat's very kind in yer, mister."[26] Testing out a trademark self that would continue to be revised and reinvented throughout his career, London follows his first query into identity with an equally crucial question about what the Kid does for a living, as if identity and work

were in fact virtually one and the same. This implied equation immediately leads the first-person narrator to address the reader directly as a
particular "you." In a remarkable gesture with interesting implications
for London's subsequent writing, the Kid then mistakes this "you" for
the police (censoring agents acting "agin" him) and goes on, when reas-
sured, to accept money from his auditor. Hailed by the reader/police/
almsgiver, London's first fictive "I" comes into being as an interpellated
subject.[27] London thus initially assumes the colloquial dialect of popular
local color as the genre best suited to carry his Frisco Kid persona—
young, Western (but urban), bold, and carefree—a set of attributes that
would remain wonderfully consistent for his loyal readers. By way of this
Kid he thus can imagine a benevolent, if subservient, transaction with
that very public. At the heart of the tale's complicated give-and-take
between "I" and "you" resides the question of mastery: by accepting
twenty-five cents in exchange for a story, the wayward narrator earns the
trust of and partially gains ascendancy over his older listener, who is
searching, it turns out, for some information to help him find his own
runaway son. Having already fictionalized himself as the Kid in the February 1895 issue of his high school yearbook, London was thus well
prepared to play the role of a young "industrial tramp" later that same
year for the respectable readers of the *San Francisco Examiner.*[28]

In subsequently writing about tramping, London quickly moved away
from this early first-person representation to occupy other subject positions. In a poem published in 1901 entitled "The Worker and the Tramp,"
for instance, London no longer accepts handouts but gives them, expressing thanks that the unemployed tramp (directly addressed as "you")
has not taken away his own job. London adopts yet another seemingly
disinterested perspective in an 1897 essay offering a typology of tramps—
"The Profesh," "The Stew Bum," "Alki Stiffs," and so on—much as a
field anthropologist might do, finishing (as usual) with an open-ended
series of unanswered questions for his intended middle-class audience
about the future of the unemployed homeless.[29]

One final example most directly bears on London's complex rhetorical positionality in his *Abyss*: the essay "The Tramp" that is sandwiched
between "The Class Struggle" and "The Scab" in *War of the Classes.*
Although first published in 1904 (in the socialist journal *Wilshire's Maga-*

zine), the essay was rejected by twenty well-known national magazines, starting with *McClure's* in late 1901 and including the *Atlantic Monthly*, whose editor Bliss Perry wrote back to London in late April 1902 that his readers did not find that "its general thesis is tenable." In a letter to George Brett written a week earlier, London referred to the essay as a "story" he had planned as part of yet another "series which I have discontinued," adding, "I have become chary of letting anyone see it."[30]

Reading "The Tramp" a century later, one can still appreciate the enormity of London's ambitions for it (as measured by the number and places of its submissions), as well as the mainstream press's intense fear of it (measured by the accumulation of rejection slips). Unlike "The Scab," this essay offers a scathing, focused indictment of the logic of capitalism that methodically explains how "the disparity between men and work" (60) in the market systematically and inevitably creates an army of unemployed.[31] Serving as the system's required "reserve fund of social energy" (66), these idle workers (past and potential) prevent the instantaneous, absolutely efficient circulation of energy (as information) that London had fantasized about earlier in "The Minions of Midas" as destroying the power of the state; now directly challenging the scientific-management belief in an "absolute standard of efficiency" (78), London insists that "without a surplus labor army, the courts, police, and military are impotent" (71), for their hegemonic role operates strictly to make up for the structural inadequacies of the system.

His indignation apparent but under control in this sharp Marxist analysis, London shifts tone a bit in the essay when he begins to consider more specifically the selection process by which some laborers keep their jobs while others are "discouraged"—they lose or fail to find work. Refusing to invoke his customary "survival of the fittest" biological explanations, London argues that unemployment is not natural (derived from heredity) but depends quite clearly on the skill level of the worker, which leads him to speculate once again on the advantages of brain labor (implicitly, his own writing) over brawn. Yet in so detailing the conditions at the "bottom of the society pit" (83), London is suddenly forced to admit that brains and even high social standing are no guarantee against failure. Marx's structural account carries London only so far, for having raised the issue of skill, he is compelled to explain the lure or "the Call of the

Road" (as a subheading in the essay suggestively puts it) in terms of a rebel's own individual choice—the discouraged worker's attempt to make a virtue out of necessity by assuming the "care-free and happy" status of a vagabond who "achieves a new outlook on life" (93). Perhaps frightened by the grim implications of so totalizing an application of Marx, London thus leaves a little room for himself and his readers to continue to imagine the road as a Whitman-esque path opening to self-discovery.

London's odd turn in the essay implies that a discouraged worker might play the (literary) part of tramp to avoid becoming one in actuality. London in fact is inclined to take precisely this view of his own past, encouraged perhaps by a remarkable set of letters sent to him independently from two of his editors, S. S. McClure and George Brett. On the author's return from England in late 1902, Brett wrote him: "There is nothing I should have liked so much as to have been with you in your Eastside London experiences. I am afraid however that I should never have been able to act the part although I have played at being farm-hand, cowboy, and a few other things of that kind when I was younger." In response to a photograph and autobiographical sketch London had sent McClure as a follow-up query letter two years earlier, the influential editor bragged in a similar vein that "I have done my share of tramping. . . . I used to know whole villages, mining villages, lumber villages, and what not." He then goes on to list the members of his editorial staff (including Ida Tarbell). Not to be outdone by the exploits of naturalist authors, friendly New York editors too could thus appeal to authenticity, turning poverty into youthful adventure, something "played at," like a summer job.[32]

Having journeyed to England in search of a compelling story, London in effect occupies a similar position in *The People of the Abyss* by approaching life on the East End streets as an occasion to examine his own labor as a writer. In the book itself London marks this occasion for his writing with a self-conscious textuality, from explicit references to contemporary British masters such as Browning, Dickens, Doyle, and Kipling, to allusions to exploration narratives such as Stanley's *In Darkest Africa*, to implied comparisons with Stevenson's *Dr. Jekyll and Mr. Hyde*—with London playing the parts of both doctor and brute.

These general allusions to contemporary British letters speak to London's desire to situate himself in a new geographic and literary terrain. But when it comes more specifically to locating himself within a tradition of writing about the poor, he tends to rely on American sources. Near the end of "The Tramp," two brief references to Walter Wyckoff and Jacob Riis are perhaps the best place to begin to understand London's book in relation to earlier efforts to represent the poor, the homeless, and the unemployed.

As the title suggests, in *How the Other Half Lives* (1890) Jacob Riis essentially assumes an outsider's middle-class perspective on the New York slums. A curious mixture of journalistic anecdote, statistics, sociology, and sermonizing, Riis's rhetoric gives readers a consistent feeling of sympathy precisely to the extent that the poor remain placed and categorized as others. Walter Wyckoff's *The Workers: The West* (1898), on the other hand, depends less on mapping the "other half" than on *being* one of them by way of the author's role play as an unemployed job seeker. In a key passage he explains a dilemma that superficially closely resembles London's own in *The Abyss*: "It was impossible for me to rightly interpret even the human conditions in which I found myself, for between me and the actual workers was the infinite difference of necessity in relation to any lot in which I was. How could I, who at any moment could change my status if I chose, enter really into the life and feelings of the destitute poor who are bound to their lot by the hardest facts of stern reality?"[33]

As the serene, composed language of Wyckoff's confession suggests, such role play is difficult because of the writer's distance from his or her subject. Unlike the more sensational stunts of new journalists such as Nellie Bly and Annie Laurie (reporting for the *San Francisco Examiner* in the late 1890s) or the fictional "experiments in misery" of Stephen Crane, Wyckoff's first-person account contains little of naturalism's documentary menace—the threat of truly becoming the very beast that the writer initially desires only to mimic. Prominently identified on the title page of his book as "Assistant Professor of Political Economy in Princeton University," Wyckoff nevertheless frequently employs the pronoun "we" (rather than "I" or "they") to suggest a common ground of interests between himself and his suffering mates. For Wyckoff (like Howells) this commonality is based on his faith in Christian fellowship that operates to transcend class division; his own "experiment in reality" enables him (despite his academic credentials, or perhaps because of them) to emphasize (beyond necessity) similarity between persons, in good liberal humanist tradition.[34]

Although London, like Wyckoff, assumes the role of the downtrodden to "dive" into the abyss, the rhetorical relation between sympathy and identity is far more complex, unstable, and tortured in his case, precisely insofar as his journey is not simply an act or performance but instead a painful reenactment of his past that erases any easy assurance of an "infinite difference of necessity." In other words, for London the trip to the East End represents a kind of atavistic return to the site of his origins, along the lines of *The Call of the Wild* or his story "Li Wan, the Fair."[35] The book's underlying atavism entails a racial return (England as the source of his presumed Anglo-Saxon ancestry) and a literary return (hence the book's allusions to those British masters). But, far more urgent, his first trip abroad to England compels London to plunge into the pit of the proletariat from which he had recently emerged and to which he could return should his writing no longer prove successful. His (paid) work as an (American) writer thus serves as the crucial line of demarcation between him and the abyss.

Understanding London's visit to England as a revisiting of a past narrowly escaped as well as a nightmarish anticipation of one still possible future helps to explain the entire first third of *The People of the Abyss*. In these opening eleven chapters, London describes at great length his efforts to get settled, fed, and bedded in the East End before going on to report on the coronation of King Edward VII, even though he had actually arrived in England only three days before the event. Deferring the coronation until the middle of his narrative made aesthetic sense, enabling him to sharpen ironic contrasts by first carefully rendering conditions of abject misery before mocking the British Empire's hollow anticlimactic show of pomp and circumstance from the perspective of the homeless poor.

Yet perhaps a more pressing reason for these many pages of orientation or settlement can be found in London's need to try out a multitude of self-consciously literary roles, to remind himself (and his readers) that he is an American professional on assignment, however loosely defined. London's work in these early chapters is to pretend to be an explorer, a detective, a high-class criminal, a shopper haggling over the price of clothes with a merchant (presumably Jewish), a stranded American sailor, a discouraged tramp. This cast of characters must be set apart from "Jack London" the author. London underscores this split by embracing soon after his arrival a Jekyll-and-Hyde "double life" (20)—the spatial separation between his staying on the streets and in casual wards (homeless shelters) and his renting a second cozy home filled with bourgeois creature comforts, a "port of refuge" that London occupies to "receive my mail and work up my notes" (19).

As the (leased) location of writing or mail call, London's flat enables him to maintain the difference between author and character that is in turn essential for affirming his work as a writer. Contemporary reviewers who took London to task for so openly running home to indulge in a Turkish bath after a particularly nasty stay at a greasy casual ward missed the point, for as Joan London astutely remarked, her father had only too recently ascended from the social pit, written himself out of it, as it were, not to feel truly relieved to be able to escape it at will—an option unavailable to the British people of the abyss.[36] Calling attention to this slumming as his own job, London can dramatize the contingency of social roles that nonetheless remain fixed for the vast majority of East Enders compelled to live out capitalism's social fiction without control over the course of its plots.

Yet as he dives deeper and deeper into the abyss, writing himself back into it, London finds it more and more difficult to sustain spatial separation between author and character, to distinguish clearly between his labor as a writer and his assumed roles, both governed by the vicissitudes of his physical body. Because he can be at only one place at one time, London must quickly decide where he stands, that is, who he is, whenever he walks out into the East End streets. After spending a sleepless night in a park, for example, London continues his role "adventuring as a penniless man looking for work" (121) and suddenly comes on "a motley crowd of woebegone wretches" (122) who had spent the night in the rain just as he had. But as soon as a policeman (declaring "Shocking!") enters the picture to roust the sleeping men, London's locus of identification shifts from the misery of the men to the surprise of the enforcer of law: "Of course it was a shocking sight. I was shocked myself. And I should not care to have my own daughter pollute her eyes with such a sight, or come within half a mile of it; but—and there we were, and there you are, and 'but' is all that can be said" (123). Before he can address his reader directly as "you," he must align himself with the police and invoke family values (his daughter). As in his first story "'Frisco Kid's' Story," the police serve to define his subjectivity—the same agency of state power, mediating between classes by way of surveillance and enforcement, to which he initially is directed in the opening pages of *The People of the Abyss* on arriving in England. London rejects the help of the police, preferring to mediate on his own. But in this episode, only after emphasizing his role as an interested spectator can he then shift to "we" and acknowledge his presence on the scene as one of those wretched homeless.

Like the vocation of the theater stage "scene-shifter" with whom he briefly shares a room (31–32), London's writing in the abyss forces him to undergo one change after another, oscillating, as in his "Boy Socialist of Oakland" newspaper publicity, between the positions of adventuring and unemployed tramping.[37] Acting like a bum to avoid becoming one, London threatens to turn into the very discouraged worker that he has only pretended to be. As in the tests of love put to Buck near the end of *The Call of the Wild*, London transforms the struggle for survival on the mean East End streets into a simulation of itself—neither accepting it as all too horribly real nor dismissing it as merely a youthful game, as his editors could do. For Buck, playing at work (during the staged sled pull) results in his celebrity, but where could simulating unemployment lead? Only by discovering some sort of honest labor taking place within the abyss could London tie his role as homeless tramp to his profession outside the abyss as a publishing author.

Precisely midway through *The People of the Abyss*, after he has dramatized problems of domestic subsistence (food, clothes, shelter) and immediately after describing Edward VII's coronation (another sort of staged, illegitimate activity), London directly explores the possibility of work within the abyss by tracing the career of one "Dan Cullen, Docker," who managed to eke out a living as a labor organizer before dying of starvation, "a lonely old man, embittered and pessimistic" (161), beaten down and blacklisted by the forces of capital.

As we might expect, Dan Cullen is Jack London himself—or rather a shadow projection showing how Jack London might turn out if he didn't watch himself. Like London, Cullen is born lowly, "self-educated" but forced "all his days" to "toil hard with his body" (159–60)—a line London would subsequently use for his 1903 autobiographical sketch "How I Became a Socialist." Like London, his mastery of books (he "could 'write a letter like a lawyer' ") enables Cullen to rise above the mass of common laborers, who select him "to toil hard for them with his brain" (160). But then London telescopes ten years of Cullen's fights for labor into a single paragraph, which quickly ends in his failure, to be followed by a moving, if sentimental, account of Cullen's pathetic death that focuses for pages on the state of his body. Although London ends his story by praising Cullen as "a patriot, a lover of human freedom, and a fighter unafraid" (166), the fate of this obscure, broken man clearly frightens him, confirming his own calling to publish books rather than organize the proletariat. There are many kinds of brain toil, and some, it would seem, are better than others.

Commemorating Cullen's heroic defeat (but hardly stopping to examine the reasons for it), London in the next chapter continues his search for work by going to the countryside to pick hops. Anticipating the back-to-the-land sentiments that would underlie many of his novels in the following decade, London turns to farming to see, following Marx, whether the "divorcement of the worker from the soil" (167) is as hopeless as the alienation and discouragement he has experienced in the East End. It is. After citing a number of grim statistics in various newspapers decrying the shrinking hop crop, London returns to his more personal mode by recounting his rural travels with "Bert, who had yielded to the lure of adventure and joined me for the trip" (172) by dressing up in his "worst rags." Even in the countryside labor takes the form of acting, now a duet instead of a solo performance.

What Jack and Bert discover while picking hops is that their toil doesn't pay: "As the afternoon wore along, we realized that living wages could not be made—by men. Women could pick as much as men, and children could do almost as well as women; so it was impossible for a man to compete with a woman and half a dozen children. For it is the woman and the half-dozen children who count as a unit and by their combined capacity determine the unit's pay" (175). Rather than explore the interesting implications of this gendered system of piecemeal payment—how the wage "unit" holds together (and exploits) the family unit or how solidarity might help overcome an otherwise destructive competition, London and his friend Bert see this humiliating episode as an affront to their manhood. In London's fictive Northland, squaws become work partners through marriage, but in the abyss, women rival men for work. Unable to keep up with the women and children, the unattached pair soon quit in frustration: "We whiled away the time and talked for the edification of our neighbors" (176). Receiving paltry pay for their labor only reminds them, finally, of the gnawing hunger in the pits of their stomachs.

Jack and Bert return to the city, and from this point on in the book London no longer bothers to hunt for a job, preferring instead to recount the grim anecdotes of other discouraged abyss workers or to quote newspaper accounts and recite large-scale sociological statistics. Becoming in effect one more "incompetent" at the bottom of the social pit, London in his failure to find work does not live up to his promise (voiced in the preface) to "measure manhood" by the individual; as a result of his failure, the book tends to fall apart, to lose the coherence that London has sustained in the first half by virtue of his dramatized presence seeking food and shelter. As the hops incident suggests, London's masculinity quite literally depends on his ability to earn a living, which in turn is closely linked to his body—a source of pride and anxiety for him throughout his narrative.

Whereas in *The Call of the Wild* Buck's body is disciplined through regulated labor, here in the unnatural social abyss, which he calls a "huge man-killing machine" (47), the body becomes the primary site of capitalism's brutal degradation, registering discouraged work's capacity to deform manhood. The most powerful passages in the entire book center on London's representations of the body: bathing, eating, aging, wasting away by disease. An alcoholic sailor, "a young sot of two and twenty" preparing for bed, stirs London to remark, "I have never seen one who stripped to better advantage," but then the homoerotic possibilities in such a scene are quickly overshadowed by London's realization that "this young god [is] doomed to rack and ruin in four or five short years" (39). In other similar early moments of negative identification, London compares his stout body (from the "husky West") with the misshapen bodies of two scrawny East End socialists (55–56) and poignantly feels the ribs of an elderly army veteran, whose "skin was stretched like parchment over the bones" (89). Even the money that London uses to treat this old man to a square meal (thereby betraying his own status as "merely an investigator, a social student, seeking to find out how the other half lived") intimately depends on London's own body: a gold coin he had sewed for emergencies "inside my stoker's singlet under the armpit" (85).[38]

As London's comparison between parchment and skin suggests, the male body is tangibly disfigured by the abyss, destroyed and corroded away, in effect, by capitalism. Exposing his "true" identity as an author who, like Dan Cullen, has traded manual labor for brain toil, London would seem to remain exempt from the brutalizing effects of such objectified inscription. He can write about the abyss rather than simply get written—stamped—by it. But insofar as London always remembers that his writing is also a form of work within capitalism (however seemingly nonmanual and American), then to that extent he cannot fully escape the consequences of his own searing analysis: like the rest of the citizens of the East End, London literally feels his "flesh" begin "to creep and crawl" (92). While the pride he takes in his body helps to emphasize the difference between the people of the abyss and himself, he is always at risk of contamination, so that he "must beg forgiveness of my body for the vileness through which I have dragged it, and forgiveness of my stomach for the vileness which I have thrust into it" (91)—forgiveness that he again begs, virtually verbatim, in the closing lines of a letter (28 August 1902) mailed from the abyss to Anna Strunsky signaling the end of their love affair (a relation I will examine in the next chapter).

London's body is so central because it serves as the dominant principle of narrative coherence in the absence of any well-defined plot or pattern for the book. The body keeps Jack and his writing together, part of a larger abstract economic and social system yet endowed with enough personal agency, personal power, to operate within that system. Given the multitude of roles that London rehearses in the abyss, the body remains his only constant, giving the various contradictory projections of self a unified corporeal dimension: stout adventuring author. Only by so containing and confining his roles in a single body can London affirm his integrity as a writer.

The site of degradation, as well as the sign of his authorial integrity, the body thus serves as the primary marker of corporate identity by which he tries to keep himself ("London") distinct from the people of the abyss ("London"). Like the room he rents to receive mail, the body becomes his sanctuary, a bounded, mobile space into which he can withdraw at times of danger. Very early in his narrative he gives way to an intense "fear of the crowd," which he imagines as "so many waves of a vast and malodorous sea" (8). He claims a bit later, after changing into the costume of a down-and-out sailor, that this fear no longer "haunted me," that the "vast and malodorous sea had welled up and over me, or I had slipped gently into it, and there was nothing fearsome about it" (15). But strange, unpublished remarks scribbled in a small notepad London kept while walking the streets of the East End suggest that his acclimation was not so easy, that simulating the underclass generated its own hazards.

The sequence of jottings begins with the curious comment "Crowd as a Fluid." Although we might expect some mediation to follow on the role of the urban flaneur, we find instead an odd set of instructions that London wrote to himself:

Follow a master & beat him at the last moment.

Tall men, get left.

Must work quietly, with an abstract look on face, or else one of pain or displeasure at the crush.

Slipping forward inside clothes, imperceptible squirm of body. The least gain will be enough to pivot a man, which will be slowly accomplished in five minutes, & very much against his will.

Keep arms down, wedge in slowly, never give a fraction of an inch.

Calls good-naturedly with man you are slowly pivotting, etc.

How I got elbow in ribs of master.

Arm behind, impossible to move forward, catch the sleeve with other hand & pull the wrincle [sic] forward.

When all are shoed [sic] back, work forward. (Horses)

When other man presses, in order to go ahead, take advantage of it yourself.

Block their legs, & trunks leaning forward they have to go back in order to regain equilibrium

Expel mind & shrink to get between—the [   ] out [   ] arms & expand chest, etc.

Wind-up—in order to succeed one must have a strong heart & stout ribs.[39]

It is difficult to know to whom "master" refers. But it does seem clear in this eerie scenario that the crowd itself holds some power over London, who can "succeed" against the masses only by asserting himself, his body, through a series of controlled, subversive gestures. A set of theater directions to himself, as it were, these notes suggest how the people of the abyss continually threaten to overwhelm London, to drown him in their collective misery that he felt so strongly and so immediately. To combat such fears, to guard his corporeal authority, London sent letters to friends and family back home to remind himself that this was only a temporary summer visit on his part. Like the counterpart dispatches from the field of industrial warfare that make up the book itself, these personal letters served to underscore London's writing in and of the social pit as a staged performance aimed for public consumption.

In the midst of his East End misery, he addressed one such letter to his wife Bessie and little daughter Joan, a photo postcard (dated three days after the letter to Strunsky) that shows him dressed up in his ragged, oversized sailor disguise, a grim look on his face, one hand stuffed in his pocket. Although in the first edition of *The People of the Abyss* London would include a photograph of himself and his buddy Bert posing in hop-picking garb, this one he decided to omit. The postcard reads:

Dear Bess & Joan:

And how do you like Daddy now? Would you gi' me a bit o' punk [hobo slang for bread] if I battered your back door?

With all sorts of love——Jack.

East London,

August 31, 1902[40]

The intense pain and degradation of the people of the abyss—London's own intense pain and suffering—are converted into the whimsy of the family man on a business/tourist trip asking for domestic recognition. Posing in the postcard, London rehearses his old cast of appealing characters—solicitous Frisco Kid, tramp on the road, adventurous Boy Socialist. Without such self-conscious playacting, London's missive from the abyss implicitly declares, these familiar roles would remain all too close for comfort. Sending his mail safely home, the discouraged worker protects his integrity, preserves his manhood.

5

Collaborating Love in and out of
The Kempton-Wace Letters

I n an early, undated note for "a socialist Novel" that was most likely typed up between 1900 and 1902, Jack London imagines a "Russian Jewess alone in the world." He then goes on to elaborate his plot idea:

> Passionate thinkers and dreamers. The propaganda and business meetings. All the welter of nationalities and ideas.
>
> Man conquers her by sheer strength and force of will, etc, in spite of herself. (Natural selection, operating on female so long, which leads her to choose strong male, etc.[)]
>
> Only, she must be conquered, mastered by his strength, unconsciously. The heriditary [*sic*] recoil against force. How her whole nature flutters madly up in revolt as soon as she is aware that force, intellectual and spiritual, as well as physical, is being used.
>
> Instance the kiss taken by strength—let this incident be the key to the peculiarity of her position.[1]

What makes this socialist? Opening with an account of cosmopolitan political activism, presumably international in scope, London's projected plot quickly gives way to a more intimate form of sexual politics. Power, intellectual as well as physical, is displayed by "Man" over "Russian Jewess," who is helpless to resist his "force of will." What allows London to move so rapidly via natural selection from socialism to love in this elemental scenario, I would argue, is his initial designation of the conquered woman as "Russian Jewess"—a highly charged identification running throughout his early work, fusing his interest in social relations and personal relations, race and gender, and, most important, as we shall see, working as a (thinly) veiled allusion to a key figure in his life and letters during this period: Anna Strunsky.

Strunsky's peculiar position as a woman and a Jew is crucial for understanding the role she played as collaborator of their coauthored epistolary novel debating the nature of love, *The Kempton-Wace Letters* (1903). The only book he produced in conjunction with another writer, *The Kempton-Wace Letters* is today probably the least-read work of "Jack London" (undeservedly so), perhaps for the very reason that the shared billing complicates our image of London as an independent self-made author. As Wayne Koestenbaum has suggested in his provocative study of fin de siecle collaboration between men, such cases of "double talk," as he calls the results of literary partnership, serve as "specimens of a relation."[2] Following the same impulse to convert personal experience into published text that governs all London's early writing, *The Kempton-Wace Letters* is thus important for challenging the assumption that his books were made by an individual working in isolation. Before, during, and after the writing of the novel, both in and out of the *Letters*, Strunsky and her fellow author attest to the collective process of publishing—getting words into print.

In his early writing, as the plot for "a socialist Novel" hints, the presence of the Jew—Strunsky in particular—served to mediate for London between politics and a more intimate set of concerns, even if such personal concerns might seem to have little to do with racial/religious designations. On the other hand, at times when we might have expected Jews to figure prominently in London's representations, they do not. In *The People of the Abyss*, for example, Jews are conspicuous primarily by virtue of their curious marginality in London's description of the British underclass. In snippets of conversation London reports overhearing in the East End, the Jews as recent immigrants emerge as simultaneously part of the British abyss but also apart from it, a focal point for the problem of work. "The Jews of Whitechapel, say, a-cuttin our throats," he quotes one discouraged laborer as complaining, while his mate is said to reply, "You can't blame them. . . . They're just like us, and they've got to live. Don't blame the man who offers to work cheaper than you and gets your job."[3]

Not one to shy away from expressing his own opinion about such matters throughout *The People of the Abyss*, London remains uncharacteristically silent during this exchange, as if he was not sure where he stood on the question—whether the Jews of the abyss were in fact "just like us" or demonized others. Were Jews part of the problem, a moneyed group in collusion with capitalists, or victims like the rest of the underclass? Where did they belong in the book's scheme of things? London's reticence is even more pronounced a few pages later, when he opens a chapter entitled "The Ghetto" with the comment, "At one time the nations of Europe confined the undesirable Jews in city ghettos" (210), yet goes on primarily to describe the physical conditions in the slum, saying "nothing about the Jews who inhabit it," as a book review in the *Jewish Chronicle* (20 November 1903) sharply criticized.[4] In this "Ghetto" chapter, London offers the most extensive and acute analysis of the effect of poverty on the institution of marriage, demonstrating how "a woman of the lower Ghetto classes is as much the slave of her husband as is the Indian squaw" (222). But he never connects such wife beating to any particular cultural context beyond his Klondike metaphors or beyond general references to the deterioration of bestial (male) human nature.

Traces of Jews are visually encoded in the photographs accompanying London's *The People of the Abyss*—a shop sign reading "Rosenblatts" (27), a photograph labeled "A Group of Jewish Children" (220), a representation of Hebrew writing painted on a coffeehouse (239). On the book's printed page, however, we find virtually no corresponding discussion. This avoidance is all the more striking given London's enthusiasm in his Northland stories for racial generalization, as well as the generic tendency of other popular social exposés such as Jacob Riis's *How the Other Half Lives* to rely heavily on racial/ethnic categories to mark sociological orders and boundaries. Insisting over and over again in *The People of the Abyss* on the contrast between Britain and America, London is unwilling or unable to account for a third sort of more cosmopolitan group—the Jews—whose seemingly shifting allegiances threatened to undermine his fundamental geographical binary opposition, thereby vexing his reformist discourse.[5]

In his valuable 1993 book *Constructions of "the Jew" in English Literature and Society*, Bryan Cheyette has focused on the ambiguous, indeterminate nature of what he calls "semitic discourse" around the turn of the century. Via a series of close readings of English writers from Matthew Arnold to Kipling to T. S. Eliot, Cheyette shows how "the Jew" was construed as embodying at once a redemptive liberal culture, transcending yet contained within an increasingly exclusivist nation-state, and a barbaric, menacing racial alterity that resisted all assimilation. Such contradictory and indeterminate constructions, Cheyette argues, turn "the Jew" into a figure of repressed identification for these writers, a double who could speak to and for the larger cultural dislocations of modernity emerging at the turn of the century. At once at the limits of society and centrally implicated in its structures of power, the undesirable cosmopolitan Jew allowed these writers to play out their own alienation.[6]

A brief but cogent set of comments on anti-Semitism by Slavoj Žižek gives a deeper psychoanalytic dimension to Cheyette's historical discussion, helping us appreciate London's representations of his coauthor in terms of this larger cultural crisis of modernity. Žižek seeks to take an analysis of ideology "beyond interpellation" via a Lacanian reading of fantasy and desire; he seizes on the Jew at key moments during his argument as a pivotal point of entry into his critique of ideological operations. Insisting that "the ideological figure of the 'Jew' is invested with our unconscious desire," Žižek goes on to show how this "symptom in the sense of a coded message" functions as a primary object of ideology in general and twentieth-century fascism in particular. The signifier "Jew," Žižek argues, works to displace and condense a series of heterogeneous social antagonisms: a figure at once wealthy and poor, powerful and impotent, foreign and familiar—like us but not us. "In short," Žižek concludes, " 'Jew' is a fetish which simultaneously denies and embodies the structural impossibility of 'Society,' " a particular kind of "social fantasy" that enables *"an ideology to take its own failure into account in advance."*[7]

I introduce anti-Semitism not to claim that London was blatantly anti-Semitic (he was not) but to suggest how his fetishizing of Strunsky specifically as Jewish served to mask certain fissures in his thinking. Although neither Cheyette nor Žižek explicitly factors gender into his analyses, Žižek's Lacanian take on ideology as social fantasy lets us see how London's fascination with—and desire for—a collaborating "Jewess" allowed him, via the question of love, to work through contradictions riddling his naturalism/socialism. In the same batch of unpublished notes in which London expressed his fear of losing his body amid the fluid East End crowds, we find another set of equally cryptic remarks alluding four separate times to a "Russian Jewess" or "Polish Jewess" that London apparently encountered on a visit to an English theater. However condensed and enigmatic, these jottings suggest what might have been at stake more immediately for London here. Musing on "this persisting life, the marvel of its descent" that could yield a second "Esther," London speculates: "And from the loins of this woman may spring a long line of strength. In America a generation hence." He then goes on to describe this woman physically in terms that continue to draw on his descriptions of his Klondike heroines, combining the features of white mothers and Native American brides: "the same prominent cheek bones," the "same brows, heavy and lifted," the "same proud breast and poise of head." Another note compares a "Polish Jewess" (presumably the same figure) to her "sister," repeating the phrases "both same Assyrian profile, both the hair, brows, etc." and then stating, "Polish girl, read and wrote Yidish [sic]—was going to New York when she could get the money—etc., etc.." Yet another passage dwells on her "black eyes, immortally dreaming" and envisions her aiming her bedraggled body "for America—this random wayfarer."[8]

Whether or not London is actually describing two distinct women (one rich and one poor) or whether he is describing one in terms of the memory of another absent figure back home, this mysterious "Russian Jewess," left out of his published account of the British slums, gives us an important insight into a more personal source for the writer's psychic turmoil during his dive into the abyss—his miserable breakup with Anna Strunsky, to whom he passionately confessed his love during the months before he sailed for England, as they were completing revision on their *Kempton-Wace Letters* and who sent him a "Dear Jack" letter while he was in England working on the socialist dispatches that would become *The People of the Abyss*. Their intense relation, professional and personal, links these two apparently disparate books—the pain, anger, and despair registered in the East End, and the more serene fictional disputations about love exchanged between two men, Dane Kempton (impersonated by Strunsky) and Herbert Wace (played by London), who is about to be married as the epistolary novel opens.

Filtered through depictions of women (Indian and white) in his Northland tales, the omitted "Russian Jewess" in his abyss notes would seem to function as a displaced version of Strunsky herself. London's refusal to ponder directly the significance of Jews in the book is thus also an effort in part to avoid the painful subject of Strunsky, whose peculiar position as a cosmopolitan, socialist, and intellectual Jewish woman allowed her to occupy the absent mediating ground between patriotic American author and exploited British underclass, both assumed as fixed entities by London. Strunsky's striking appearance—beautiful black eyes, Assyrian profile, and "proud breast"—heightened her exotic appeal for London. During their literary collaboration over the previous two years, Strunsky, like the "immortally dreaming . . . random wayfarer" with ambitions to move from England to America and produce a race of her own, had come to embody for London a cluster of complex associations— on race, on socialism, on women—that both energized and threatened to destabilize his writing.[9]

Up to here in this book, I have been closely reading a discrete number of "primary" texts authored by Jack London in light of a variety of turn-of-the-century cultural formations. But at the risk of indulging in intimate biography for its own sake, we need to consider how and why London and Strunsky wrote each other into their lives—via their personal correspondence and their mutual authoring of a single finished work—as well as why London might have sought to write her out during his composition of *The People of the Abyss*. The story of their collaboration, it turns out, may be more compelling than the contents of the book that they coproduced and copublished.

It is important to understand that from the start of their relationship—"a white beautiful friendship" as he described it to her—London assumed Strunsky's Jewishness as a fundamental part of her identity rather than merely some peripheral detail. For example, when first recounting the genesis of his collaborative project to his friend Cloudesley Johns, London began:

"Didn't I explain my volume of letters? Well, it's this way: A young Russian Jewess of 'Frisco and myself have often quarrelled over our conceptions of love. She happens to be a genius. She is a materialist by philosophy, and an idealist by innate preference, and is constantly being forced to twist all the facts of the universe in order to reconcile herself with her self. So, finally, we decided that the only way to argue the question out would be by letter. Then we wondered if a collection of such letters should happen to be worth publishing. Then we assumed characters, threw in a real objective love element, and started to work."[10]

Later I will have occasion to analyze this account of the novel's origins more fully, but two points are worth mentioning here. First, London takes a philosophical quarrel between them and quickly converts it into a division within her, shifting any ambivalence of his own onto the woman. Second, London implies that the woman's divided nature stems directly from Strunsky's cultural makeup. When thinking about Strunsky, London consistently draws this connection. A few months later, for instance, he introduced her (in writing) to Elwyn Hoffman, another aspiring writer friend, closing his letter by again emphasizing: "She loves Browning. She is deep, subtle, and psychological. . . . She is a Russian, and a Jewess, who has absorbed the Western culture, and who warms it with a certain oriental leaven." Mailed on his return from the East End, just as Strunsky was planning to meet his Macmillan publisher, George Brett, in New York, a letter written by London to Brett to convince him to take *The Kempton-Wace Letters* offers a similar, if somewhat more perfunctory, assessment of London's collaborating partner: "I am sure you will find her charming. She is a young Russian-Jewess, brilliant, a college-woman, etc."[11]

Before 1910, London rarely, if ever, used the term "Jew" in his letters to identify any of his male acquaintances. But his persistent identification of his female friend as a "Russian Jewess" suggests a combination of traits—intellectual, cultured yet exotic, feminine—that bears a certain resemblance to the Orientalism by which he represented the Indian brides in his Northland stories as occupying a position outside the white man's totemic clan. Just as the squaw in the Klondike helped London in his fiction to define himself as an Anglo-Saxon male on trail, so does his identification of Strunsky as foreign, Jewish, and a woman of letters help sharpen the principles driving his literary naturalism.[12]

But Strunsky's Jewishness was more to London than an object of allure to be shared exclusively with his male friends. Less than two weeks after first striking up a correspondence with her beginning 19 December 1899, he boldly sent her a story with a Jewish character named Jaky and was duly chastised by her for his stereotyping: "Only not all Jews haggle and bargain," a criticism he himself quoted back to her in a subsequent letter, claiming a mutual misunderstanding. In another letter mailed a few weeks later, he listed as his "influences" Karl Marx and Israel Zangwill, the popular English novelist noted in the 1890s for chronicling the rich life of the very East End ghetto that would remain so invisible in London's own account of the abyss. And as if to emphasize the point, he also enclosed in the same letter a review of a Mary Antin book, following a single line of quotation with a deliberate comment directed at Strunsky herself: " 'Like most modern Jewesses who have written, she is, I fear destined to spiritual suffering.' How that haunts one!"[13]

As Strunsky's response to the character "Jaky" makes clear, while resisting London's stereotyping she was quite willing to engage in a kind of identity politics of her own. London's socialist inclinations emerged from nativist, Western, working-class politics (particularly strong in northern California and Washington State), whereas her socialism derived from a European model largely made up of secular middle- and upper-class Jewish intellectuals like herself.[14] From the start of their relationship both London and Strunsky felt this ideological difference—a division marked most dramatically by the question of race. In the most perceptive contemporary review of *The Son of the Wolf* (published in the journal *Dilettante*, February 1901), for example, Strunsky astutely called attention to the young author's "bionomic bias" and singled out "pride of race" as the dominant "motif of the book." But beyond merely describing London's totemic equation of white man with the Wolf clan or simply puffing the book as a favor for a friend and fellow collaborator, Strunsky felt compelled to take him to task for his views, identifying herself in the review as a "democratic cosmopolite" deploring "race distinctions" as "arbitrary and artificial." Yet despite this vigorous condemnation, she was intrigued by London's representation of love as combining the "technicality" of "modern sociology" with the passion of poetry, and she closed her review by praising him as a "Red God."[15] Clearly Strunsky was just as attracted to London's otherness as he was to hers.

London's willingness to have this remarkable woman read his work, her willingness to criticize it (both in private and in public), and his respect for her critical opinions together quickly paved the way for their ambitious plans to collaborate on the writing and publishing of a book—a surprising experiment for an author who tried throughout his life to cultivate a literary reputation as a Lone Wolf, a self-made independent writer. As London's curious notes for "a socialist Novel" suggest, moreover, such collaboration (as projected onto an imaginary plot) also entailed a kind of struggle for control, intellectual as well as physical, between "Man" and "Russian Jewess" that culminated in their falling in love and simultaneously producing a book about love.

We therefore have a number of complex stories to follow here: their personal relationship as it emerges in the eighty-odd letters he sent to her between 1899 and 1903; their working relationship while coauthoring a book as represented in these same letters; and the entanglement between these personal and professional concerns as one sort of letters was getting converted, or rewritten, into another—the published epistles that constitute the fictional *Kempton-Wace Letters*. We can detect traces of their contending for power by carefully examining the novel itself, particularly when we analyze how a coherent narrative comes to be jointly constructed out of the letters that London composed and Strunsky composed in their respective guises as Herbert Wace and Dane Kempton. But given London's lifelong inclination to use himself (and his comrades) as the subjects of his texts, it makes more sense to begin by reading his private correspondence with Strunsky to appreciate how he positioned himself as a writer in relation to her own formidable intellectual presence.

His letters to her develop through a number of successive stages, beginning with his initial exchanges (from late 1899 to mid-1900, when they began their collaborative project) in which he largely speaks in highly idealistic terms about literature and literary values. Following these were less idealistic, if more intimate, exchanges (from late 1900 to early 1902) about their book in progress; a time of intense passion (early 1902 to mid-1902) as their book neared completion and he left for England; and the aftermath of their love (late 1902 to mid-1903), a period when their novel was being prepared for publication (May 1903), soon after which London fell in love with another woman—his future wife, Charmian.[16]

From his very first letter to Strunsky, London's mail is strongly inflected by gender, assuming for himself and his new reader a subject position in sharp contrast to the chummy, practical sort of fellowship apparent in the letters he was sending to his aspiring writer friend Cloudesley Johns during this same time. The letters to Johns exchange tips about the writing game viewed fundamentally as a profession and discipline, the domain of skilled male workers. Reading these letters between men and then encountering London's first letter to Strunsky dated 19 December 1899, one cannot help but be struck by London's ability to alter his written self-representation so dramatically—a gift for accommodating audiences that he displayed brilliantly throughout his career.

Addressing his new acquaintance as "My dear Miss Strunsky," London begins by presuming a degree of intimacy that depends less on her person than on their mutual love of literature: "Seems as if I have known you for an age—you and your Mr. Browning." In some thirty-three previous letters to Cloudesley Johns trading information about rates of pay, the editorial policies of various magazines, and methods of composition, Mr. Browning is not even mentioned once; the canonical poet's citation in the very first line of his very first letter to Strunsky clearly signifies London's ambition to enter into another sort of discourse, with "Browning" functioning as the code word or coin of the realm for precisely that world which London had never directly known: a middle-/upper-class, genteel, and feminized late-Victorian culture of letters that still dominated American publishing at the turn of the century. A literary celebrity in his own right, Robert Browning circulated through this culture of letters via fan clubs in England and the United States that had been established to honor the man (who died in 1889) and his poetry.

Acutely conscious of being shut out from such a genteel culture, London chooses to emphasize his otherness rather than try to hide it in his early letters to Strunsky. Written just two days later, his second letter (dated 21 December 1899) opens, for instance, with this confession: "Surely am I a barbarian, lacking in cunning of speech and deftness of touch. Perhaps I am only a Philistine. Mayhap the economic man incarnate. At least blundering and rough-shod, lacking even that expression which should properly voice my thoughts." Recalling the painfully strained mannerisms of his earliest literary efforts, London's inverted syntax and quaint diction ("Mayhap") blatantly contradict the uncultured "stamp of self" he is trying to impress on Strunsky; no primitive would write so preciously. While in this letter he goes on (more directly) to claim that "I am like a fish out of water," his concluding image of himself as "a stray guest, a bird of passage, splashing with salt-rimmed wings through a brief moment of your life—a rude and blundering bird" lavishly signals (as if in a bad imitation of an Elizabeth Barrett Browning sonnet) his bid to trade in his brutish naturalism (wolves) for a more domesticated, feminine sort of nature (fish and birds) that he assumes Strunsky must possess. By virtue of her cosmopolitan absorption of Western culture, warmed by the Orient, surely *she* was no Philistine.

But as in the case of the Jewish "Jaky," Strunsky would surprise him. London discovered to his delight the "preposterous" fact that she enjoyed Kipling (see letter dated 27 December 1899). He also learned from early on (29 December 1899) that she was not reluctant to criticize the stories he sent her, so sharply pointing out "where I missed and why" in one story that London humbly responded with, "It is you who are the missionary"—an extravagant bit of praise in stark contrast to the hectoring, bantering, and playfully argumentative tones he often adopted in his letters to his male friends. Clearly Strunsky was not just one of the boys, a paler version of himself, but neither was she the girl London thought she was. The continuing resistance of this "missionary" to London's imposed gender constructions, we shall see, would compel him to reconsider master/slave relations in terms of ideologies of bourgeois love.

The Strunsky-London friendship was further complicated by the fact that beyond her status as "Russian Jewess," Strunsky was also an aspiring writer just like London himself. Whereas such a mutuality of interests produced in his correspondence with Johns mixed feelings of identification, professional commiseration, and competition, with Strunsky London once again registered difference in their positions as writers. Presuming from his very first letter (19 December 1899) to "sum" her up as a "woman to whom it is given to feel the deeps and the heights of emotion in an extraordinary degree," London automatically invests her with "soul"—the "material" needed to make a "career" in writing. What remains to be seen is the question of her drive to succeed or "dig." This (masculine) ambition London encourages directly by praise and indirectly by offering to help her with "the more prosaic but none the less essential work of submitting Ms." A month later (31 January 1900) he would be promoting himself as a self-taught amateur in his autobiographical sketch to Houghton Mifflin, but here he wants to assume the role of an experienced mentor who has already mastered the editorial ropes of the writing profession.

In such a forthright manner London thus imagines in this initial letter—a more intimate sort of letter of inquiry than those he sent publishers—a clear division of labor between the woman's spiritual/emotional natural resources—Strunsky's poetic "material"—and his own prosaic skills at accessing publishing. This gendered division in turn allows him to propose by implication a kind of exchange between writers beyond the enclosed manuscripts that they traded back and forth: as "economic man" he will teach her about "rates, availability, acceptability, etc.," while as Russian Jewess she will help him gain entrance to the "transcendental feeling" that he assumes is invested in her and in her warm appreciation of culture. Thus in his subsequent early letters, London must "throw myself at the mercy of the Court," make Strunsky "uneasy" (21 December 1899) by so nakedly representing himself as a lost soul, "aimless, helpless, hopeless," with "the best . . . stamped out of me" (29 December 1899). In this way he hopes to use her moral authority over him to help convert his spiritual lack (what had been "stamped out") into literary gain (the writer's "stamp of self").

Acting, in effect, as London's Father (or mother) Confessor, Strunsky in turn asks him to be her "taskmaster," spurring her to hard labor—a role he humorously embraces with some relish: "I love power, to dominate my fellows. I shall stand over you with a whip of scorpions and drive you to your daily toil. Like Pharoah [sic] of old, I shall hold you in bondage" (13 February 1900). However playful, London's figuration of himself as pharaoh not only (yet again) fixes Strunsky as Jewish but also anticipates the psychomachy of *The Call of the Wild*—the whipping/clubbing/driving of the dog Buck on trail delivering letters, which culminates in his enslavement to his master's love. London's astonishing bondage metaphor here suggests an equally curious distribution of power between woman and man: the wealthy college student Strunsky knows how to feel, but is unfamiliar with work, whereas poor London knows how to work but has been emotionally brutalized by the social abyss. Writing together, perhaps the two aspiring authors could consummate a joint venture that would make up for what each lacked. And what better subject than heterosexual love, conceived by Western writers from Plato on as a search for lost wholeness?

The intensity of this early correspondence would soon give way to a more pedestrian series of exchanges. But the complex psychic economy of their relationship would remain in place. By 26 December 1900 London had moved from "Miss Strunsky" to "Anna" to "Comrade Mine"— a more intimate form of address that operated, as in his scenario for "a socialist Novel," to merge political and personal relations under the question of possession ("mine"). Although London first met Strunsky at a lecture given in fall 1899 by fellow socialist Austin Lewis and although they shared a deep interest in progressive politics, in his letters to her London rarely addresses the issue directly, preferring instead to treat the subject only as an adjunct to more intimate literary matters.[17] Otherwise we might be inclined to think that London most passionately affirmed his commitment to socialism by falling in love with a socialist. But in another letter (31 July 1900) also referring to Strunsky as "comrade mine," London aims to gloss over the problem of sexual politics as well by insisting that because "a real unity underlaid everything" between them, there could be "no inner conflict" in their friendship. However different, they were equals. Yet a month later (30 August 1900), after they had already decided to collaborate on their book of letters, London is worrying about Strunsky's "impetuous way" and asks that they get together and "map out" the book before they commence, a request that he nervously repeats a few days later (9 September 1900).

With the introduction of their publishing project, the question of control doubles in complexity. For we must not only follow their plans for collaboration as expressed in London's private letters but also examine the master/slave relation as it is fictively rendered in the other set of *Letters*, the philosophical give-and-take between Herbert Wace and his friend Dane Kempton.

I am far more interested in how *The Kempton-Wace Letters* came to be written, as well as how it came to be read in relation to London's break with his wife Bessie Maddern, than I am in the final product itself. Although it is unfair to dismiss the book as "boredom incarnate" as one contemporary reviewer cruelly put it,[18] as a novel of ideas on the nature of love it is hardly compelling, with London (as Herbert Wace) insisting over and over again, from the point of view of a rational scientific materialist, on love as strictly a biological necessity to propagate the species, while Strunsky (as Dane Kempton) was insisting in letter after letter, from the viewpoint of a romantic idealist, on love as a transcendent, poetic fusion of souls—the same part London assumed for her in his early private correspondence.

Such a sharp division between materialist and spiritual notions about love and marriage was hardly startling at the time. In his systems theory analysis of the semantics of love, Niklas Luhmann has suggested how in the course of the nineteenth century choosing partners on the basis of "romantic" love led to "an institutionalized understanding for enraptured passion."[19] This entrenched code was in turn challenged early on in the century by thinkers such as Schopenhauer, who dismissed the ideology of romantic love as a mechanism for social management—a demystification reinforced later in the century (post-Darwin) by evolutionist assumptions about the biological imperatives controlling human behavior, including sexual selection. By the end of the century, when Kempton and Wace begin their fictional debate, romantic ideology has managed to survive, Luhmann argues, but only "at a high cost," its eventual exposure as an illusion. In the new century romantic love, now transfigured, fulfills a more therapeutic function as "the validation of self-portrayal"[20]—the role love finally plays for London in his relation to Strunsky, as we shall see.

Despite its stilted inertia, their novel does progress through a number of variations on this basic debate between idealism and materialism, addressing in turn the evolution of man from "hunter of beasts" to "singer" (43–44), the division of labor in modern and ancient marriage (90–109), the biology of sexual differentiation (110–20), the role and regulation of private passion in a modern secular democracy (154, 188), the persistence of polygamy (175) and wife beating (echoing the discussion in *The People of the Abyss*), self-transcendence via labor (194–95, echoing *The Call of the Wild*), and the difference between women as mates and as mothers (210), among other interesting subjects.[21] But their exchanges never really move toward any dialectical synthesis. They lead instead to a polarized set of simple binary oppositions, labels and slogans that in effect are more rigid, more narrow, and less telling than the complex shifting positions occupied by London and Strunsky in their private correspondence.

A far more promising approach to the novel, as I have been suggesting, focuses less on the content of its ideas than on the imaginative leaps required by London and Strunsky to express them. My interest lies, in other words, on the complicated *relation* between private and public letters, between London as declaring "himself" to Strunsky and as Herbert Wace corresponding with Dane Kempton about love. For London the move from private representation to public is not much of a leap. Lifting verbatim his self-introduction as "economic man" in his very first letter to Strunsky, London novelizes himself as Herbert Wace, a young iconoclastic professor at the University of California at Berkeley hard at work completing a political/sociological treatise entitled "The Economic Man" (148). While there may be a certain amount of wish fulfillment here, London's impersonation of a materially inclined socialist professor on the verge of marriage is certainly not a big stretch, especially because his professed arguments in the book about love as strictly "sex comradeship" (69) so closely resemble the unromantic "bionomic" reasoning he used to talk himself into marrying Bessie Maddern (on 7 April 1900, the publication date of *The Son of the Wolf*) amid his charged epistolary commerce with Strunsky.

But Strunsky's leap is another matter. In an astounding move whose origins we really have no way of knowing, she becomes a he, Dane Kempton, of Anglo-Saxon extraction, living in England, and, better still, an older father figure for Wace. This gender shift has profound implications. First, by playing Kempton, Strunsky continues the role of moral "missionary" that London assumed for her in their private letters, but now with the additional imaginative burden of literalizing that position in the embodied figure of a surrogate "foster-father" (12). Second, by shifting personal pronouns from "she" to "he," Strunsky must in effect give up her side of the equation, displace her growing emotional investment in her writing partner onto a more abstract debate *about* love in which an intellectual oedipal struggle stands in for heterosexual passion. Third, given this imaginary philosophic parry and thrust between two men, the voice of the engaged woman virtually drops out, deferred until the end of the book. The ostensible object of this ongoing father-son exchange, the imaginary fiancée Hester Stebbins, emerges in her own voice (via Strunsky) only at the novel's close to write the final two fictional letters: a "Dear Herbert" letter (as Strunsky wrote London in the East End), and a final note addressed to Dane Kempton explaining why she broke off the marriage.

As far as possible we must carefully try to coordinate the timing of London and Strunsky's private mail with the progressive composing of their public *Letters*—how Strunsky decided in November 1902 to rewrite that "Dear Herbert" letter, for example, shortly after she had sent London his own "Dear Jack" one.[22] But for now I want to call attention to a sort of confusion on London's part between these two forms of writing. Like the blurring in *The People of the Abyss* between London the author and London the city, here the question concerns which sort of "letters" are under consideration. When London somewhat vaguely writes her that "by your letter I see more clearly than ever what a mess the whole thing has been," quotes two lines from the novel, and then comments, "O Anna, it is all so unjust!" (15 November 1900), their professional affairs threaten to spill over into their personal ones. At another point in their correspondence he addresses her directly as "Dane Kempton" ([? March 1902], p. 287). That London might be more unclear than Strunsky on this issue makes sense given the relative ease with which he could slip in and out of Wace, as opposed to Strunsky's more daring and difficult impersonation of Kempton.

As in all his early work, London would seem to court this confusion between private feelings and public texts precisely insofar as such a conflation served to energize his writing. To publish emotions would allow him at once to command his words and be commanded by them, to elide the differences between submission and control. In his enthusiastic initial response (15 September 1900) to her first Kempton letter, for example, London speculates that "the very realization of our personalities will not permit us to wander from the predestined course," but it is a bit unclear whether he is talking about the "personalities" of the authors or the characters. This ambiguity would seem to be cleared up a few sentences later when he insists that "the living breathing souls we have created shall master us, and dictate to us, mere instruments of their manifestation." Yet he would then seem to take a little of that mastery into his own hands when he admits to Strunsky that he slightly revised her prose, only to assure her that "I must not cramp you" and that "we must be ourselves. So see, girl, that whatever alterations I make, I make with this understanding." Be yourself, (Russian Jewish) girl, when fictively acting as my (white) father. Such a twisted notion of laissez-faire inspiration quickly turns to anxious excitement emerging again from London's desire to guide the plot. He suggests to Strunsky that she not give too much away about Kempton but let him be "goaded" through "love" and "fear" of Wace—"the madness of position" taken by the young man—"to lay naked before us his most sacred possession."

Presumably that "goading" would be done by Wace himself—or rather by London acting for him. But Strunsky, acting for Kempton, had ideas of her/his own. As hinted in his first letter to his foster son, Kempton would in good time disclose a "sacred possession," but less by virtue of the son's prodding from a position of "madness" than by the father's desire to shake up the son. The question, of course, both in the book and in their letters about the book, centers on control: in an epistolary novel jointly constructed by written exchanges, who is responsible for the course of the plot? How does a coherent narrative take shape between letters, as it were, under such a collaborative experiment? In plotting, knowledge—made manifest, withheld, or deferred—is power; being herself, Strunsky introduces the matter of Kempton's "sacred possession" on her own terms and in a way that strives to transform their bland rehearsal of abstract ideas into a familial drama—a more compelling, more tangible site to explore competing ideologies of love.

Strunsky takes the initiative here to particularize familial roles perhaps because her imagined gendering in the novel is so problematic. Although in the penultimate draft of the novel Dane Kempton signed his first letter to Wace as "your friend," in the final draft Strunsky replaced "friend" with "devoted father," presumably to bolster an identity already rendered suspect.[23] In the opening paragraph of this initial letter, Kempton had announced that Herbert's impending marriage gave him "pride in your fulfillment, more as a mother would, I think, and she your mother" (1). Kempton's (trans)parent gender crossing persists in the novel until Wace's very last letter, in which the wayward son bid farewells to "you dear old fluttery, mothery poet father" (243). Such provocative moments threaten to erase altogether the distinction between letters and *Letters*, laying all too bare London's multiplying desire for Strunsky as mother/father/mate—the parental authority and missionary which he never knew and which he struggled to invent in his frozen Northland landscapes peopled with American Indian brides and patriarchs.

To stabilize the epistolary fiction—to keep it such—Strunsky adds familial drama into the novel's plot at three key junctures that sharply interrogate Wace's motives for marriage: first, Kempton's admission to a buried love of his own, a "sacred possession" that turns out to be his unrequited passion for Wace's own dead mother; second, young Wace's subsequent confession, prodded by Kempton, of romantic first love; and finally, Hester Stebbins's rejection (as a kind of punishment) of Wace as a heartless suitor—a confirmation of Kempton's idealist views on marriage and proof in effect that the father, not the son, was right all along.

These simple but highly charged plot turns need to be read with some care, because they suggest how the Kempton-Wace debate, beneath all its philosophical posturing about the nature of love, has more urgently been exploring the significance of the family in the construction of such ideologies. Both Herbert and Hester are described as parentless from an early age, the bachelor Dane Kempton having raised Wace as a surrogate son after his parents died. His sister Barbara (invented by Strunsky) assumes only a secondary role, exemplifying for Kempton a true marriage based on romantic love. Fulfilling the Old Testament injunction to leave the father and take a husband in his stead, the coming marriage of Hester and Herbert, then, will reconstitute the missing family, with husband and wife now expected to play parental parts as well. But Strunsky's revelation (55) of Wace's dead mother Ellen as Kempton's own unrequited love suddenly adds another dimension to the familial drama, introducing a second triangle long submerged in the past—dead biological father, dead mother, and Kempton as a rival lover who was Herbert's current age when he fell madly in love with Ellen and lost out to Herbert's eventual father. Rehearsing "An Odyssey of the North" (1899) and anticipating *The Sea-Wolf* (1904), this triangle of woman and two rival lovers complements the novel's more philosophical and sedate triangulated exchanges between sage Dane, young Herbert, and earnest Hester.

The relation between these two triangles is complex indeed, further complicated by the London-Strunsky friendship itself. Resisting the imposed role of sage father, Strunsky endows Kempton with (remembered) life as a vigorous young lover. She thereby partially transforms discourse about love between two men into a love story between a man and a woman, who as Herbert's dead mother affords Kempton the chance to channel his unconsummated lost passion into a passionate defense of transcendental romance. Bringing the mother Ellen back from buried memories, Strunsky gives an edge to the intellectual father-son oedipal rivalry. In a gesture that matches London's own habit of linking ideas directly to personal experience, Strunsky affirms that the moral authority with which Kempton speaks stems from his own love, not merely borrowed philosophical abstraction. By inserting Ellen so forcefully into the plot, Strunsky additionally makes up for the relative invisibility of the intended Hester, letting the dead mother centrally motivate the past narrative as a way of compensating for the fiancée's peripheral status as a disembodied object of epistolary exchange between father and son in the present.

From London's early Northland tales to *The Call of the Wild*, females function mainly to affirm bonding and rivalry between males; compelled to play one of those men—a father, no less—in her fictive collaboration with London, Strunsky in effect comments on this patriarchal traffic in women, complicating London's triangular schemes by giving voice to the woman. In so doing she helps turns a plodding exchange of inert ideas, a treatise designed to showcase London's philosophical pretensions, into a work of imagination—a novel.[24]

The revelation of Kempton's "sacred possession" Ellen also provokes Wace near the end of the book (207–11) into an intimate personal disclosure of his own, as he confesses to his father a series of three early romantic passions that ostensibly help account for his current skeptical

Male Call

materialism: his worshipful first love as a fifteen-year-old for a professor's "coquette" daughter (aged twenty-two); his physical, "elemental" lust at twenty for "a mad, wanton creature, wonderful and unmoral and filled with life to the brim"; and, finally and most dramatic, a more mature passion for "another man's wife, a proud-breasted woman, the perfect mother." In a phrase that uncannily echoes his dedication to *The God of His Fathers*, Wace/London goes on to sing the praise of this unrequited mother-lover: "So long as there are such women on this earth, that long may we keep faith in the breed of men" (210).

Let us move for a moment from the novel back to the pair of novelists. Having safely transposed his own recent status as husband (to Bessie Maddern) onto another man's wife, London fictively enables this forbidden, "proud-breasted woman" to become a version of Strunsky herself, just as Strunsky in imagining Ellen as Kempton's long-lost love transparently transformed herself into the mother of Herbert and Jack, dead but not entirely forgotten. "Oh, Dane," he writes in the novel to Kempton (Strunsky), "she was glorious, but she was another man's wife. Had I been living unartificially, in a state of nature, I would certainly have brained her husband (a really splendid fellow), and dragged her off with me shameless under the sky. . . . As it was, I yearned dumbly and observed the conventions" (211). No "closet naturalist," Wace in experiencing such intense frustration can thus speak "authoritatively" about the need "to substitute reasoned foresight and selection for the shortsighted and blundering selection of Mother Nature" (211). As in the case of his foster father, unrequited love, not logic, dictates the "madness" of his position in this debate. The scentific materialist is exposed for the failed romantic that he is, leading Wace (London), as Niklas Luhmann's analysis has suggested, to a more modern preoccupation with heterosexual love primarily as a source for self-validation.

It is difficult to determine when, exactly, this confessional passage late in the novel was composed. But presumably London had already sent his private version to Strunsky on 26 December 1900, a letter that marks for London a desperate deepening of their "white beautiful friendship." Beginning by confessing "the blues," a mood he always measured by his inability to do "a stroke of work," London goes on, apparently more impersonally, to bemoan the tyranny of the masses: "I grow, sometimes, almost to hate the mass, to sneer at dreams of reform. To be superior to the mass is to be the slave of the mass. The mass knows no slavery; it is the task master"—the same phrase Strunsky had used earlier in the year (13 February 1900) requesting London's literary guidance. As in his plot sketch for "a socialist Novel," London in this letter also draws an idiosyncratic connection between social and sexual politics, as he then makes explicit:

"But how does this concern you and me? Ah, does it not concern us? We may refuse not to speak, yet we speak brokenly and stumblingly—because of the mass. . . . I remember, now, when I was free. When there was no restraint, and I did what the heart willed. Yes, one restraint, the Law; but when one willed, one could fight the law, and break or be broken. But now, one's hands are tied, one may not fight, but only yield and bow the neck. After all, the sailor on the sea and the worker in the shop are not so burdened. . . .

I could almost advocate a return to nature this dark morning. . . . What you have been to me? I am not great enough or brave enough to say. This false thing, which the world would call my conscience, will not permit me. But it is not mine; it is the social conscience, the world's, which goes with the leg-bar and chain."

The Northland's law of club and fang, the Law of the Father inscribed by letters and internalized as self-discipline, has turned into something far more devious and difficult to combat for London: the bourgeois institution of marriage, those iron conventions that have transformed Herbert Wace into such a cold, rational materialist. Although in the white silence of the Yukon he was naturally free to imagine men on trail ravishing Indian brides, in the Southland London felt compelled (along with Strunsky herself, presumably) to obey the codes of civilization, explicitly treating the subject of marital infidelity only in his last completed novel, *The Little Lady of the Big House* (1916). From this point in their collaboration until London left for England in the summer of 1902 to dive headfirst into the abyss, the law of marriage would loom large as a prohibitory force, calling into question London's faith in self-mastery. More and more urgently during this period, London would be compelled to redirect his desire for Strunsky into slavish work (the joint making of *The Kempton-Wace Letters*, among other projects in progress), producing as a result some of his most powerful pieces of writing (the second and third volumes of those Northland tales), including a series of letters to Strunsky herself that explore the problem of love far more intensely than their veiled, epistolary fictional counterpart. From "Comrade Mine," Strunsky would be addressed as "My Little Collaborator" (24 July 1901) and simply "Dear You" (3 October 1901 and afterward), while London would begin to sign his letters as "Sahib" or "Your very miserable Sahib" (7 June 1902)—a charged name combining intimacy, formality, and exoticism that functioned to contain the multiple tensions of their developing love for each other.

Alternating with more mundane, informative letters about their collaborative project, these letters address a number of intimate concerns—what could be shared between two people so different as were they (3 April 1901), how such a "white beautiful friendship" was to continue, and the relation between internal impulses and external dictates. To cite just one especially remarkable letter (11 February 1902) that begins with this question of external "dictations," London prefaces a defense of his decision to witness an execution with a passionate outburst that uses her protest against his decision to sharpen and to validate his own sense of his manhood.

London's letter takes him far beyond the ostensible matter of a particular criminal's sanctioned hanging by the state to explore the deepest psychological reaches of that state. Asserting that "the woman in me pleads, but my manhood reasons," London (in anticipation of the second half of *The Sea-Wolf*) internalizes Strunsky's plea as a feminine principle within himself that must be conquered if London is to "secretly respect myself." The Kempton-Wace debate has turned inward, with London seemingly playing both parts. Although in this letter and others sent to Strunsky during this period London tries to understand the "paradox" that their intimacy is based on difference, that they are "coldly independent of each other," "neither of us compromising, neither of us giving over or diminishing," the very articulation of this difference threatens his autonomy, so that he must quickly turn away from her, convert their power struggle into an occasion for self-mastery: "Do you catch me? I know not why, but the thing so shapes itself that it is not you I must face and consider, but myself. All that I have stood for, and preached and thought (which is I), rises up before me to judge." Implying that Strunsky could not fully understand him because she is a woman, London goes on in a powerful passage to identify his "inmost self" specifically with his life among men, moving from their heterosexual love to a kind of self-love manifesting itself via homoerotic companionship, imagined by London as the grounds for narcissistic projection:

How can I tell you?—tell you of the things slowly and subtly grown in me, of the long upbuilding of what I am, of my last and inmost self from which I cannot get away. Why to tell you this, were to have you live with me from the cradle, to dream with me my boyhood's fancies, to do things with my hands and face things with my face, to buck with men, to think as I have thought at masthead or solitary wheel, to drink long nights and days away, to sleep under blanket with men that were MEN, to learn to grow sick at cowardice and to honor a brave man above an honest man, to honor men unafraid—and how can you understand when I cannot tell you.

Suggesting yet another meaning for "buck," this passage clearly looks forward to the rough love play between male dog and male master in *The Call of the Wild* (composed later that same year), as well as the brutal intimacy between men as dramatized in *The Sea-Wolf*, as I will discuss in the next chapter. But for now I want to emphasize how the question of (self) judgment, internalized as manly conscience, takes on enormous import for London as a sign of his standing in society in general, an issue triggered by his defiant desire to witness a legal death. The intensity with which he argues against Strunsky's fearful concern that the execution will coarsen him suggests how he has made their illicit and unconsummated love into an occasion to accept, as a man's man, the letter of the "Law"—carried by London (with a capital *L*) well beyond the institution of marriage to encompass the operations of the state itself: "When you dare to walk home by sidewalks lighted by the Law, then are you a party to the crime committed by the Law when it hangs a man. . . . By living in this community of people you help support the Law which this community makes. . . . I, for one, stay with it, and staying with it I am neither afraid nor ashamed of it. . . . Not that I hold a hanging above your favor . . . but that there is something else which I must hold above all if I would hold you or anyone or anything at all." So ends this striking letter, a confession to Strunsky that imagines their frustrated love, his own quest for self-respect, and the juridical practice of the modern state as all operating under the same inexorable Law.

In practical terms, London's fearless embrace of the Law gets translated into his naturalist code of ethics, which in turn is expressed by his compulsion to work. In a brusque letter to Strunsky written just a week after this confession, London complains that he is "head under heels" with moving, whereas in a 2 June 1902 brief note to his writing partner he similarly protests that he is "head over heels in work," with "work" clearly substituting for "love" in the colloquialism. As testimonials to his productive prowess, London proudly details to Strunsky word counts, displaced tokens of his affection. But it would be a bit misleading to imply, using a crude psychoanalytic model, that writing for London during this period served simply as a sublimation for his sexual desire, since as I have contended, Strunsky and London fell in love in the very process of collaborating on their novel as much as their collaboration served to channel their passion. The relation between life and letters is not causal (one way or the other) but homologous.

More to the point, this writing in (but against) the Law developed concurrently during London's white friendship with Strunsky, with *The Kempton-Wace Letters* as the published consequence of their relationship. Referring from early on to the "creation" and "grow[th]" of "the whole thing" (15 September 1900 and late September, respectively), the novel for London thus represented the tangible public product of their partnership, a surrogate child. On the verge of his departure for England, London can finally declare his love openly in terms of their newly completed book: "We've done something, little one, you & I. I hold you in my arms" (18 July 1902). As London explained to Cloudesley Johns two years earlier in accounting for the origins of the epistolary fiction, arguing with a brilliant "Russian Jewess" about love, immediately considering whether such an intimate debate might be "worth publishing" as a novel, then assuming characters and throwing "in a real objective love element" (how "real" London would only too soon discover), and exchanging more correspondence about these letters are all analogous activities, interchangeable versions of getting into print—continuous mail delivery. What to do with intense conversations (spiritual and intellectual) with a beautiful, exotic genius? Invent a fictional scenario for your talk, write it up between you, and get it out. No communication is too intimate for publication.

London's reaction while in England to Strunsky's personal rejection offers the clearest indication of this tendency to subsume books and people under the single governance of publishing. Responding to the news that London's wife Bessie was again pregnant—a real child as opposed to the textual fruits of their literary intercourse—Strunsky accused London of insulting her love by lying to him about Bessie, presumably the fact that he was still having sexual relations with her despite his loving Strunsky.[25] London angrily responded from England with a pair of distraught letters (25 August and 28 August 1902) dramatically acknowledging that "the Sahib is dead, and forgiven as the dead are forgiven." After mentioning his latest word production for *The People of the Abyss*, London bitterly goes on in the first letter to quote his comrade's words back to her, set off by quotation marks to render them a kind of fiction. Telling her to "work back nine months," London a bit cryptically alludes to their having "held speech upon a very kindred subject," a vow they jointly made that London now reads as a promise to withhold news from her, not as a pact to remain celibate, as his writing partner charged, presumably out of jealousy.

Collaboration would seem to have its limits; treating their shared speech in terms of love, professional partnership, and Dane Kempton's "sacred possession" all mixed together, London can quickly move on to the next bit of mail awaiting his delivery. Although he complains near the end of the first letter that if he didn't love her then "the thing" they spent months on would be "purposeless," by the end of the second letter to her, London is enthusiastically describing his current *Abyss* writing. A month later, still in England, he opens another letter (28 September 1902) by proudly announcing, "The book is finished!" then apologizes for his harsh behavior during their breakup, and closes with "and now it is all over and done with. So be it. Henceforth I shall dream romances for other people and transmute them into bread & butter." After reiterating the fact of closure ("Did I tell you I had finished the book?"), London ends with a request: "Continue writing me, please. My mail will be forwarded."

Puzzled by the ambiguities of this letter, critics have debated whether the "it" that London has sealed for good refers to the "romance" of his love or his socialist descent into the abyss.[26] But for London, what's the difference? Having the book of love closed on him, as it were, London furiously writes to finish off his own volume, knowing his mail will always be forwarded, his past safely behind him as he races to obey yet another summons (what would literally become *The Call of the Wild*). Rebuffed in love, the male ego rebounds to meet its next challenge; if London ever stopped to consider fully the consequences of his writing, then he might not have been able to continue working so hard and so long.

Perhaps giving under the strain of playing London's father (both in and out of fiction), Strunsky for her part decided in the fall of 1902 to write a preface to their novel, a long series of letters written by Hester Stebbins representing the woman's own painful perspective on rivalry, this time female. Taking her hint from London's own confession in the novel of an earlier forbidden love, Strunsky introduces yet another triangle by having Hester contemplate the married woman who first captured Herbert's heart. Never published, this prologue threatens to open up, largely with the slip of a crucial single word, what London would confine to the fictional book itself; for Hester in her prefatory letters calls Herbert "Sahib," the personal code name that had previously signified the most intense moments of their epistolary intimacy outside the novel. For Strunsky this collaborative project could not be finished so cleanly or neatly.

While Strunsky was still trying to revise and rewrite their relationship, London turned his attention to promotion, making sure Macmillan would "push" the book. Although London claimed to his publisher Brett that he was "thoroughly in accord with this plan" (11 December 1902), his response to Strunsky a week earlier (6 December 1902) violently criticized the idea of a prologue, which by foregrounding her love would "destroy" the book as "letters on love" and turn it into a "broken-backed, unconsecutively argued hodge-podge." In the end, the two men—London and Brett (like Wace and Kempton)—joined forces to shut Hester/Strunsky off, explaining their decision to remove the offending prologue for business as well as aesthetic reasons. Experienced professionals in the writer's market, the two men understood the "general reading public" (see London's letter dated 20 January 1903) in ways that the soulful Russian Jewess could not. Although from the start of their relationship Strunsky had tried on occasion to resist this gendered division of labor, here she complied, signing off on the unpublished prologue, some fifty years later, by admitting that she was grateful for their good advice. From the long retrospect of 1958, clearly a woman's pretext did not belong in the turn-of-the-century philosophical debate between father and son.[27]

Sharing his promotional concerns with Strunsky as their book was readied for its May 1903 publication, London would make the textuality of their affair explicit: "No, Dear Anna, I am neither in joy nor sorrow. I closed certain volumes in my life on a certain day in London. These volumes will remain closed. In them I shall read no more" (letter dated 20 December 1902). It is important to see how these sort of book metaphors that control their relationship are not cynically imposed by London after the fact of her rejection but run throughout their friendship, such as when he bluntly encouraged her shortly before he left for England to advertise herself: "All the world's copy, for that matter, and you are exceptionally good copy. I would ask no better" (1 April 1902). Although this curious praise may strike us as demeaning or mocking, for London to see and be seen as "good copy" represents the truest validation for himself as well as of his love for Strunsky.

White beautiful friendships and the emotions that accompany them make sense only if they are published; everything is fair game for publication, and nothing is immune from mail call, for only mail call lets you feel connected and in charge. In the very *first* letter to "My dear Miss Strunsky," filled with polite formalities and feminine decorum, London ends his cheeky efforts at summing her up with an astonishing admission to this effect. In a request for face-to-face communication that would in turn lead quickly to their working together on *The Kempton-Wace Letters*, London writes, "Candidly, I may some time steal you or certain portions of you for exploitation between covers, unless you hasten to get yourself copyrighted." Although from the moment of his marriage the following April London felt prohibited from exploiting Strunsky between bedcovers, book covers could be just as good or better, depending on who would hold the copyright.[28]

Male Call

The flip side of the urge to publish is not privacy (no longer possible in the new century's writing game, it would seem) but dramatized anonymity. To help mark the closure of their affair, London embraced a proposal by George Brett, conveyed through Strunsky (who had recently returned from New York) to bring out *The Kempton-Wace Letters* anonymously, with the hope that concealing the book's authorship would fuel speculation and spur sales. Insofar as a blank author's page was clearly preferable to an acknowledged collaboration with an unknown, the Lone Wolf's trademark would just this once be withheld for a potentially more rewarding show of secrecy. Anonymity would heighten interest in the mystery of authorship. While the book never reached sales close to *The Call of the Wild* or *The Sea-Wolf*, the promise of a roman à clef was enough to pique the curiosity of many readers, even those reviewers who understood such anonymity as a marketing gimmick—a strategy "with an eye to some extra advertising," as one early July 1903 notice observed. Turning from the abstract contents of the novel, reviewers mused (as I also have done) on the more compelling question of the novel's production—single-author theories versus theories of collaboration, speculation about the gender of the writer(s), educated guesses (based on analyzing literary style) as to the "real" identities of Wace and Kempton. One reviewer goes so far as to propose and then reject Jack London as the novelist, sensibly concluding that "he would hardly pose as an anonym."[29]

Although the story behind the novel's authorship was gradually leaked to the press by London himself, presumably in yet another marketing ploy (as one review intimated), the book suddenly assumed full responsibility for its authors in August 1903, when the separation and impending divorce between London and Bessie Maddern became public news. The prohibitory force of the Law that London had so vigorously interrogated in his love letters to Strunsky had now taken on a literal meaning. In filing restraining orders and complaints for divorce the following summer, London's wife would use *The Kempton-Wace Letters* to justify her legal actions, claiming what the press had already publicized: that the iconoclastic materialist views on marriage expressed in the novel by Herbert Wace were actually London's own and that London had become romantically involved with another woman, his writing comrade Anna Strunsky.

This somewhat contradictory pair of explanations circulated in newspapers during the summer of 1903, although journalists had got the wrong woman, for London by then had recovered from Strunsky's 1902 rebuff to fall in love with another friend and soul mate, his future wife Charmian Kittredge. But the truth of London's love affairs is less interesting here than their press coverage; following rapidly on the heels of the sensational publication of *The Call of the Wild* in July 1903, news of the celebrity's marital problems would serve as a "terrific boom" for *Kempton-Wace* sales, as one reviewer cynically remarked. No longer anonymous, London is now understood to have written "the End of His Own Love Story," one headline blared, while his coauthor Strunsky is introduced to the public as "the Champion of Passion." Shifting back and forth between transparent text and equally transparent author, journalists confirmed what the writer himself had always insisted as part of his quest for recognition: that "Jack London's Career Affects his Writing," as one typically understated British newspaper account politely put it.[30]

To friends and to George Brett, London protested that his "conscience" was clean and that while his fiction was one thing, his life was another.[31] But surely the now famous author couldn't have been too surprised at the gossipy treatment of *The Kempton-Wace Letters* by the press, given the logic of his own lifelong efforts at self-promotion. Whether or not Strunsky ever saw it, a typed poem tipped into London's own personal copy of the novel, titled "The Passionate Author to His Love" and playfully signed "Puck" (presumably a post-Sahib incarnation), announces London's desire to deliver himself up for publication.[32] In all its complexity of tone and range of allusion, let it stand as the best commentary on the collaborative making of the book.

> Come write to me and be my Love,
> And we will all the profits prove
> That furnace sighings, signed and sealed,
> And vows epistolary yield.
>
> Empty the coffers of thy heart;
> Its every throb and thrill impart;
> Search every secret, holy nook;
> 'Twill make, Sweetheart, a lovely book.

And I will make thee vow for vow,
And in my letters mention how
By thoughts of thee I'm sweetly harried,
Despite the fact that I am married.

Thou'lt write how to my arms thou'dst fly
If 'twere not for the legal tie;
And I how straight I'd fly to thee
If from my fetters I were free.

These tender things we'll put in print.
Sweetheart, there may be millions in't!
The public simply can't resist
"Love Letters of a Socialist."

We'll turn our passion to account,
And realize a large amount.
If of the plan thou dost approve
Come write to me and be my Love.

6

Between Men of Letters : Homoerotic
Agon in *The Sea-Wolf*

The Sea-Wolf culminates London's intense drive for prestige, expressed throughout his first decade's work in terms of various master/slave power relations that threaten to thwart his quest for individuation. The tangled relations between mastery, subjugation, and identity, I have suggested throughout this book, center for London on the problem of masculinity, which manifests itself in his early writing by way of a number of formalized ideological structures—the business of publishing (or mail call), racial kinship (the Northland tales), professionalism (*The Call of the Wild*), social class and nationality (*The People of the Abyss*), and institutions of love and marriage (*The Kempton-Wace Letters*).

Such categories organize difference for London to help him fix identity: white, professional, American, husband, and son. But in *The Sea-Wolf* these markers are only partially available to mediate manhood, which London is compelled to confront more directly, imagining men at sea acting with and against one another without relying on clearly recognizable social scripts. While the novel retains traces of London's earlier interests in race, labor, and social class, these issues remain overshadowed by London's main concern—what it means to be a man in the company of men. Particularly in the narrative's initial absence of women as objects of triangulated desire and exchange, London's sea story reconfigures masculinity in far more daring, unstable, and dangerous forms than does his previous work, pushing him into unfamiliar terrain (much stranger than his invented Northland), where manhood can no longer be entirely understood in relation to patriarchal order or narcissistic self-projection. Domination and submission in this new sort of community must undergo continual revision, as "masculine" and "feminine" roles in the novel continually shift positions, getting defined and redefined in relation to the question of power. For this brief, uncertain period in his career—the first half of 1903—London finds his manhood, homoerotically charged, within interactions between different sorts of men possessing different sorts of strengths and weaknesses. Only in the guise of a dog story, Buck's love for his master John Thornton, could London previously represent any such passion between males.

In his recent revisionary account *Gay New York*, historian George Chauncey has examined sexual practices among working-class men in the early twentieth century, demonstrating decisively how "manliness in this world was confirmed by other men and in relation to other men, not by women." Dissociating gender performance from sexual practice, Chauncey locates within these relations an interplay between effeminate (submissive) and masculine (dominant) males. He argues that "the determinative criterion in the identification of men as fairies was not the extent of their same-sex desire or activity (their 'sexuality'), but rather the gender persona and status they assumed." Dominant males conversely could gain more status, become *more* manly, by physically taking fairies—"sexual activity defined not by the gender of their partner but by the kind of bodily pleasures that partner could provide." The logic that makes "sexual orientation" ("hetero" versus "homo") the norm for understanding gender is a remarkably recent middle-class invention firmly entrenched in American culture only after the 1920s, Chauncey concludes.[1]

In his analysis of this turn-of-the-century, all-male "erotic system" of power relations, Chauncey singles out "three groups of men who were exceptionally disengaged from the family and neighborhood systems that regulated normative sexuality: seamen, prisoners, and the immense number of transient workers (or hoboes) who passed through American cities before the 1920s."[2] This trio of fraternal roles matches perfectly a series of identities and episodes at the center of London's sexually formative years, 1893–94: his shipping out to sea at the age of seventeen, tramping with Kelly's Army of the Unemployed the following year, and subsequent jailing in the Erie County Penitentiary for vagrancy, where he confessed to being the "meat" of a "powerfully-muscled man"—"a brute-beast" whose eyes nonetheless revealed to the youth "humor and laughter and kindliness."[3] What most biographers take as London's initiation at the age of seventeen and eighteen into naturalism's law of club and fang thus suggests a more pointed set of sexual introductions into this all-male world of power relations, where prestige, not "heterosexuality," determined one's manhood. In composing *The Sea-Wolf* ten years later, London, on the brink of publishing success and with his marriage failing, chose to revisit this world to test his own status as a now mature man.

Two letters from London to his publisher George Brett help fix the boundaries of this period of writing.[4] On the verge of beginning the novel, London wrote to Brett on 20 January 1903 detailing his plans for a new sea story filled with "adventure, storm, struggle, tragedy, and love." This (heterosexual) love will be present from the start, London insisted:

> The love-element will run throughout, as the man & woman will occupy the center of the stage pretty much all of the time. . . . The human motif underlying all, will be what I may call *mastery*. My idea is to take a cultured, refined, super-civilized man and woman . . . and throw them into a primitive sea-environment where all is stress & struggle and life expresses itself, simply, in terms of food & shelter. . . . The superficial reader will get the love story & the adventure; while the deeper reader will get all this, plus the bigger thing lying underneath.

London is describing a classic naturalist fable to follow on the heels of his nearly completed *The Call of the Wild*.

But this is certainly not *The Sea-Wolf*, at least not its first half. Presumably still under the sway of the Buck-Thornton bond and recalling his intimate experiences with men ten years earlier, London deferred the introduction of his heroine Maud Brewster until precisely midway through the narrative. He thereby created a far different sort of story than he first imagined, with "a primitive sea-environment" defined less in terms of a struggle for "food & shelter" than a solitary man struggling for "mastery" against other, less civilized men, especially the satanic ship's captain, Wolf Larsen. If there is a "bigger thing lying underneath" for deeper readers to discover, it will be another sort of "love-element" that London construed for himself in the absence of a woman.

The second letter to Brett was sent six months later on 24 July 1903, with "the sea novel about half-done." Still operating in the proleptic mode, as he was wont to do with Brett, London promised that even though he did not "know what to make of it . . . it will be utterly different in theme and treatment from the stereotyped sea novel." As in his previous letter, here too London mistakes his own intentions, for the introduction of Maud at this point in his composition functions strictly to stereotype, by way of conventional gender categories, an otherwise unbearable growing tension/intimacy between Wolf Larsen and the novel's narrator, Humphrey Van Weyden. *The Sea-Wolf* thus sharply divides into two halves marked by the entrance of a generic woman—a division that is identified only to be misrecognized by London, who in writing his sea novel operated under the same sort of "savage repression" that Larsen and his crew operate under in their "new and elemental environment" at sea.[5]

In the pages that follow I will closely examine this "elemental environment," especially in terms of *The Sea-Wolf*'s divided plot structure. First, I will establish a network of contexts for the novel in relation to precursor texts, London's life, his own previous writing, as well as his growing ambitions, showing how London worked these contexts into the overdetermined opening chapter of the novel itself. Then I will turn to the first half of the narrative, focusing on the interaction between Van Weyden and Larsen. Finally I will look briefly at a series of events in London's life during the summer of 1903—his falling in love with Charmian Kittredge, the reception of *The Call of the Wild*, and his being pressured by *Century* magazine editor R. W. Gilder to tone down his novel—to suggest how the second half of *The Sea-Wolf* effectively undoes the first half, betraying in the process the narrative's intense homoerotic investment.

That *The Sea-Wolf* entertains such radical possibilities at all may seem a bit surprising, given the utter conventionality of the sea novel at the turn of the century as a popular genre designed to transform boys into men. Along the lines of Dana's *Two Years before the Mast* (1840), Kipling's *Captains Courageous* (1897), Norris's *Moran of the Lady Letty* (1898), and any number of sea narratives by the prolific British writer W. Clark Russell (who had corresponded with London as early as 1892),[6] the plot and characters of *The Sea-Wolf* would seem at first glance to conform perfectly to the familiar literary formula: effete, aristocratic first-person narrator Humphrey Van Weyden suddenly finds himself at sea at the mercy of tyrannical, brutish ship captain Wolf Larsen, who subjugates his captive to a bruising series of initiations whereby the sissy Van Weyden, affectionately dubbed "Hump" by Wolf, is toughened, tested, and ultimately proves himself as a self-reliant man.

But unlike the protagonists of these precursor texts, Van Weyden is no innocent youth in need of a disciplining father. Instead, he is a thirty-five-year-old distinguished literary critic who spends half his time on ship discussing great books and great ideas with his tormentor, whereas during the other half he witnesses graphic violence and gets violently manhandled himself. *The Sea-Wolf* thus enables London to continue the philosophical debate he began with Anna Strunsky in *The Kempton-Wace Letters*, with a crucial difference: the discussion is no longer between surrogate father (a role enacted by Strunsky) and rebellious son contemplating marriage to a third party. Instead, the contest between idealist and materialist is waged in the open between two strong-willed individuals whose intense feelings for each other take the form of high-minded intellectual disputation. Ostensibly feminine, letters turn out to afford yet another way to prove manhood. The Hump-Wolf relation signals London's ambition to write a popular novel of ideas that could at the same time (unlike *The Kempton-Wace Letters*) admit the power of physical intimacy between men. Following the emphasis on corporeal integrity that dominates *The People of the Abyss*, London locates Larsen's materialist philosophy as much in his body as in his words, with the body and speech linked, as we shall see, by way of the mouth—the site in the novel of sexual excitement (oral intercourse) that eludes stereotyped systems of gender.

The peculiar mixture of pretentious bookishness and brutality by which masculinity is interrogated and affirmed in *The Sea-Wolf* distinguishes it in important ways from a novel like *Captains Courageous*, which in depicting the rough adventures of an American millionaire's fifteen-year-old son has more in common with London's early juvenile fiction *The Cruise of the Dazzler* (1902). In so deviating from his coming-of-age literary models, London thus offers a deviant, far more interesting reading of turn-of-the-century American manhood. A postadolescent look at men at sea, *The Sea-Wolf* has bigger fish to fry than showing simply how boys grow up to lead the pack, to assume the patriarchal reins of society. Abandoning the bildungsroman format that traced Buck's development in *The Call of the Wild*, in *The Sea-Wolf* London works by more improvised, open-ended narration that enables quest-romance and questioning conversation to mix together.

To begin to account for the curious combination of dogmatic philosophizing and spectacular violence that fuels his sea novel, we need to consider more generally London's choice of a new field of writing in early 1903, directly following his composition of *The Call of the Wild*. As I have indicated (and what we should have come to expect), autobiography powerfully motivated London's literary interest in the sea, allowing him to replay his 1893 experience sailing and seal hunting on the *Sophie Sutherland*—his own entrance, at the age of seventeen, into the adult world of work. As John Sutherland has shown in detail, London retraces this experience with some exactitude, opening his novel on "this particular January Monday morning," a reference to the same date—Monday, 23 January 1893—that the *Sophie Sutherland* indeed set sail from San Francisco Bay.[7]

Yet more crucial than the actual experiences that closely inform his fictional plotting, the setting of the sea afforded London a chance to revisit the scene of his first triumph as an author, since his life on the *Sophie Sutherland* was itself the basis for London's very first story to get into print, his 1893 award-winning sketch "Story of a Typhoon Off the Coast of Japan." From this originary moment of publication, the scene of the sea reappears at key moments in his early writing, which suggests how by 1903 the vocations of "sailor" and "author" had become closely associated for London. On the verge of international success, with a decade's worth of publishing behind him, the genre of the sea novel thus offered London a chance to tell stories about his own career as a writer— a retrospective process that coincided with London's growing celebrity around 1903, as I discussed in my opening chapter.

London's ambitions for *The Sea-Wolf* extended beyond professional self-revision. By explicitly identifying his narrator Van Weyden as an influential literary critic, actively engaged as the novel opens in adjudicating the reputations of authors such as Edgar Allan Poe, London means to examine his own potential place in Anglo-American letters. Understanding how sea fiction had come to occupy an important position in literary tradition—from Dana, Melville, and Poe to Kipling, Conrad, and Crane—London takes the sea as his subject to gain entrance into this select company. London calls Larsen's ship the *Ghost* precisely to underscore the apparitional presence of past masters in his chosen field of writing, which carried a ready-made cultural capital far greater than anything he could generate from his own imaginary Northland. Repeatedly referring to his new project from the start as simply his "sea novel," London aimed to move beyond magazine stories and even serialized fiction to make a more permanent mark in American letters.

The Sea-Wolf thus represents London's first (and last) bid for canonical status. As I have previously insisted, up to this point in his career London mainly had been concerned with breaking into print, defined as the competitive field of contemporary professionals struggling for access to publication. But drawing primarily on Milton and Shakespeare by way of *Moby-Dick* (a relatively obscure work in 1903), London tries in *The Sea-Wolf* to effect a merger between mass culture and high art, with Wolf Larsen as a kind of fashionable turn-of-the-century naturalist rendition of Lucifer somewhat akin to today's heavy-metal versions. Yet if Wolf Larsen in the end turns out to be no Captain Ahab, and first-person narrator Van Weyden, surely no Ishmael (and clubbing seals, no hunt for the great white whale), the important differences between these two texts may have less to do with London's artistic limitations than the very way his rendering of quest-romance so unabashedly streamlines and updates a novel like Melville's. Whatever deep anxieties London shares with Melville about manhood, these anxieties hardly extend to the process of composing the novel itself, since London seeks to read and write himself into a literary tradition by way of a benign sort of popularizing rather than an aggressive act of appropriation. For all of its macho pretensions, *The Sea-Wolf* thus offers a model of canon formation that does not wholly depend on oedipal contestation between precursor fathers and sons.

To appreciate the complex interconnections between London's autobiographic experience, his writing career, and his aspirations for the canon, all in relation to representations of homoeroticism in the novel, we must go to a scene at the heart of London's interest in the sea—the traumatic fear of drowning, from which Van Weyden is initially saved and brought aboard the *Ghost*. The scene of drowning recurs with unnerving frequency throughout London's early writing, and not just in narratives explicitly set at sea. His first published tramp tale " 'Frisco Kid's' Story" (1895), for instance, recounts the death by drowning of the Kid's pal Charley to a nameless auditor who turns out to be Charley's distraught father. Some eight years later, while masquerading in *The People of the Abyss* as a tramp himself—an indigent American sailor, no less—London initially imagines the crowds of the East End as a "vast and malodorous sea" that threatens to submerge him in the underclass. And late in *The Call of the Wild*, we can recall that the bad masters Hal, Mercedes, and Charles fall through a hole in the ice to meet their watery demise, whereas in the key episode of *A Daughter of the Snows*, published the previous year (1902), the hero braves icy river rapids to save a stranded mail carrier.

In all these examples, drowning signifies social death, so that being saved from such a fate represents a reprieve from the abyss of failure. Add to these examples the autobiographical account of London's early drunken attempt at suicide by drowning (related in *John Barleycorn*) and we can begin to grasp the powerful hold this scene had on London's imagination: what it meant in terms of his fear that he might never amount to anything, might never make a name for himself. Opening with a scene far more graphic and intense than the similar moment of being swept away that inaugurates the plot of *Captains Courageous*, *The Sea-Wolf* begins by depicting a fog-shrouded collision between a local Bay Area ferry and a "Leviathan" (5) steamboat that plunges the narrator into cold water. As other critics have noticed,[8] this opening trauma closely resembles London's metaphoric drowning in *The People of the Abyss*, but with one important difference. Whereas in his socialist exposé London imagines himself becoming engulfed by the crowd and therefore losing his identity, in *The Sea-Wolf* the threat is inverted: "I was alone. I could hear no calls or cries—only the sound of the waves, made weirdly hollow and reverberant by the fog. A panic in a crowd, which partakes of a sort of community of interest, is not so terrible as a panic when one is by oneself; and such a panic I now suffered. Whither was I drifting? . . . I was alone, floating, apparently, in the midst of a gray primordial vastness" (9).

Here, social death threatens by too much individuation rather than too little. *The Sea-Wolf* thus picks up where *Moby-Dick* left off, with the orphaned narrator awaiting rescue, awaiting reintegration with community after the apocalypse. Humphrey Van Weyden is so panicked by the thought of his isolation, in fact, that he confesses, "I shrieked aloud as the women had shrieked" (9). Later I will look carefully at the role played by those shrieking women in the collision scene leading up to Van Weyden's panic about being submerged in the solitude of the sea. But first we need to consider at some length one more of London's early treatments of drowning—his lurid horror tale "A Thousand Deaths," published in 1899 but written in 1897. Dismissed by most London critics as mere hackwork,[9] this science fiction potboiler carries enormous implications for what I have been calling *The Sea-Wolf*'s postadolescent, post–*Moby-Dick* recovery mode, helping us see what direction Van Weyden's sudden "drifting" might be taking him: what new "community of interest" might soon become available to him.

"A Thousand Deaths" begins briskly in medias res: "I had been in the water about an hour, and cold, exhausted, with a terrible cramp in my right calf, it seemed as though my hour had come. . . . Now I gave up attempting to breast the stream and contended myself with the bitter thoughts of a wasted career, now drawing to a close."[10] Like Van Weyden, this first-person narrator too comes from wealthy, "good, English stock," but unlike his counterpart, this privileged son, who "perpetuated the wildest and most audacious folly," has been "disowned by my people." Forced to leave home, the narrator has embarked on "one long peregrination . . . to find myself at last, an able seaman at thirty, in the full vigor of my manhood, drowning in San Francisco bay because of a disastrously successful attempt to desert my ship." With the exception of this Poe-like imp of the perverse by which the gothic tale's fallen aristocrat has landed in water, the two narratives thus open with virtually identical scenarios: drowning men (not boys) facing premature death, uncertain, lost, floating between two worlds.

Fading in and out of consciousness (like Van Weyden), the narrator is rescued from the bay by "a gentleman's yacht" captained, coincidentally, by his estranged father, who initially fails to recognize the son. In keeping with the tale's overheated gothicism, the father turns out to be a mad scientist bent on using his newly found "assistant" for a series of "delightful" experiments of "cold-blooded cruelty" in which the son is variously killed—by poisoning, strangulation, suffocation, electrocution, and so on—and then revived by the father. When the son reveals his true identity early on, the father responds that since he had given him life, who had better right to take it away? Feigning "unbounded enthusiasm" in this work of his father and his two black henchmen, the narrator gains his revenge by conceiving his own experiment: when he is awakened by "the strident voice of my father" summoning him for another round of torture, the son activates a device that reduces his tormentor to a "fantastic heap" of ash (thus echoing the ending of Poe's horror story "Valdemar"). His revenge exacted, the first-person narrator concludes on a note of release: "A little pile of elementary solids lay among his garments. That was all. The wide world lay before me. My captors were not" (83).

The autobiographical outlines of this graphic patricidal fantasy are painfully clear. Weeks before submitting this story (to *Scribner's*, of all places!), Jack London received a pair of astonishing letters from his presumed father, the itinerant astrologer Professor W. H. Chaney. Strenuously denying that he was his father, Chaney responded to London's inquiries with sufficient vivid bluntness to match the horror tale, offering a number of other possible candidates for London to look up, insisting that he did not "disease" London's mother Flora, nor did she "disease" him, and claiming that he was "impotent at that time, the result of hardship, privation & too much brain-work"—an explanation that carries profound implications for London's own decision, following in Chaney's footsteps, to work by his brain (as a writer) and not by his body.[11]

London's immediate response to Chaney's denial was to mail off "A Thousand Deaths" to one of the most prestigious publications in the country.[12] In a pattern that would continue for the rest of his life, London thus takes a traumatic event in his experience and transparently converts it into the stuff of popular fiction: the astrologer who repeatedly rejects his patrimony becomes the cruel mad scientist, whereas the humiliated, illegitimate son becomes the victim of continual torture who finally gains release by besting the father at his own game. I have traced the story and its autobiographical implications at such length because by choosing to rehearse—as if in repetition-compulsion—the same sequence of drowning, rescue, torture, and release that structures *The Sea-Wolf*, London would seem to be replaying this patricidal fantasy, with Wolf Larsen now occupying the role of the tyrant who denies his son even as he sadistically tortures him. But as I will argue, it is London who will disavow the father in the novel; London makes the opening of *The Sea-Wolf* follow "A Thousand Deaths" so closely precisely to construe Wolf Larsen in contrast to such an oedipal mode of generational strife.

London began interrogating that oedipal model with the publication of "A Thousand Deaths" itself some two years after he initially wrote the story. As we have seen, London's aspirations for a career as a professional writer were effectively coterminous with Chaney's letters of denial. In May, June, and July 1897, the son discovered his illegitimacy, was rebuffed by his presumed biological father, wrote a gothic tale of horror in imitation of Poe (another abandoned son), failed to publish said story, and then left for the Klondike. On his return the next year he composed a series of new stories centering on "The Son of the Wolf." The surname "Chaney" was thus replaced by the designation "Wolf"—the symbolic totemic clan by which London sought to restore his place in patriarchal order. As my chapter on London's three Northland collections has suggested, London reconstructed such an order by successively moving from white sons to white mothers/red wives and finally to tribal elders in an effort to legitimize his manhood—to find a permanent address for his mail.

Yet when we shift from the symbolic content of his stories to their material context, as London himself always did, we discover that "A Thousand Deaths" may have been more vital an affirmation of his standing in patriarchal order than his first "Son of Wolf" stories. While he was starting to compose *The Sea-Wolf* in spring 1903, London published a retrospective account of his apprenticeship that credited "A Thousand Deaths" with saving his (literary) life. Entitled "Getting into Print," this anecdotal advice essay (as I discussed in chapter 1) reenacts a kind of primal scene of publication: an ambitious Northland story ("To the Man on Trail") is deemed to be worth only five dollars, whereas the "hack" horror tale earned the struggling young author forty dollars—a sum that let him continue writing. From such legendary origins, the rest is history. The autobiographical impulse to so dramatize his first "getting into print" while he was composing the sea novel suggests again for London how *The Sea-Wolf* rereads "A Thousand Deaths" in order to allegorize his career as well as his personal rejection by Chaney: life and work connected in this case by the need for recognition by the f/Father. Just as *The Call of the Wild* uncannily anticipated its own triumphant reception by virtue of Buck's apotheosis, so too was the author of "A Thousand Deaths" saved from the same sort of "wasted career" that he feared for his first-person narrator, whose fictional rescue from drowning anticipated London's own rescue almost two years later by the editors of *The Black Cat.*

Which brings us back to Edgar Allan Poe and the question of the canon. "A Thousand Deaths" was not published in *Scribner's,* as London naïvely intended in 1897, but in a newly established periodical of pulp fiction named after a famous Poe short story. Although London professed to Cloudesley Johns to disparage such a "hack" publication, he was attracted early on to its prize money. The name of the magazine and its heavily promoted contests helped to institutionalize the author Poe as a popular icon of the gothic imagination, reconceived at the turn of the century as a kitschy piece of mass culture driven by the promise of easy money for writers/contestants. Yet at the same time, the author Poe is also beginning to show up in new literary histories written by professors (such as Barrett Wendell from Harvard University) proposing to establish "American literature" as a legitimate field of academic study. Taking their cue from the French, these genteel arbiters of taste rediscover Poe as an unappreciated, if quirky, romantic genius who was great before his time.[13]

In a complex cultural process that might have delighted the trickster himself, Poe is simultaneously turned into pulp and canonized as a master—an apparent split between highbrow and lowbrow that Jack London sought to negotiate in his own sea novel and in a second critical essay he published in 1903 a few months after "Getting into Print." Called "The Terrible and Tragic in Fiction," the article uses Poe as a case study to explore the possibility of combining popular success and lasting fame in Anglo-American letters. Ironically juxtaposing Poe's desperate pleas to publishers for money against the fact that in 1900 one of his first editions sold for over two thousand dollars, London puts the problem succinctly:

"The public read Poe's stories, but Poe was not in touch with that public. And when that public spoke to him through the mouths of the editors, it spoke in no uncertain terms."[14] In the remainder of his essay London goes on to champion "rebelliously aspiring" Poe and the commitment to the "terrible and tragic" that his writing represented (60), offering along the way an interesting sociological account of the contemporary bourgeoisie's hypocritical fear of awe-inspiring fiction. For a moment London imagines two distinct audiences perpetuating Poe's name—magazine readers and the buyers of his books—but he rejects this key explanation in favor of a more conventional naturalist attack on the public's thirst for safe, sentimental love stories.

Yet even here London is less interested in endorsing the courageous example of Poe, the "powerful effect" of his writing, and his famous dream for a new magazine containing "nothing namby-pamby, yellowish, or emasculated" (64), than in trying to figure out how to avoid Poe's fate, conceived by London as a kind of marketing failure. Despite "a proved demand for the terrible and tragic," Poe is unable to cash in during his lifetime and must await canonization after the fact. Assuming from the start that "the public" and "the mouths of editors" are synonymous, London regards with mild nostalgia Poe's antebellum hope for a special kind of readership—a hope akin to Hawthorne's "Custom-House" appeal "to the one heart and mind of perfect sympathy" or to Melville's similar epistolary construction of Hawthorne as his own ideal reader.

But for London at the turn of the century, readers simply amount to "the public," materially inscribed by the editorial apparatus of publishing; any "bids for place and permanence rather than for the largest circulation" (such as his own sea novel) must directly admit this public and the editors through whom it speaks (64). Although London in his early essays enjoyed mocking these editors, he understood that their word was final. In response to such a hard fact, from reading Poe London learned how to autobiographically encode his person in his fiction to protect himself from a largely anonymous mass market of readers.[15] But the sheer transparency of London's encryptions suggests how much he needed to be recognized in public and not simply savored by a select, ideal few in private. Although in his first letter to Brett about *The Sea-Wolf* London discriminates between "superficial" and "deeper" readers, the logic of publication collapses the two under the single aegis of the editors, whose "mouth" voices the will of a monolithic "public."

London's Poe piece appeared in *The Critic*, the sort of highly specialized professional trade journal that had been printing his advice essays since 1899. But his fictional counterpart Humphrey Van Weyden in *The Sea-Wolf* publishes his "analysis of Poe's place in American literature . . . in the *Atlantic*" (2)—the site of London's breakthrough Klondike story "An Odyssey of the North" that led to the publication of his first collection of tales, as I have previously discussed. Despite this early triumph, London was never very successful at placing his critical prose with the *Atlantic Monthly*, whose editors were decidedly cool to his socialist inclinations. Making his first-person narrator write for the *Atlantic*, London signals Van Weyden's investment in a genteel culture that London could view only from the outside. Yet if his own essay on the terrible and tragic disparages this highly influential culture as sentimental and feminine, London's representation in his novel (via Van Weyden) is more ambiguous, since Van Weyden will use his superior knowledge of highbrow letters as a weapon to combat Larsen's rule by physical intimidation. In some ways literary criticism is more powerful than fists, we will discover, along with Hump and Wolf.

Thus the first chapter's pointed reference to Poe, followed by the narrator's drowning so soon after, not only enabled London to incorporate his thoughts on the canon into his novel itself and to reprise his career by way of "A Thousand Deaths" and all the intense autobiographical baggage that went with it, but also established yet another related context for understanding the ensuing struggle between the two men: the ostensible gendering of letters. This crucial division between "masculine" and "feminine" is itself set in the more general context of modern society's division of labor, as the novel opens with Van Weyden smugly applauding his specialized skills as a critic who need not concern himself with how to operate the ferry on which he is traveling. Standard interpretations of *The Sea-Wolf* take for granted that Van Weyden's dabbling in literary criticism is a feminized occupation associated with the soft, "sissy" existence he led at home living with his mother and sisters. In this view the idealism of letters remains in stark contrast to the physical, brutally material world of men that he encounters on board the *Ghost*. For Van Weyden, idealism and materialism can be negotiated and integrated, specialization overcome, only with the help of a woman.

Yet London's representation is far more interesting and complex, for from the very first paragraph of the novel, he imagines reading as an aggressive, macho activity. Triggering the entire plot, Van Weyden crosses the bay returning from a weekend with his friend Charley Furuseth, who would "toil incessantly" in the summer but who would "rest his brain" in the winter months by grappling with Nietzsche and Schopenhauer. Beyond the pretentious habit of name-dropping that marks so much of the novel, London here in the figure of Charley Furuseth imagines a division of labor by way of seasons that allows manhood to be maintained year-round through a certain kind of muscular bookishness: the leisurely consumption of notoriously difficult (and misogynist) German philosophers. But the kind of texts that London identifies as manly (philosophy versus poetry) is perhaps less important than the bravado with which Furuseth is said to read—a style that cuts across seasons and places him squarely between Van Weyden's expert, genteel literary criticism and Larsen's self-taught, primitive philosophizing.

The mediating link between Hump on land and Wolf at sea, Charley Furuseth plays a key role throughout the narrative, recalled affectionately by the narrator whenever his own authority as a man is at risk. Vividly invoked at one point as "lounging in a dressing-gown" and delivering "pessimistic epigrams" about Van Weyden's presumed drowning, the narrator's intimate friend is especially important in the first half of the novel as a model for civilized, literate masculinity in the absence of any women to come between Van Weyden and his captor. With the introduction of writer Maud Brewster in the second half of the novel, a clear division of labor is restored, both in terms of an economy of gender, as I have suggested, as well as an analogous economy of letters, with famous author and her appreciative critic teaming up to overcome the threat of Larsen. With Maud around, Charley becomes less important for Van Weyden to remember so fondly. But to gloss the first half of *The Sea-Wolf* entirely in terms of the second half would be a mistake, since the novel's early verbal parry and thrust between men suggests a far more unstable and volatile series of homoerotic struggles for mastery.[16]

Male Call

If literature cannot be so simply equated with being a sissy, then how else is femininity defined in these early chapters of the novel? Before Hump ends up on the *Ghost*, the role played by women is quite specific: they scream. During his description of the sinking ferry, Van Weyden encounters a "red-faced" man with "artificial legs" who urges the narrator to "grab hold of something . . . and listen to the women scream" (6). In the course of the next page Van Weyden registers this screaming no less than four separate times, focusing less on the noise than on their wide "open mouths," which resemble "the jagged edges of the hole in the side of the cabin." Reminded of "the squealing of pigs under the knife of the butcher," Van Weyden finds himself "feeling sick and squeamish," even as he remarks that the sinking "was just as I had read descriptions of such scenes in books." In a moment of panic he goes overboard, begins to drown, spies his rescuers, blacks out, and wakes up on board ship to find himself being revived by two sailors, one of whom roughly massages "my naked chest" (13), while the other soon after dresses him in a "bloodstain[ed]" shirt and a pair of trousers with one "abbreviated leg" (16).

This drowning clearly represents a birth trauma that enables Van Weyden to reemerge as a man among men on the *Ghost*. Unlike the novel's subsequent two moments of transition that similarly occasion the hero's symbolic regeneration—the arrival of Maud Brewster and their Adamic escape to Endeavor Island—this begetting takes a literal turn by virtue of the text's obsessive fixing on the women's bodies. Letting mouth stand for vagina, London fuses genital sex ("the knife of the butcher") with the act of birthing, so that women function simultaneously in this scenario as objects of heterosexual desire (however distasteful) and as mothers. Once Hump arrives on Wolf Larsen's ship in a fog, however, such a conventional oedipal configuration vanishes. As the women sink into the sea, they leave in their wake a far more nebulous set of relations: there will be knives and there will be mouths, but who controls them will now be up for grabs.

Sweeping women from his text and replacing them with Wolf Larsen and his crew, London is compelled to reconceive radically manhood itself. For in oedipal logic, without women there can be no fathers. This is not to say that Larsen and his sailors have abandoned the phallus: interactions between these men are driven by a kind of hyperphallocentricism, as we shall see. Nor in making women disappear does London relinquish the gendered categories of "masculine" and "feminine." Quite the contrary. Forced to conceive such categories outside of "male" and "female," London redistributes them between men in a way that brilliantly exposes the question of mastery at the heart of such categories, as Chauncey's historical analysis of early twentieth-century male sexual practice serves to confirm. More than London might have imagined in his January letter to Brett, more so than *The Call of the Wild* or *The People of the Abyss*, *The Sea-Wolf* is about *social* mastery, politics represented in rather raw terms. Accepting as a given the equation between masculinity and aggression, femininity and submission, London turns these perfectly traditional cultural associations inside out, relocating them in relation to shifting identities marked by social class, vocation, and, most important, bodies that can both give and take intimate expressions of power.

London had previously imagined a world without women in his very early, curious story "The Strange Experience of a Misogynist" (1897), written at the same time as "A Thousand Deaths." His first-person bachelor, a "young fellow of twenty-eight or thirty," is haunted in a dream by the melody "Reuben, Reuben, I've been thinking what a good thing it would be / If the women were transported, far beyond the northern sea," to discover on waking that his dream has come true: "The femininity of the earth is no more!!" one newspaper headline blares. Initially rejoicing, the narrator soon finds how the absence of women rends the fabric of society by disrupting labor relations. Women's disappearance, both as consumers and producers, throws men out of certain jobs, creating "new profession[s]" for others. Fearing that "we soon would be reduced . . . [to] taking in each other's washing," the narrator paints a grim picture of moral disintegration: "The men became insulting and riotous in their demands for more wages and less hours. The toiling capitalists, discovering that they also had no families to labor for, became indifferent. . . . Life nor property were no longer held sacred and a reign of pillage and slaughter ensued."[17] Eventually dismissed as a bad dream, this vivid nightmare (which makes the narrator vow to get married) is effectively replayed six years later on the *Ghost*, but now less as an apocalypse than as a troubling opportunity.

Two points are worth emphasizing about this story in relation to the subsequent sea novel. First, London realizes that women stabilize the social order not simply morally but also materially in terms of work. Second, he understands that without women, certain feminine jobs such as washing would still have to be done. *The Sea-Wolf* pursues the implications of this insight by gendering sailors' work on board ship. Initially taken on as a cabin boy, Van Weyden starts out as an assistant to the Cockney cook Thomas Mugridge, who is repeatedly marked with numerous "effeminate features" such as "slim hips" (13) and a high "discordant falsetto" (59). But in keeping with the logic of London's "Misogynist" tale, Mugridge's body (which makes Van Weyden's own flesh crawl) does not express his innate femininity as much as call attention to his job doing women's work. The prime site of domesticity on the ship, the cabin/kitchen feminizes Van Weyden as well as Mugridge.[18] As an assistant to Mugridge, Van Weyden begins as the most womanly, a position that allows Mugridge to play master by lording it over his newly assigned underling.

London complicates matters in *The Sea-Wolf* by further linking gender performance to social class in a way that again exposes the question of power governing "masculine" and "feminine." Although Van Weyden insists that Mugridge's repulsive sleaziness bespeaks a "hereditary servility" (16), the ease and speed with which the cook assumes a position of superiority over Van Weyden as soon as the gentleman is hired suggest otherwise. London's brilliance here is to see, following his analysis of the British underclass in *The People of the Abyss*, how industrial capitalism has rendered the nonworking aristocracy useless in much the same way that the unemployed proletariat is useless. With a "soft skin . . . like a lydy's" (15–16), as the fawning Cockney puts it, Van Weyden is feminine by virtue of his idleness. Van Weyden is repulsed by the greasy cook because in this regard they are so similar; he can temporarily afford to pity the pathetic Mugridge only after he, Hump, has worked as a man, which, we shall see, has less to do with sailing than with holding his own verbally against Larsen. The interplay between cook and assistant is so much more volatile and interesting in the early stages of the novel than later on, because once Van Weyden surpasses the cook, then "feminine" and "masculine" no longer function as mutually constituted categories of power forged between them as they vie for Larsen's approval. Despite imagining class and gender as socially constructed and fluid, then, London also fixes clear boundaries on such mobility, so that Van Weyden can rise, whereas Mugridge cannot.

The grounds for Van Weyden's ascendancy touch on class and labor but primarily lie elsewhere. To begin with, he is reborn on the *Ghost* immediately to witness a funeral. As others have noted, this opening death and burial at sea replays the ending of London's first publication, "Story of a Typhoon Off the Coast of Japan," which closes with a brief reference to the disposal of the body of the "bricklayer."[19] Yet a far more immediate set of associations can be gleaned from London's description of *The Sea-Wolf's* dying sailor: "a large man" covered in black hair "like the furry coat of a dog" with a mouth "wide open" (18), whose corpse in the next chapter is unceremoniously flung into the sea "like a dog flung overside" (34). By this curt funeral, we may surmise, London bids farewell to his canine hero Buck, with the implication that he will not be retelling that same story, for Van Weyden can no longer depend on hard work or tender play, as in *The Call of the Wild*, to realize his manhood. Announcing early on "and thus it was that I passed into a state of involuntary servitude to Wolf Larsen" (32), London's first-person narrator would seem to reinvoke the structure of captivity narrative that had driven Buck's quest for the freedom of the wild. Yet with the dog flung overboard, Hegelian master/slave dialectics take a different turn, as Van Weyden's "servitude" to Larsen becomes increasingly invested with emotions more complex and confused than the starker feelings of loyalty, adoration, hatred, and pride that motivate Buck.

How do we understand these emotions in relation to traditional social roles? Just as John Thornton is explicitly compared at one point to a good father who cares deeply for his canine children, it might be argued that Wolf Larsen acts as the castrating bad father who must be destroyed, just as the mad scientist is reduced to ashes in "A Thousand Deaths." Nicknamed the "Old Man" (19) by Mugridge, Larsen himself would seem to assume this part. Early on he repeatedly mocks the "scholar and dilettante" (42) Van Weyden about his inability to earn an independent income, so that the gentleman/sissy must financially stand on the dead "legs" of his father (26)—a phallic barb that clearly recalls the ferry's

Male Call

moment of sinking in which the red-faced man on artificial legs warned Van Weyden to listen to the women and "grab hold of something." London has Larsen repeat verbatim this caution to "grab hold" (37) as a wave crashes over the deck of the *Ghost*—a scene that gives the literary critic at once his nickname "Hump" and a wounded, swelling leg, another pair of obvious phallic contrivances (with many more to come) by which Larsen and his crew call attention to Van Weyden's male lack. For "the making of you," Larsen insists, Van Weyden will clearly need "to stand on your own legs" (27). But how these legs are fashioned and whether they are at the expense of Larsen's own beautiful body may not so easily fit into any conventional coming-of-age narrative scheme.[20]

For one thing, while the content of Wolf Larsen's admonitions may be harsh, his tone is not. Like Milton's Lucifer, London's too has a sense of humor. From the start his interaction with Van Weyden takes the form of a playful affection (which he never shows Maud once she arrives)—a teasing, tender banter rather than a harsh taunting, a mode that he tends to reserve for the rest of the crew. This sort of fond verbal interplay is easy to miss in the novel, given the displays of physical violence directed at Hump by which Wolf intimidates his captive. But even here Van Weyden expresses a fascination with Larsen's body as a repository of male power somehow located outside his tyrannical person—in effect, power operating as a free-floating phallus already castrated. Against a standard psychoanalytic paradigm that posits sadomasochism as yet another rehearsal of father-son strife, Van Weyden's attraction, I will suggest when we look closely at these passages, is less driven by envy than by his strong urge to take Larsen at his word: to grab hold of something.[21]

To begin to make sense of this command, we need to return to the dead sailor whose funeral presides over *The Sea-Wolf*. The key here is that he is specifically identified as the captain's "mate." One of the first things Larsen says to Van Weyden is, "My mate's gone, and there'll be a lot of promotion" (26). However apparently disdainful and cold, Wolf's search to replace his lost mate thus structures the entire narrative, at least its crucial first half. This quest means that Van Weyden will attain manhood not by replacing the father (becoming, in effect, his own captain via diligent labor, instant fame, or what have you) but by learning how to be the captain's mate—a position defined simply as being close to Larsen.

As his promotion of Hump suggests, the captain cares little what nautical skills his candidates may possess. The role of mate in the novel does not follow a hierarchy of work, in other words, but a hierarchy of emotions, as the job really entails being the companion of the captain, who derives pleasure from abusing his crew and is excited when he gets abuse in return. London thus disavows an oedipal model that treats ego formation as a process of identification—killing the father to become your own—in favor of a model (without depending on women) in which the ego develops by attachment (and aversion), the desire *for* another man rather than to *be* another man.[22] In this regard Wolf Larsen is less a tyrannical or benevolent parent than a continuation of the wolf "brother" who had helped lead Buck away from Thornton into the wild at the end of that story.

Here is the particular striking, unmistakable significance of Larsen's status as a "Wolf." In his analysis of early-twentieth-century, working-class gay culture, Chauncey points out that a dominant male who sexually preyed on other men was called a "husband," "jocker," or "wolf," whereas the subjugated male was known as "fairy," "punk," or "sissy" (Van Weyden's initial designation). The "wolf" was a distinctive kind of man, primarily of working-class origins (like Larsen), who prowled in search of sexual satisfaction. Discussing this erotic system of "wolves and punks," Chauncey goes on to insist that "although some men treated fairies in the same way they treated prostitutes, not every relationship between a man and a fairy was brief, coercive, or loveless."[23] A Wolf could have an extended, intimate liaison with a sissy and be counted no less of a man for it.

Even if he cannot admit it, London's Wolf wants what Hump wants—communion. Such attachment works mainly by talk, the means by which Wolf and Hump discover what they have in common and how they differ. Whereas Van Weyden initially panics at the thought of his isolation, fearing a loss of community, Larsen pretends to revel in his individuality, professing to value himself as a self-begotten and self-contained monad without regard to anyone or anything surrounding him. I say "pretend" because for such a supposedly antisocial loner, Wolf Larsen sure enjoys bending people's ears, especially Van Weyden's. The captain is (almost literally) starved for conversation; when Hump arrives, Larsen finally

finds someone who, by virtue of his experience as a man of letters, can significantly "appreciate, as no other listener," the "vividness and strength"
(20) of his language. Looking for someone to conduct the funeral service,
Larsen initially mistakes Van Weyden for "a preacher" (23), but it is
Larsen himself who plays that part, thanks to his "thrillingly imperative"
(29) public speaking—what Van Weyden a bit later appreciates as "the
primal melancholy vibrant in his voice" (105).

Unlike *Moby-Dick*, which dramatizes Ahab's removal from human
community by repeatedly pushing him into soliloquy (and thereby straining the constraints of the novel's first-person form), London always imagines his captain talking with his narrator, even if these conversations are
about how contemptuously Larsen regards his fellow human beings.
Ahab is so remote that not even poor cabin boy Pip can fully claim his
attention; in soliloquy he speaks only to himself. But London wants his
Wolf to be heard by others. Despite what he says, Larsen's impulse to
debate with Van Weyden thus suggests that his tiresome naturalist philosophy cloaks a far more elemental need for London: converse at all costs,
or in other words, grab hold of something.

This is not to say that the Hump-Wolf relationship transcends Hegelian master/slave dialectics to arrive at some egalitarian, all-male uto-
pia filled with Whitman-esque soul-sharing or the spermatic squeezing
of hands celebrated by Melville's Ishmael. *The Sea-Wolf's* interactions
among men are hierarchical, panicked, discordant, abusive, and brutal—
contestation that culminates in the failed mutiny that takes place in the
confusing darkness of the forecastle (chapter 14). My point is that these
sailors are continually trying to connect with one another. Their intimacy is most often occluded by way of contagious violence, which tends
to collapse the distinction between aversion and attraction, as Van Weyden himself begins to register: "Brutality had followed brutality, and
flaming passions and cold-blooded cruelty had driven men to seek one
another's lives, and to strive to hurt, and maim, and destroy" (120).
Since Jack London and his men cannot allow themselves to admit openly
the homoeroticism stoking their agon, its possibility must be construed
by other means, as D. A. Miller has argued in another context: "When
homosexuality is entrusted to the totalizing, tantalizing play of connotation, the only way to establish the integrity of a truly other subject posi-

tion is performative: by simply declaring that one occupies such a position and supporting the declaration with a strong arm."[24]

Such shared spectacles of manhood in the novel extend beyond gross displays of physical violence to embrace other sorts of performance, including, most important, sheer talk: strong disputes, as well as the softer "gossip" (61, 103), innuendo, and "tittle-tattle and tale-bearing" (120) that collectively circulates throughout the *Ghost*. The very first night on the ship, for instance, Van Weyden listens to a heated debate among the crew's seal hunters about whether baby seals could swim at birth—an interesting topic that glosses Hump's own predicament. But I am less interested in the content of their debate than in the way London renders their passionate intercourse in material terms, treating speech as at once threatening and sickening. He stresses the men's "vociferating, bellowing," "their voices surg[ing] back and forth in waves of sound," their "arguing and roaring like some semi-human amphibious breed," until "the air was filled with oaths and indecent expressions" mingled with the thick murky haze from the tobacco that they "incessantly smoked" as they argued long into the night, while for sleepless Hump, "my imagination ran riot" (41–43).

Merging together talk and smoke as primitive, tangible, and confusing, like the "moist obscurity" (1) of the fog that leads to the ferry's collision, this passage helps us see the obsession with orality that is at the heart of the novel. From the opening "screaming bedlam of women" (7) to the narrative's concluding (heterosexual) kiss, *The Sea-Wolf* graphically depicts dozens and dozens of mouths in action. In chapters 2 and 3 alone teeth are set on edge (twice), jaws drop to freeze into a diabolical grin, a "terrific denunciation" is "swept" out of "Wolf Larsen's mouth" (21), tongues are bitten (figuratively), mouths are opened to speak, and the seal hunters "gave mouth to a laughter . . . like a wolf-chorus or the barking of hell-hounds" (33). London seems unable to abstract speech from the mouth, as if talk were only one manifestation of a wider range of more fundamental oral activity—cursing, biting, grinning, sucking, chewing, bellowing, swallowing, and spitting—all (per)versions of the stock naturalist trope "Eat or be eaten."

As we might expect, the most prominent example of oral power is reserved for Wolf Larsen himself. When Van Weyden first spies the captain from the water, he "seemed to be doing little else than smoke a cigar," staring at the water in "deep thought," Narcissus-like, "smoke issuing from his lips" (10) until he casually glances at the drowning Van Weyden and decides to rescue him. When Hump then first encounters him on ship, Larsen's actions are a bit more aggressive, as he furiously paces the deck "savagely chewing the end of cigar" (18). The next *ten* times Wolf Larsen is described, it is explicitly in conjunction with his "ever-lasting cigar" (37), which disappears as soon as Maud arrives on the scene.

To paraphrase Freud, sometimes a cigar is just a cigar. But certainly not in this case. Yet the transparent schematics of London's phallicism belies its complex function here. Given the narrative's fixation on the mouth as a material orifice, we cannot simply assume that the cigar is an external projection of Larsen's essential manhood, since it could just as likely be thrusting into him—into his mouth—from the outside. Like the repeated references to knives that mark these early episodes, like the terrible "oaths that rolled from his lips" (20) that Van Weyden finds so electrifying, Larsen's cigar is a weapon that shows his contemptuous power over other men, suggesting how the phallus on board the ship is not a fixed possession but rather a mobile sign of mastery, defined as relational—manliness that moves back and forth between men. Larsen's cigar in his mouth thus calls attention to the phallus as a kind of cover-up, counterfeit, or stand-in, exposing the very lack from which *all* these men suffer and seek to counteract by beating, shouting, and stabbing.[25] Vestiges of patriarchal structure remain, but not even the ship's captain is man enough to fill the role of the lost father completely. Wolf's interest in Hump getting some legs takes on a more poignant cast once we see how London has so openly and so relentlessly represented masculinity's black hole for all on board the *Ghost*.

Oral intercourse between men effectively controls the logic of the narrative's first half in specific ways that make sense, I trust, beyond glib metaphor.[26] Even the infamous knife-sharpening foreplay between Mugridge and Hump is resolved by way of words that enable Van Weyden to stay on top. If we look more closely at Van Weyden's early descriptions of Larsen's person, we can discover how and why mouthed words have such an effect. As I have indicated, the captain rules on this "miniature floating world" (33) not by the authority of his office or by the power of his philosophical convictions but by sheer force of personality. Yet how the novel constitutes personality is by no means self-evident. In our first extended look at Larsen, the narrator begins by describing his cigar chewing and then moves on to convey "my first impression or feel of the man" (18) by a series of yoked contraries (the rhetorical term is "synoeciosis"): massive, yet not massive; like a gorilla, yet not gorilla-like; strong with the "essence of life" yet which "writhes in the body of a snake when the head is cut off" (19). In the course of two paragraphs, Van Weyden repeats the word "strength" no less than nine times as he strains to capture Larsen's power.

This is pretty lame prose, even by London's standards. I suppose it could be argued that the strain in the language here says more about Van Weyden than about Larsen. The famous literary critic is simply tongue-tied in the presence of Wolf, a linguistic awkwardness that speaks eloquently to the mesmerizing effect the captain has on other men. Up to this point in my discussion, I have read the novel fairly transparently, not stopping to distinguish between London and his first-person narrator. From a New Critical formalist perspective, it would be a mistake to ignore how London has constructed Hump as a self-contained character whose personal limitations emerge in the course of his narration. In this view Hump, not Jack London, is responsible for the strains in the text. But such a temptation to restore control to the author at the expense of his character ignores the degree to which London is heavily invested from the start in his first-person critic, whose "feel of the man" (Larsen) tends to be endorsed rather than ironized by London throughout the narration.

Irony of the Jamesian sort was never London's strong suit. In so sharply dividing his authorial energies between Hump's passive witnessing and Wolf's domineering philosophizing, London would seem to be unable to decide at any given moment which of the two men he most intimately desires to impersonate, at least until Maud Brewster arrives midway through to help diminish the significance of Larsen. In the absence of a woman, there were clearly certain advantages to pretending to be a sissy, for London as well as his first-person narrator. This narrative split between who sees for the author (Hump) and who speaks for him (both Wolf and Hump), like the analogous problem of personality, stems from the way Larsen's person is represented in the text. After struggling with the word "strength" nine times, Van Weyden takes another shot in the next chapter at a "first impression": "I received my first impression of the man himself, of the man as apart from his body and from the torrent of blasphemy I had heard him spew forth" (24). Whether this remark reflects Van Weyden's limitations as a storyteller or the truth of Larsen's peculiar status is less important here than the crucial way such a description imagines personhood as dissociated: there is speech, there is body, and there is "the man himself" existing apart from speech and body but presumably the single source for both.[27]

Approximated by the term "strength," the "man himself" specifically means Larsen's manhood—the force "alive in itself" that writhes in the snake after its head is cut off. This self-contained essential manhood applies to other men on ship as well. For instance, the "timid frankness and manliness" (14) of Johnson, who serves as a kind of Starbuck to Larsen's Ahab, reaches its breaking point when he struggles against a brutal beating by Larsen and his sadistic mate Johansen, as witnessed by Hump: "Of course there was no hope for him . . . but by the manhood that was in him he could not cease from fighting for that manhood" (114–15). Instead of fighting for his "life," which would be a more predictable naturalist gloss on the will to survive, we encounter "manhood," not self-preservation, at the circular center of his being. Even Hump's manhood works this way as a mysterious thing apart: recounting his taunting by Mugridge, he permits "my manhood to look back upon those events" and feels shame, claiming that "in the pride of my manhood I feel that my manhood has in unaccountable ways been smirched and sullied," only to dismiss immediately this disturbing puzzle by the awkwardly cavalier "All of which is neither here nor there" (46).

Manhood is thus at once hypostatized and figured as a phantom on board the *Ghost*. Simultaneously objectified and mystified, the "man himself" of each of the crew again points to phallic power in the book as in flux, to be possessed and dispossessed between men—postcastration and postoedipal—by way of knives, missing legs, open mouths, and comparisons with writhing, decapitated snakes. While talk and body cannot wholly stand for his manhood, only through talk and the body (especially the relationship between the two) can such strength manifest itself; hence the narrator's initial straining to put it in words. I have already discussed at some length how the speech acts of Larsen and the crew collectively work as a primitive ejaculatory force in the novel, and I will return to the question of oral intercourse at the heart of the power struggle between Van Weyden and Hump. But first we need to consider the role played by the body in the book—not as manhood's locus but as the object by which the viewing male can express his desire for such manhood.

As the narrator's tongue-tied stabs at rendering Wolf's strength suggest, the act of seeing in *The Sea-Wolf* is impotent precisely to the degree that the act of speaking grants power in the novel. In this regard, Larsen's body is especially worth looking at. Van Weyden discusses the captain's body three times, each more remarkable than the last. In the next paragraph after fragmenting Larsen into three parts (manhood, speech, and body), Van Weyden begins to dwell on Wolf's "large and handsome" eyes. Declaring "it was my destiny to know them well," Van Weyden launches into a lavish description that ends: "Eyes . . . that could grow chill as an arctic landscape, and yet again, that could warm and soften and be all a-dance with love-lights, intense and masculine, luring and compelling, which at the same time fascinate and dominate women till they surrender in a gladness of joy and of relief and of sacrifice. But to return" (25).

A better (and less interesting) writer, on rereading this passage, might have crossed it out and started all over again. Letting himself go overboard, London allows these breathless lines to stand, calling attention to his excess by that wonderful "But to return," a phrase that signals the narration's loss of command. What has happened, of course, is that in rendering the corporeal beauty of Larsen's manhood, in treating the "masculine" as itself beautiful, Van Weyden is forced to feminize himself, presumably since only a woman could appreciate Wolf as a manly lover. To the extent that his eyes dominate and fascinate others who gladly surrender to him, the captain is "masculine" and these others are "feminine." Occupying such a position in relation to Wolf makes it hard for Hump to keep "myself in control" (26), as he admits. The mere sight of Larsen unmans Van Weyden.

In standard accounts of the "male gaze," it is assumed that power accrues to the viewer by the act of seeing, whereas the object of spectating (usually a woman) is diminished. But London reverses this scenario: the object of the gaze assumes control by virtue of being looked at, whereas the gazer relinquishes power—in effect becomes a woman—by such uncontrollable staring.[28] The next two extended physical descriptions of Larsen work the same way. After making the captain's bed (his duty as cabin boy), Hump remarks (twice), "I caught myself looking at him in a fascinated sort of way" (98) as Larsen tinkers joyfully with one of his nautical inventions. Bending over backward to insist that Larsen is beautiful "in the masculine sense," the narrator focuses on the "smooth-shaven" "fair" face of his comrade and master in a way that distinguishes him from the rest of the grizzled, brutish crew.

Van Weyden's fascinated account also serves later to differentiate the captain from the "feminine" (142) beauty of the attractive sailor "Oofty-Oofty," who is described as breathing "as placidly as a woman" (134) in the forecastle at the beginning of the crucial mutiny episode. Thrown overboard by a crew member, Larsen climbs back on board via a self-begotten, dripping rebirth and descends into the forecastle to check on which of his rebellious men are only pretending to sleep. Ostensibly to provide a repeated point of contrast to Wolf's "masculine" (142) beauty, exotic Oofty-Oofty's "pleasing" lines are curiously invoked soon after the mutiny's violent display of "entwined bodies" in which various members of the crew physically attack Larsen—"the soft crushing sound made by flesh striking forcibly against flesh" (135)—but fail to kill the tyrant because they lack a knife. Even at their most brutal, amid what effectively amounts to an attempted gang rape, male bodies thus remain passionately beautiful objects to behold.

During this mutiny Hump silently and secretly witnesses the intense clash of bodies, as he has done all along on the ship, but passively refuses to take sides and ends up, significantly, following his master back on deck rather than staying with the rebels. What follows is in many ways the most crucial scene of the book—not simply for its graphic depiction of Larsen and the homoerotic charge it gives Van Weyden but also because it marks an important change in their relationship. Greeting Hump with a "whimsical smile," the injured captain asks him to nurse his gaping wounds, having been bitten on the leg by one sailor—the ultimate in oral aggression. At his first sight of Larsen's naked body, "stripped and bloody," Van Weyden simply remarks, "[It] quite took my breath away" (142). Claiming to "appreciate" the "wonder" of "the perfect lines of Wolf Larsen's figure" by virtue of the "artist" in him, Van Weyden finds that he "could not take my eyes from him" as he dresses his wounds (143). Once again, the beholder is powerless to resist the "terrible beauty" of the male body. Marveling at Larsen's manhood, Hump describes his rippling muscles under his flesh in much the same terms that he had described that writhing, decapitated snake.

Unlike the two previous scenes, however, here Larsen explicitly notices Van Weyden's staring, so that the object of desire, knowing he is such, now assumes the subject position. Eye contact becomes mutual. Caught in the act of seeing, Van Weyden can only stammer in embarrassment that "God made you well," pointing to Larsen's own perfect body as the best proof for the existence of God, contra his captain's atheism. But Larsen turns the ensuing theological banter (purpose versus utility) into an occasion to "command" Hump to touch and feel his "muscles . . . softly crawling and shaping about the hips, along the back, and across the shoulders." By such a smoldering, barely repressed act of caressing, Hump finally succumbs to Wolf's opening imperative to grab hold of something. Having previously taken intense physical pain (squeezing) from Larsen, Hump learns to give physical pleasure. "When my work [as a doctor] was done," the captain in return decides at this instant to make him his "mate," noting that Hump is "a handy man" despite the fact that he knows nothing about navigation. Even though Van Weyden protests with a corny line right out of a grade-B Hollywood movie (" 'I won't be mate on this hell-ship!' I cried defiantly"), his mating with Larsen is now complete—a promotion that culminates their mutual quest for communion (141–45).

As this extraordinary scene suggests, the sissy Van Weyden finally gets his legs, so to speak, not by being tested against nature's elements or fending off Mugridge but by finding pleasure in the sight and feel of another man's body, who is himself pleased by such pleasure. The vocational categories of "artist" or "doctor" or "nurse" can only partially account for the (repressed) joy that Hump and Wolf find in this encounter, during which the growing intellectual intimacy between these two men takes on a literal, material dimension. It is important to remember that while Hump is touching Wolf, he is also arguing philosophy with him, for it is only through their developing verbal intercourse that London can eventually allow himself to imagine such physical congress. In this strenuous exercise of minds, Larsen repeatedly tries out his naturalist doctrine on Hump, as he had tested it physically on his crew, whereas Van Weyden in effect talks his way into Larsen's affections by vigorously striving to convince him to abandon his nihilism.

The pair's dialogue during this scene may seem to deflect our attention away from their physical interaction. But conversation from the very start of the novel has been represented as a sexually stimulating activity, originating as it does for London in the body itself—the mouth. Most commentators on *The Sea-Wolf* spend a great deal of time analyzing the philosophical import of these conversations, but their conceptual content seems far less interesting than do the heated passions motivating the exchange of ideas. Hump and Wolf thus engage in their own, slightly less crude version of the bellowing and roaring of the seal hunters whose disputation imitates the behavior of their prey. For all the supposed distinction between competing philosophical systems in the novel, these systems end up amounting to pretty much the same thing. Given the way that talk primarily expresses the will to power, idealism and materialism are simply two sides of the same coin dramatizing the same intense scene of persuasion.[29]

Here we begin to grasp the importance of Van Weyden as an established literary critic, already possessing a certain kind of legs of his own. Unlike the feminine occupations of nurse or artist, the role of the man of letters is aggressive and penetrating, in perfect keeping with the atmosphere of intimidation by which Larsen reigns on the *Ghost*. Van Weyden can hold his own with his captain by virtue of the manly art of intellectual debate and criticism that Larsen himself is starving to engage in. Early in their intercourse, for instance, Van Weyden boldly takes advantage of "the intimacy of the conversation" to omit the deferential address "sir" (49)—a subversive omission that the captain misses because he is so excitedly contesting Wolf's claim to read "immortality in your eyes."

Whether the subject is Darwin (69), Browning (82–83), Omar Khayyám (107), or Shakespeare (111), Van Weyden triumphs over his master by virtue of his superior experience and skills as a reader. Exposed as a limited, self-taught misreader of these authors, Larsen dutifully accepts edification by the expert bookworm narrator. In the very process of professing to disparage such specialization in favor of a more harmonious integration between bodily toil and brain work (as managed by Hump's role model, Charley Furuseth), London thus ends up affirming the conquering force of letters—the basis of the communion between Wolf and Hump, despite Hump's insistence that he has "nothing in common with him" (68). Before the mutiny Van Weyden calls attention to his remoteness from the ship's "flaming passions and cold-blooded cruelty" by purportedly contrasting such brutality with far less threatening instances of male interaction: "the cutting sarcasm of Charley Furuseth," and "the nasty remarks of some of the professors during my undergraduate days" (120–21). But such a revealing comparison works precisely in reverse, for the relation between Larsen and Van Weyden indeed more closely resembles a shifting student-teacher set of exchanges than any oedipal father-son conflict.

Van Weyden aims to maintain the dominant role in their relationship by presuming to read Larsen and the other members of his crew as texts. To teach Larsen how to read gains Van Weyden respect (and frees him from manual labor), but explicating him directly gives him narrative control. In this regard, reading explicitly takes on a phallic and sexual function. Recognizing how misdirected "lust" in Mugridge manifests itself when the cook viciously stabs another sailor, Van Weyden immediately remarks, "I could read the workings of his mind as clearly as though it were a printed book" (88). Although, again, we might suppose that London is drawing a contrast between a bloody knifing and a critical reading, such a juxtaposition suggests how both are expressions of sexual potency that fill in for male lack.

Physical violence (stabbing, squeezing, beating) and literary criticism (reading and disputing) thus represent analogous, occluded attempts at homoerotic bonding. And even though Mugridge's psychology may present a different (but no less complex) text than Larsen for Van Weyden to decipher, the narrator's role as phallic reader in both cases remains the same. Directly prefacing the knife-sharpening episode that takes place between Mugridge and himself, for instance, Van Weyden recalls some verbal sparring with Larsen, who is drawn out by Hump to articulate some crude but important insights about Herbert Spencer: "I felt an elation of spirit. I was groping into his soul-stuff as he made a practice of groping in the soul-stuff of others. I was exploring virgin territory" (81).

Penetrating Larsen's virgin mind, the practiced critic openly reads his master like a book. In doing so he effectively puts words in his mouth— words that function at once as the ejaculated "soul-stuff" of manhood bursting out or "shooting off" (as Larsen calls Johnson's defiance, 112 and 114), as well as Hump's own manly "stuff" going in: the lessons in interpretation that form the basis for their increasing "intimacy" (95). Like Larsen's public cigar smoking, these traded words show power on the ship as dynamic and relational. Larsen is thus perhaps more right than he knows when he dismisses "the possibilities of millions of lives" that are "in our loins" (68), for we have come to appreciate how manhood shared between men, "turning over . . . soul-stuff" by "speech" that "cut and slashed" (84), as Hump puts it, carries its own special kind of pleasure.

This pleasure reaches its climax, I have suggested, during Hump's nursing of Wolf's wounds in chapter 16, a scene that directly follows the aborted mutiny. These key middle chapters clearly represent the most dangerous and disturbing section in the novel, for until Maud Brewster arrives (in chapter 18), London must confront questions of power raised by the crew's rebellion, Van Weyden's allegiance to the captain, and his subsequent promotion to the "position of mate" (146)—an office that enables him, despite his momentary protest, to "sit in the high places" (145) of the ship as Larsen's right-hand man. If the satanic captain is such a tyrant, why stay with him? London finesses this troublesome question by introducing two key scenes in chapter 17 that serve to naturalize the issue of social mastery at the center of *The Sea-Wolf*: a brief description of seal hunting—the ostensible mission of the *Ghost*, relatively invisible up to this point in the narrative—and an extended description of a violent storm that replays London's "Story of a Typhoon Off the Coast of Japan."

The description of seal slaughter offers the first explicit indication of what sort of job Hump can do after his promotion. With Larsen's guidance, Hump has quickly moved up the ship's pecking order, graduating from feminized cabin boy (peeling potatoes, making beds, nursing the sick) via an aggressive, masturbatory self-display—the knife-sharpening duel with Mugridge (an episode that details "handy" manual labor of another sort). As Larsen's new mate, overseeing the skinning and counting of seal pelts, Van Weyden suddenly discovers he possesses "executive ability": "This handling and directing of many men was good for me" (155). As Buck is transformed in *The Call of the Wild*, so this new occupation toughens Hump such that "I could never again be quite the same man I had been." But in contrast to London's dog story, here the captain's companion works primarily by brain, not body, while it is his previous physical labor as cook's helper that is dismissed as feminized. Crediting Wolf with "open[ing] up for me the world of the real," Van Weyden realizes his potential as a true man by managing other men—a task he proudly performs, like all his other roles on the *Ghost*, with "a wild desire to vindicate myself in Wolf Larsen's eyes" (157).

The work of seal killing not only confirms the "real" motive behind such labor (to be a man in the eyes of Wolf) but also points to this labor's "real" end: "And north we travelled with it [the seal herd], ravaging and destroying, flinging down the skins so that they might adorn the fair shoulders of the women of the cities" (155). The entire crew of "the hell-ship" and its infernal quest is thus suddenly framed by a larger context that links economic imperatives to "the satisfaction of woman's vanity and love of decoration," as Hump had similarly characterized seal hunting to Larsen earlier in his narration during a "flood of speech" that "burst from me" (99). Once captain and mate have been paired, the novel aims to move beyond the claustrophobic confines of the ship, opening up the "world of the real" by associating the savage drive of the men with the imperialist expansion of capitalism (as in *Moby-Dick*). But in *The Sea-Wolf* this familiar association between market and manhood is assumed from the onset to depend on the desires of women. By such a curious introduction of a "natural" femininity (female vanity) *outside* the ship, London prepares for the arrival of Maud Brewster, the woman who must inevitably come between Wolf and his mate.

But before Maud can replace Larsen as the means for Van Weyden to vindicate his manhood, London introduces into his plot a tremendous storm—"Old Mother Nature's . . . hind legs" (158), Larsen calls it, in presumed contrast to the dead father's phallic legs. Like the seal hunting, this storm serves to naturalize questions of mastery, turning attention away from passionate struggles between men to reimagine power and violence as forces of (Mother) nature.[30] But even here the problem of social mastery creeps back in, as we can see by comparing his 1893 rendering of this typhoon with the version he wrote ten years later for *The Sea-Wolf.* The most striking difference between London's first published sketch and his mature novel lies in their use of personal pronouns: with only one brief exception, the narrator of the 1893 sketch constantly and remarkably refers to "we," submerging the self in a kind of communal groupthink, whereas the far more individualized narrator Van Weyden positions himself as an "I" in relation to the storm as well as the other members of the crew who battle it.

Community is thus taken for granted in the 1893 sketch in ways that London must work to establish ten years later, beginning with Van Weyden's rebirth from the threat of a solitary drowning. Turning from a model based on free-for-all violence among men, London more and more confines his focus in the first half of the novel to the interplay between captain and mate, so that social bonding is conceived in terms of a single male-male couple—a shift that again prepares for Maud Brewster and the narrative's subsequent affirmation of normative heterosexuality. In the novel's storm scene, for instance, London leaves Wolf and Hump alone on the *Ghost*, along with Mugridge, while all other members of the crew are out at sea hunting. Although the presence of Mugridge during this vivid scene might suggest a return to the complex circuit of emotions (fear, jealousy, hatred, disgust, and so on) triangulated between captain, cook, and helper in the early chapters of the novel, Van Weyden prefaces his account of the storm simply by saying, "I saw more of Wolf Larsen than ever . . . and left on board were only he and I, and Thomas Mugridge, who did not count" (156).

Hump's blunt assertion about Mugridge not counting is more cruel and shocking than any of the physical punishment the pathetic Cockney has taken from Larsen, whose contempt at least is a perverse form of attention, unlike Van Weyden's utter refusal here to acknowledge Mugridge's value as a person. Earlier he had replaced his loathing for the repulsive creature with a kind of understanding and pity, declaring, "I shall be able to appreciate the lives of the working people hereafter" (61) by virtue of his own mistreatment. But Van Weyden cannot afford to continue to feel any such sympathy, which would imply some lingering identification between the two men. Hump's implicit grasp that Mugridge is feminine primarily because he is treated like a woman—that both women and the poor are rendered powerless and abject by the social control of those who rule—can no longer make any sense once the narrator learns how to become a man himself, a process that entails bossing other men. Mugridge must be discarded precisely because he is an *unnatural* woman created by social conditions, unlike the forces of Mother Nature and globally expanding female vanity that now occupy London's attention in advance of Maud Brewster. Symbolically castrated by the shark who bites off his foot (a parody of the cosmic insult aimed at Ahab, perhaps), the queer Cockney, "bleeding at the mouth" with his "offending" shirt in tatters (201), is finally sacrificed (literally thrown overboard) a few chapters later in the presence of Maud—a last bit of "man-play" (204), Larsen profoundly calls it, that marks an end to the *Ghost*'s graphic violence between men and, with it, the end of all homoerotic contest. With a real woman now on board, the representation of mastery will take a decisive turn.

Maud Brewster's arrival midway through the novel is announced with a flourish by a member of the *Ghost*: "May I never shoot a seal again if that ain't a woman!" (176). With this vow that utters the master signifier "woman," we can all but hear a palpable, massive sigh of relief escape Jack London's lips and find its way onto the novel's printed page. Only moments before her sudden appearance, Hump's passion for Wolf had reached its most feverish pitch, as he confesses during a murderous fit of rage: "I felt almost irresistibly impelled to fling myself upon him" (175–76). Rescued from the shipwreck of a "mail steamer" (182)—"disabled," of course!—Maud comes to rescue narrator and author from the wreck of their ghostly manhood, to give their mail a more natural destination. As the seal hunter's vow suggests, such a restorative project is connected to Van Weyden's previous remarks linking men's savage will to power with women's vain desires. But now the implication is that a woman on board could counteract such global savagery; by some curious logic the desires *of* women have turned into the desire *for* a woman—desire that London assumes will by definition supplant the sailors' homoerotic violence. Male lack under phallic patriarchy is thus reimagined as simply stemming from a lack of women; in relation to the first half of the novel, Maud serves less to call forth the crew's desire for women than to negate the men's desire for one another. Literally this means that London must take away what he has given. A few pages after Maud's arrival, Van Weyden prepares the lady's boudoir, "her head resting on a pillow I had appropriated from Wolf Larsen's bunk" (180). One mate comes to replace the other, one love story canceling out (as London's letter to Brett put it) "the bigger thing lying underneath" that was threatening midway through the narrative to push its way to the surface.

What looks like desire for women therefore more closely resembles a need for them; to invoke the terms of Hump and Wolf's intimate debate, it is a question of utility rather than purpose. This need first emerges early on, when Van Weyden attempts to escape his bondage to Larsen by signaling to a passing boat aptly named *"Lady Mine"* (30).[31] Women thus represent the only way off Wolf's hell-ship—more precise, women who function as things to be possessed. Here possession is not so much acquisition as a form of internalization, for to have "lady mine" would be to get in touch with something tender inside onself that could rein in phallic aggression. Whereas previously the slippery categories "masculine" and "feminine" are patently and painfully understood in the novel as raw manifestations of the struggle for power, now the "feminine" is driven underground, if you will—an internal "side" awaiting expression and integration with the "masculine" self.

Preparing the way for his heroine Maud, London explicitly shifts gender from social to psychological foundations in a famous passage that directly prefaces Larsen's self-begotten emergence from the sea and subsequent bloody gang assault by his crew. Spurred by Mugridge's passing remark that he never had a mother, Van Weyden suddenly realizes "that I have never placed a proper valuation upon womankind" (128). Ruminating on his own mother and sisters, Hump next considers the absence of mothers on ship, finding it "unnatural and unhealthful that men should be totally separated from women and herd through the world by themselves. Coarseness and savagery are the inevitable results." Without women, he concludes, "there is no balance in their lives. Their masculinity, which in itself is of the brute, has been overdeveloped. The other and spiritual side of their natures has been dwarfed," turning them into "a company of celibates, grinding harshly against one another." Van Weyden even wonders if "they ever had mothers" (129).

This passage is usually cited by sympathetic critics such as Sam Baskett to affirm Jack London's profound respect and understanding for women—the means by which he could achieve psychic balance and overcome his macho tendencies. In this view the first half of the novel's interplay between Wolf and Hump, which cannot be reduced "simplistically to homoeroticism," Baskett cautions, is in effect corrected by a more holistic and wholesome integration of gender that leads the way to the second half's "ideal androgynous relationship": male-female balance externalized and written large as a dynamic heterosexuality. Confidently speaking of "genuine masculinity" and "genuine femininity" as fixed entities, Baskett can go on to assume that both man and woman are "androgynous" in a positive, progressive way so that "the label of homosexuality," as he calls it, will remain "invalid" for interpreting this novel.[32]

In addition to accepting as givens perfectly stereotyped conventions equating womankind with spirituality, Baskett's case for androgyny ignores the massive confusion at the center of London's celebration, for in this passage Van Weyden moves back and forth between women as mothers and women as wives as if these two subject positions were entirely interchangeable. This key passage thus serves to restore the oedipal paradigm that has been missing on board the *Ghost* ever since the ferry's women, screaming like stuck pigs, figuratively give birth to Van Weyden and then sink into the sea. But such a restoration comes at the expense of reason. If the problem is celibacy, then presumably having mothers on board would not help, but if the problem is lack of maternal influence, then the assumption is that wives are simply surrogate mothers. Conflating the crew's celibacy with absent mothers, London's narrator goes so far as to suggest that these men are in fact "a race apart, wherein there is no such thing as sex; that they are hatched out of the sun like turtle eggs" (129), with the assumption that their self-begetting and their unnatural adult "grinding" with one another are one and the same.

But just because these men don't honor or remember or even have mothers does not mean that they must be without sex. Baskett endorses such a bizarre piece of logic when he credits Van Weyden with realizing that "masculinity with no admixture of feminine qualities is asexual." We must wait to see just how sexual the "normal" relationship between Hump and Maud will turn out to be, compared with the intimacy displayed between men. But perhaps more to the point here, "sex," as I have been arguing all along, is not something which these men possess biologically as much as the actions which they perform with and against one another.

Sex clearly need not be mapped onto a grid of stereotyped gender difference, but this is exactly what Baskett's argument must assume, following London's lead in the second half of the novel. Associating notions of "true femininity" with the novel's own ideological construction of "womankind" as a sort of abstract female principle, at once eternal and internal, Baskett simply duplicates London's savage repression that permits the mere arrival of a female to undo all he had previously done to represent the agon between captain and mate. The woman on board thus matches the woman inside, and all is right with the world once more.

What most critics assume to be a moment of epiphany in the novel, I take to be the beginning of the end. With the introduction of "woman," Hump can be born again, this time as a "genuine" man defined solely now in relation to a woman. I say "woman" because the heroine is not even given a name when she first comes on board, for her immediate function in the story depends strictly on her status as woman, not on her personal identity. Personality, in fact, would initially interfere with London's systematic attempt to restructure his narrative and reorient its characters by way of gender alone. Without even knowing who she is, Van Weyden immediately marks the difference her presence makes. "A being from another world" (177), this creature smiles (she has a mouth, as the men do), but "as only a woman can smile" (177). Such abstract insights give the toughened Van Weyden a new kind of charming awkwardness, once he begins "realizing what a delicate, fragile creature a woman is" (178): not just this one in particular (he hardly registers her individuality), but womankind in general.

Inserted into the narrative with a kind of clinical precision, London's generic woman quickly enables Van Weyden to abandon his position as captain's mate in favor of a new role—woman's protector.[33] Labeling Larsen "a brute, a demon" (179) to this newly arrived third party, Hump "resolve[s] to prevent her seeing the brutality" (179) on the ship. Formerly a helpless witness and participant in this contagious violence, Van Weyden abstracts himself from it by pledging to shield someone else. The novel's master/slave dialectics, represented as quest-romance, thus yield to a new sort of love triangle, with the woman now serving to mediate between men, to redirect their demonized intensity away from each other.

Elaborating the work of Jonathan Katz, Anthony Rotundo, and other historians, George Chauncey had argued:

> If homosexuality did not exist in the early nineteenth century, then neither did heterosexuality, for each category depends for its existence on the other. The very capacity of men to shift between male and female love objects demonstrates that a different sexual regime governed their emotions. "Normal" men only became "heterosexual" in the late nineteenth century, when they began to make their "normalcy" contingent on their renunciation of such intimacies with men.[34]

The rise of "heterosexuality" in middle-class culture around 1900 depended on exactly this sort of renunciation, which London so graphically and dramatically renders in *The Sea-Wolf* with the introduction of Maud Brewster. Giving up his "Wolf" for a woman, forsaking the pleasures of the body for more spiritual joys, London in effect turns his back on his working-class origins to affirm his allegiance to an emergent set of middle-class norms.[35]

Although the captain-mate relationship has been based on attachment/aversion, as I have stressed, the Maud-Hump relationship begins to resemble a case of identification. Larsen helps London here by treating her exactly as he had initially treated Van Weyden, introducing his new captive on board with a public interrogation aimed at exposing their class similarity: "I suppose you're like Mr. Van Weyden there, accustomed to having things done for you" (195). This remark follows a brief taunting of Hump by the captain addressed specifically to Maud, during which he mockingly praises his mate for having now gained "legs to stand on," points to the knife Hump is carrying in his belt, and teases (with a hint of jealousy) that "he can scarcely control himself in your presence. He is not accustomed to the presence of ladies" (193–94). Once a source of pride, the *Ghost*'s all-male version of manhood suddenly is made to look a bit silly in front of a woman.

When the woman finally gets a chance to speak, Wolf himself is mocked in return, framed in a way that ostensibly dramatizes the vast difference between Maud and Hump. When asked the inevitable question about earning money by her own labor, the woman offers a setup of patriarchy—"I remember my father giving me a dollar once, when I was a little girl, for remaining absolutely quiet for five minutes"—only to drop the bombshell on Larsen and Van Weyden that she "earns eighteen hundred dollars a year."[36] This fact makes her a "woman . . . worth looking at" (196–97), Van Weyden dryly notes. Just as a homoerotic pairing gives way to a heterosexual triangle, so too does the ship's hyperbolic phallicism give way to the less primitive power of the capitalist market, which gives the woman who can "turn out commodities" (197) a different sort of individuated legs than the ones Van Weyden has so brutally suffered to forge. Neither aristocrat nor common brute, Maud is resolutely middle-class, an independent professional bent on success.

Yet the particular way this woman earns her money crucially works to reestablish mutual identification between her and Hump. She receives her full proper name in the novel at the exact moment she announces her profession, when her allusion to a "typewriter" suddenly triggers Van Weyden's recognition: " 'You are Maud Brewster,' I said slowly and with certainty, almost as though I were charging her with a crime" (197). "The name and its magic" mean nothing to Larsen, but Van Weyden already knows her as a published poet, a famous woman of letters, while she in turn recognizes him, by virtue of his previous critical appreciative review of her writing, as Humphrey Van Weyden, "Dean of American Letters, the Second" (198–99).

However preposterous, this astonishing "typewriter" recognition scene—the scene of a crime, Hump suggests—reinforces gender as a stabilizing system of difference that allows for identification by treating the profession of letters, now set in the context of middle-class genteel culture, as an analogous division of labor. Gender and letters, in effect, become one and the same: man and woman work together as part of a larger whole to support middle-class normative heterosexuality, a circuit that for London is mirrored in the relationship between admiring male critic and female writer—the only genuine source of procreative, moral power. Sharing letters in common, critic and author—doubles in effect—can thus establish true congress with each other, by way of published poems and reviews, before they even meet on the ship.[37]

Once the aggressive means to probe the captain's "soul-stuff," letters now operate to exclude Wolf Larsen, for critic and poetess soon conspire "in secret alliance" (208) to defy their captain even as they appear to humor him by continuing to "discuss literature and art" (209) in his presence. During these specialized professional exchanges, the uncomprehending Larsen doesn't "count" (199) any longer, as he himself acknowledges, repeating Van Weyden's prior dismissal of Mugridge. Acting as Hump's "kindred intellect and spirit," Maud remains "in striking contrast to Wolf Larsen" (213). Although the captain's splendid body, speech, and manhood remain dissociated from one another, Maud's "body and spirit" are in perfect accord, harmonized by her poetry: "Describe her verse, as the critics have described it, as sublimated and spiritual, and you have described her body" (212). To such an ethereal creature—Woman with a capital *W*—Van Weyden readily submits as "her willing slave" (193). By this telling oxymoron London seeks to undo Larsen's bodily hold on Hump's manhood. Only by making the new (critical) object of (heterosexual) desire so bloodless can London drain Wolf of his power over the narrator, whose manly energies are now spent on slavish appreciation, protection, and praise.[38]

For London's conventional love triangle to work, Larsen has to be willing to play the game, attracting Maud and being attracted to her in return. Although London makes some half-hearted efforts in this direction by suggesting how Maud is "fascinated" (213) by Larsen's mesmerizing eyes, the captain's end of the bargain is most often simply assumed by way of Van Weyden's own formulaic assertions: "I was jealous; therefore I loved" (215)—the classic affirmation of mediated desire. For his part, Larsen seems more jealous of Maud than amorous for her. London does plot a predictable scene of ravishing, yet Larsen's attempted rape is curiously cut short not by any last-minute rescue by Hump but rather by one of Wolf's blinding headaches, which increasingly render him more and more impotent as the novel progresses. Trying to aid Maud, Hump finally does manage to stab his tormentor, a "superficial" (253) knife thrust now safely contained by the novel's newly erected heterosexual framework. As Joan Hedrick shrewdly observes, this headache feminizes Wolf in a particular way, in effect turning him into a frightened newlywed who begs off her husband's advances by claiming a sudden pain in anticipation of the pain of sexual intercourse.[39] Given Larsen's interaction with his men in the first half of the novel, it is difficult to imagine him taking any physical interest in this woman.

At least one of London's contemporary readers also found the Maud-Wolf part of the triangle difficult to swallow. Writing to London in 1911, one of his socialist admirers, the gay writer Maurice Magnus, asked if heroes such as Wolf Larsen and Burning Daylight were in fact each too much of a man to ever be with a woman. For Magnus, this powerful male libido in the absence of women is "greater and more splendid to all mankind," the "secret of the priest's celibacy." Avoiding the trap of "it takes one to know one," London gamely replied by insisting that even though he has "studied the sex problem" very "thoroughly and scientifically," he "never dreamed of drawing a homosexual male character," in part simply because "those who figure vitally in that problem constitute too small a percentage of the human race to be an adequate book-buying inducement to a writer."[40]

Regarding homosexuality as a scientific "problem" and/or an inadequate "inducement" to publish (his ever present concern), London concludes his letter by asserting, "Flatly, I am a lover of women." It might as well be Humphrey Van Weyden himself speaking, for once Maud arrives on the scene to redirect the narrative's energy, Larsen is then treated in similar terms as a kind of problem or case study for the two heterosexual lovers to contemplate. In this new allegory of letters, male critic and female author join together to reduce Wolf Larsen to the ontological status of a character, glossing him by way of a series of literary analogues that trope him to oblivion—as a "male Circe" (243, an odd comparison worth pondering), and a proud "Lucifer" (365; see also 95, 249)—until he expires, like Poe's Valdemar, a "disembodied" (357) spirit communicating from beyond the grave.[41] Although earlier in the novel the penetrating force of critical exchange between men enabled Hump directly to probe Wolf's soul-stuff, here shared canonical allusions serve to relocate Larsen as a third party outside the lovers' own increasingly exclusive binary intercourse. In the end the blind and paralyzed Larsen, dwindling to sheer verbiage (first lips that speak, then a writing hand), is left to reiterate to Hump, with a "twisted smile," his desire "to eat you" (343). For his part Van Weyden jokingly (but honestly) can credit his newly acquired strength to "taking" the medicine of "Wolf Larsen, in large doses" (321), although he had earlier complained to his captain about suffering from "indigestion" (216) in his presence.[42]

Cut down to size, Larsen begins to lose his grip on Hump soon after Maud's arrival, so that London can no longer sustain even the semblance of a love triangle. The novel quickly narrows to a domestic romance as critic and author withdraw ("like good comrades" [246]) to the aptly named Endeavor Island to be reborn as a kind of archetypal bourgeois couple reconstituting society from scratch amid a hostile natural environment. Even though Larsen disrupts their cozy private retreat, the island setting is about as far removed from the *Ghost* as possible, for on land Hump no longer need contend with unnatural men at sea.[43] As Maud declares after helping her partner kill seals, "It's just like home-coming," with Van Weyden now performing masculinity for "my woman, my mate" (292) alone. Realizing in this scene that "I could not play the coward before her eyes" (286), Hump tells Maud, "What I need is a longer club" (289).

A cross between *Robinson Crusoe* and the Hollywood comedy *It Happened One Night*, the Endeavor Island scenes offer a textbook demonstration of heterosexual decorum preparatory to marriage in which individuality is maintained by way of stable categories of "masculine" and "feminine," whereas intimacy is celebrated as a form of mutual possession that mirrors each's self-possession. In this respect the couple's separate sleeping huts on their enchanted private island are perhaps less a concession to the prudish tastes of London's readers than an epitome of the novel's logic in the second half, which finds in the solitary man-woman dyad the means to reaffirm an autonomous selfhood sorely tested by Wolf Larsen and his contagious violence in the narrative's first half.

Even without the continual presence of an outside rival, mastery in this dyadic heterosexual structure continues to accrue through the woman, as the gaze is restored to its proper controlling function: "Maud's eyes were shining with anticipation as they followed me. She had such faith in me! And the thought of it was so much added power. . . . I had but to look at her, or think of her, and be strong again" (315). Unlike Hump's previous uncontrollable fascination with Wolf's body, in this scene, as Maud and Van Weyden together begin triumphantly to reerect the *Ghost*'s masts (cut down by Larsen), the shift from looking to thinking suggests how the couple's reciprocal admiration is primarily conceptual, for their passion serves, as in the epistolary exchanges between London and Strunsky in *The Kempton-Wace Letters*, to validate the self-contained power of the lover. Thinking is just as good as looking for Van Weyden, because the phallus is no longer a mobile sign, dynamically negotiated between men, but safely fixed, as the notorious, prolonged, and rather technical remasting scene suggests. Like their analogous seal-clubbing adventure, Maud can help her mate wield and display manhood (in this case gently guiding the ship's mast "over the hole," 348), as long as she remains the conceptual "fulcrum" of a conventional system of gendered difference, resolving the man's "problem of lifting oneself by one's boot-straps" (316)—London's central preoccupation throughout all his first decade's writing. Manly self-reliance, it turns out, depends on the presence of a woman.[44]

As the cure to the problem of masculinity, Maud Brewster thus represents not only the turning point in the novel but also a crucial turning point in Jack London's entire career. Her arrival halfway through *The Sea-Wolf* coincides quite closely with London's own decisive experiences during the summer of 1903—falling in love with his future wife Charmian Kittredge in June, achieving worldwide recognition in July with the book publication of *The Call of the Wild* (serialized beginning June 20), and negotiating in August with *Century* magazine editor R. W. Gilder the hefty four-thousand-dollar serial rights to *The Sea-Wolf* as the novel reached midcompletion. As we might expect, London worked his relationship with Charmian into the plot itself via a reference to a storm that served to merge their recent first sexual encounter with Maud's imminent arrival, both cast in terms of his twin publishing triumphs (1893 typhoon sketch and 1903 dog story): "Gales we encountered . . . and, in the middle of June, a typhoon most memorable to me and most important because of the changes wrought through it upon my future" (157). These memorable June "changes" refer at once to his new celebrity as a writer and his new relationship with Charmian; if London's origins as a professional author (in 1897) are coterminous with his discovery of illegitimacy, the father's disavowal, and the son's revenge in fiction ("A Thousand Deaths"), then his fame (starting in 1903) is coterminous with the discovery of one's soul mate for life, Charmian. Thinly veiled as Maud, Charmian would serve as Jack's own "one small woman," an identity Maud herself embraces in the novel's conclusion as "my father's name for my mother" (355). *The Sea-Wolf* thus charts London's turn from the death of the father to the finding of the oedipal mother/mate, with the intense homoerotic interplay beween Hump and Wolf (neither father nor spouse, exactly) functioning as the uneasy, unstable passage of transition.

To appreciate the influence of Charmian on the writing of *The Sea-Wolf*, we need to look briefly at the love letters London sent her during their summer affair, beginning 18 June 1903—eloquent testimonials to heterosexual passion in their own right. The first thing to note about these letters is that they show signs of having been carefully *prepared* by Charmian herself. Although Anna Strunsky was content simply to save London's love letters, Charmian took it on herself to transcribe his intimate letters to her, removing salutation and signature, at the very least, and arranging their sequence to form a kind of plot of her own. In the absence of London's original letters, presumably destroyed by her, we have no way of knowing the extent of Charmian's retyped revisions. But these copies do suggest how in so brilliantly sensing the significance of London's emerging fame, Charmian became from the very start of their relationship her mate's editor and typewriter—a word at the turn of the century that could refer to the person as well as the thing. A reference to a typewriter in the novel, recall, triggers the mutual recognition of Brewster and Van Weyden as public figures, a famous woman and man of letters. Understanding their private affair as yet another grounds for publication, Charmian in effect outdoes her mate, taking on the role of promotion that he had previously taken on all by himself.

While the complex, lifelong relationship between Jack and Charmian is beyond the scope of this study, his summer 1903 letters to her (written midway through composing *The Sea-Wolf*) help shed light on his construction of gender in the novel. As I discussed in the last chapter, London's love letters to the socialist Anna Strunsky written during the previous two years (1900–1902) are preoccupied with exploring his beloved's difference, which he persistently defined in terms of Strunsky's status as a "Russian Jewess." Struggling with her perceived otherness—at once fascinating, remote, exotic, and compelling—London finally decided that only someone exactly like him, another man, could truly understand his joys and sorrows, with the assumption (also underlying their coauthored *Kempton-Wace Letters*) that love as passion leads in the end primarily to self-validation. His early letters to Charmian also voice a similar need for a companion just like himself, which London expresses as his "dream" of "the great Man-Comrade" who "could grapple with the fiercest life"—a desire he had also admitted in a letter to Cloudesley Johns as early as 17 April 1899. Offering a pretty fair description of Wolf Larsen (minus his pointed sadism), London rapturously confesses to Charmian that such "closeness . . . whereby the man and I might merge and become one for love and life" might no longer be possible but that in their very "kinship" she herself had become that identical "very One."[45]

Charmian as London's perfect "Man-Comrade"—the lovers can sustain this astonishing conclusion only by assuming some built-in structural difference already always existing between them, as a 1 September 1903 letter from London makes crystal clear: "We are so alike in so much, that, as you have remarked, perhaps we are too alike to be for each other. But there is a great difference between us, which in connection with our likeness, makes us preeminently for each other, and that difference is your essential femininity and my equally essential masculinity. There is where our great unlikeness comes in. You are, when all is said & done, of women the most womanly; and I, I hope, am somewhat of a man." For London, Charmian thus fulfills precisely the same function that Maud Brewster fulfills for Van Weyden: a safe means to realize manhood apart from other men. In contrast to those critics like Baskett who argue for the author's androgyny, a concept that internalizes difference even as it rigidly maintains essentialized categories, here London severely polarizes essential gender oppositions precisely to preserve each partner's individuality. In this regard Charmian's often-noted role as New Woman (played to some extent by Maud as well), boxing and riding horses with Jack, is less an assertion of feminism than a copy of conventional masculinity made possible by London's sudden faith in the natural foundations of gender difference itself. Straightening Jack out, Charmian can satisfy her mate's ideal of a "Man-Comrade" only by being the most womanly of women.

Standard psychoanalytic accounts of love between men treat homosexuality as a form of arrested oedipal development in which the subject cannot progress beyond narcissistic self-love. As Michael Warner has persuasively shown, such a perspective assumes that gender must be the primary category for organizing difference.[46] In his love letters to Charmian, Jack London completely buys into this logic but nonetheless manages to suggest a surprising alternative: that narcissism is actually sanctioned by traditional heterosexuality and not homosexuality. The "compulsory" nature of heterosexuality thus may have less to do with the perpetuation of patriarchy per se, as feminist theory has proposed, than the fact that conventional gender structures permit men to love themselves without having to confront this desire. The woman lets the man think he is irresistible to himself. Narcissism is thereby restored once gender as a system of patriarchal difference is reinstated. Unlike other turn-of-the-century naturalist authors dedicated to remasculinizing their profession, Jack London at least is brave enough in his writing to admit his need for a companion just like himself (thereby collapsing the distinction between identification and attachment), even if in the end his fictional alter ego Wolf Larsen is demonized and blinded (castrated) for presuming to take physically another man as his mate outside the regulations of gender.

Earlier in this chapter I suggested that in sinking the screaming women who help give birth to Van Weyden on board the *Ghost*, London closed off oedipal rivalry between men. With the arrival of the ideal woman Maud/Charmian midway through the novel and in London's own life, we might expect a resumption of such a normalizing schematics, yet where do we locate the disciplining father in the second half of *The Sea-Wolf*? Certainly not in Larsen and his crew, who are deemed unnatural by Hump/London precisely for lacking mothers and wives. I would argue that the censoring father returns not as a character inside the text but rather as a controlling presence from the outside in the guise of Richard W. Gilder, the powerful *Century* magazine editor. In a galling, impertinent letter sent to Macmillan editor George Brett in late August 1903 that bragged about his previous blue-penciling of Twain's *The Adventures of Huckleberry Finn*, Gilder insisted on revising many of the *Ghost* scenes in the novel and previewing the second half before agreeing to pay London to serialize it.[47]

The oedipal triangle is thus reinscribed by way of the institutional apparatus of publishing itself. From the very start of his career London always knew that if he wanted to get into print, he would have to play by the rules of his editors. Yet having signaled his aspirations for the canon at the start of his sea novel, having earned a national reputation by virtue of the publication of *The Call of the Wild*, and having secured a life mate in Charmian, London would seem to have been in a better position to stand on his own legs, to borrow Wolf Larsen's perpetual taunt of Van Weyden. By summer's end 1903, Jack London had finally made enough of a name for himself to assume some artistic autonomy (if only to be affirmed by symbolic gestures). But alluding to "the changes in my life which have just been occurring," London replied to his editors' request in a reassuring letter to Brett on 2 September 1903, giving "Mr. Gilder" "my full permission to blue pencil all he wishes" because the author is confident that the novel's "characters themselves, will not permit of anything offensive." Editorial pressure is thus incorporated into the novel itself by way of characters' internal principles of restraint, as if the mouths of editors (to recall London's essay on Poe) and fictional protagonists speak the very same language. Coinciding with the arrival of his future wife and personal amanuensis, adviser, and publicist Charmian, the regulatory system of gender introduced into the plot by Maud Brewster also registers London's assent to an analogous editorial regulation.[48]

Helping together to market Jack London, Charmian and his publishers worked for the next thirteen years to keep their man popular: London's strongest (if not deepest) lifelong interest. In this sense the Maud-Humphrey romance in *The Sea-Wolf* is less a reflection of their own love affair than a blueprint rehearsing how they would live the rest of their lives before the public eye as well as in their (semi)private Sonoma ranch retreat. Publication quickly became the very model for such celebrity, as Jack and Charmian learned how to comport themselves as if they were charismatic characters in one of London's popular bestsellers.[49] Given the presumptuous daring of the first half of *The Sea-Wolf*, it is difficult to regard the second half of the novel as anything but a failure of nerve on London's part—not for politely desexualizing his charming couple to prevent offense but for relying on them at all to refashion the meaning of masculinity.

Yet perhaps this failure is necessary, for in so systematically depending on Maud to unman his men at sea, London directs attention to the very queerness he seeks to normalize. In his letter to Brett, Gilder himself would seem to have recognized something more elementally repulsive in "the dead level of almost sickening brutality in the first draft of the first half of the story as submitted" beyond its staged violence (which, after all, has always been largely acceptable in American life and literature). If Wolf Larsen is Lucifer, it is less by virtue of his nihilism, egotism, or sadism than his transgressive sexuality, which threatens to undermine foundational cultural assumptions about the making of manhood. Abandoning his captain so that he could in effect run his own ship, London turned away from the most powerful and disturbing implications of his own work to transform his sea novel into serialized magazine romance, his commitment to conventional middle-class heterosexual order sealed by his lovers' closing kiss. On the strength of the *Century*'s serial publication, on the strength of his now famous name, London was able to sell over fifty-five thousand advance copies of *The Sea-Wolf* even before the book reached stores—an eloquent testimony to modern mass marketing that could so efficiently disseminate the popular author's stamp of self.[50] Once the question and quest that haunted his writing, Jack London's mail/male call had begun to sound like the answer.

Epilogue : Celebrity

A little more than a year after *The Sea-Wolf* appeared as a book, London published "The Sun-Dog Trail."[1] This story marks London's farewell to Sitka Charley, the Anglicized Indian trail guide, and with him a certain kind of stark naturalism. An official letter carrier, Charley is again identified as being as good as "white," although he has never learned to read or write. Instead of reading letters, as the tale opens Charley is attempting to read pictures, illustrations torn from popular magazines and newspapers. Puzzled by such representations, he engages in a discussion with the tale's first-person narrator, a professional artist or "painter-man," as Charley calls him, who is interested in Charley's opinions precisely because the illiterate Indian is assumed to be a "sheer mastery of reality," an "unbiased judge who knew life only, and not art." As in *The Call of the Wild*, labor is thus sharply divided between carrying words and reading them, with the aim, once again, to purify the mail and render the mailman unconscious of his messages.

But when the white painter-man tries to teach the red man about the art of popular illustration by comparing it to a "man writing a letter" as viewed through a window, Charley responds with a story of his own. However untainted at heart, Charley is not above financial considerations, having accepted the mysterious offer of a white woman to go on trail for 750 dollars a month: "I, too, go on and on, because I am strong on the trail and because I am greatly paid." Charley and this woman are soon joined by a third person, constituting the familiar configuration of Indian, white woman, and white man, all in obsessive pursuit of a fourth, a white "stranger-man." The motives of these "baby wolves" remain unclear to Charley, who quickly learns that money is not enough to make him happy. But he is nonetheless willing to share their relentless obsession, leading his two white masters, "toil-mad" and "hunger-mad," in search of "black spots" moving against "the snow and the silence," until staggering and crawling they catch up to these black marks and kill their human prey. When the painter-man asks him the meaning of his experience, Charley calls it an "end without understanding," a "piece of life" like the man at the window whose letters remain seen from the outside— destination unknown, content unknown.

Rarely again would Jack London so self-perceptively cast his work in such painfully elemental terms: toil, hunger, weariness, pursuit, and death, all framed by the opening and closing image of a man writing. During London's final decade, the two dramatic mainstays of his naturalism—power and suffering—would instead come increasingly to reside in that very self-consciousness, itself a function of Jack London's growing celebrity as an author. In much of his early correspondence with editors such as George Brett, London put his career in an anticipatory light, requesting advances for work not yet done. But as my discussions of *The Sea-Wolf*, his advice essays, and the preface to *War of the Classes* have suggested, by 1903–4 he began on occasion to turn retrospective, searching his past work and its reception for new ideas—for new ways to recast himself in relation to his readers.

Although it makes little sense to insist on a single moment or clear origin for such a trajectory, one obvious place to start would be his novel *White Fang* (1906) insofar as it takes up the concerns of *The Call of the Wild* (1903)—the book that initially won him international fame. Although London insisted to Brett in late 1904 that his "hot" idea for a new novel was a "companion" and not a "sequel,"[2] the fact that his imagination was spurred by a newspaper article entitled "The Call of the Tame: An Antithesis" (itself triggered by London's *Call*, no doubt) suggests a circuit of exchange or a feedback loop between producers and consumers that points to contemporary Hollywood.

My interest in *White Fang* thus lies precisely in its function as a sequel, a work written specifically in relation to a previous successful one. If *The Call of the Wild* can be read as enacting the author's professional anxieties, the need for discipline and self-control to gain recognition for his work, then the subsequent story of a wild beast's domestication at the hands of his masters can perhaps best be read allegorically as expressing London's understanding of what happens once such public recognition has been achieved. Taming exacts its price: although White Fang may show some of his old spirit in the end by saving his adopted masters from an escaped prisoner bent on murder, the wolf-dog remains a defanged family pet more akin to Lassie than Buck, despite London's best efforts to retain some of the beast's wildness.

More germane, perhaps, is the market-driven logic of the sequel itself, whose commercial success depends on an audience's prior familiarity with that work's predecessor. Audiences approve of sequels because it gives them more of the same, with ever so slight variations, so that producers can minimize the risk of failure. What sells once will sell even more the second time around. My point here is not to insist that the sequel is necessarily inferior to the original version—*Batman Returns* is arguably better than *Batman*, with both movies perhaps eclipsed by the aptly titled *Batman Forever* (promising sequels ad infinitum). Nor am I suggesting that London did not have good reasons for imagining how a wild wolf might become a dog. But the writing of *White Fang* does underscore London's willingness to let his literary career be so shaped by his past performances in an attempt to guarantee continuing acceptance from readers already in place. On the title page of book after Macmillan book, London saw himself as "Author of 'The Call of the Wild,' 'White Fang,' Etc." Those critics who complain that London has been unfairly typecast as a writer of dog stories would do well to consider how London, in conjunction with his publisher and his readers, helped to fix his literary reputation.

That reputation, with modifications and variations, becomes the central subject of a trio of big novels that London published in a brief three-year span: *The Iron Heel* (1908), *Martin Eden* (1909), and *Burning Daylight* (1910). One after the other, each novel's main character, magnified and glorified, plays out a different imaginary career for London—socialist revolutionary fighting plutocracy (Ernest Everhard); scorned artist succeeding too late (Martin Eden); and, perhaps most interesting, Klondike gold miner turning capitalist speculator turning gentleman farmer (Burning Daylight). All three novels are united by more than idealized autobiography; many of London's earliest productions, we have seen, are clearly autobiographical—and thinly veiled confessions at that. But in these novels, autobiography has become a public affair for London, for what now most concerns him and energizes his writing is the celebrity status of his own creations.

As I have already suggested in my introduction, London mixes politics with glamour in *The Iron Heel* to powerful, if peculiar, effect. While common sense might dictate that Everhard's adoring wife is a poor choice for a narrator to convey an apocalyptic vision of a protofascist state, London more profoundly grasped otherwise, understanding how serious political ideas and personal charisma in the twentieth century can be linked (and leveled) precisely as public expressions of power. Similarly, in the case of *Martin Eden* it does little good to chide London, as did his daughter Joan, for misleading readers into thinking he was endorsing Eden's individualism instead of condemning it, when once such egomania is displayed in the open (when the artist gains recognition), then endorsement and condemnation can no longer remain very distinct, blurred by publicity itself. For both Martin and Jack, any attempt to write off celebrity or gain some perspective on it by taking it as one's explicit (literary) theme ends up simply feeding the fan's desire for more publicity.

In this respect *Burning Daylight* is the most revealing of this set of midcareer novels, because London revisits scenes of past success in an attempt to imagine a less public alternative for his future. One of his last productions set in the Klondike, the novel opens with the nicknamed character "Daylight" already a local Yukon celebrity, much like "The Boy Socialist of Oakland" figure played by London early on in Bay Area newspapers. At once commenting on and seduced by Daylight's irresistible charm for both men and women, his flair for "spectacular, melodramatic" entrances, Jack London at one point curiously remarks of his alter ego: "He was a slave to himself, which was natural in one with a healthy ego, but he rebelled in ways either murderous or panicky at being a slave to anybody else."[3] Presumably it is fine to be enslaved by some imaginary version or stamp of yourself, as long as you retain control over it.

The (panicky) hope here is that "self" and "anybody else" can be clearly distinguished; yet given Daylight's "fatal facility for self-advertisement" (108), as London calls it, the location of Daylight's mastery is problematic to say the least. Making a show of rejecting romantic love as well as the dictates of social convention, Daylight may be less "the lone he-wolf" (26) than he insists. Over and over again in the novel London verges on insight, only to fall back into sheer astonishment that duplicates the self-consuming position of celebrity itself. London follows his "self-advertisement" analysis, for instance, by shifting his attention to the magical effects of Daylight's personality: "Things he did, no matter how adventitious or spontaneous, struck the popular imagination as remarkable" (108). Suddenly we are off again on a rehearsal of Daylight's great feats: showing up first in the "heartbreaking stampede to Danish Creek," killing a "record baldface grizzly," winning a canoe race, making tremendous poker bets, and so on and on, all the trademark scenes of London's previous Northland fiction rolled into one.

Unable to understand his character's "fatal facility," London is left simply to plot it, following closely the success of his own literary career. Striking it rich in the Yukon (as London did with *The Call of the Wild*), Daylight relocates to San Francisco, where he uses his wealth to go into large-scale financial speculation. Assuming some crucial continuity of identity between adventurer and capitalist based on Daylight's daring gambler spirit, London in fact suggests in the novel's middle section how his hero's "self" is more fundamentally integral by virtue of its public consumption: "And once more the papers sensationalized him" (125). The man once renowned as "Adventurer of the Frost" now gets written up for his investment prowess, appearing on "the breakfast table of a million homes along with the toast and breakfast foods," London puts it with remarkable acuity, dramatizing late capitalism's commodification of news. More than simply part of the game, publicity begins to look like the game itself, replacing the writer's body as the source of his authorial integrity.

Even though Daylight realizes (via his narrator's paraphrase) that "work, legitimate work, was the source of all wealth" (157), like Buck in *The Call of the Wild* he quickly discovers that capital need not depend on labor once it is free to circulate in the market. Growing cynical, getting burned on a big business deal, exacting revenge, Daylight is finally saved from himself by way of an ending that represents London's solution to the problem of celebrity. Turning his back on the fast life, Daylight finds the love of a good, simple woman (who happens to be under his employ as a stenographer, much as Charmian worked to type Jack's manuscripts), moves with her to the Valley of the Moon in Sonoma County (as London had), and lets his business go bust, insisting that only "paper" will be destroyed and not "the gold I dug out of the Klondike" (325).

Love, land, labor: London's solution seeks to restore what fame had taken away by returning to those core values informing his early writing. Yet insofar as celebrity operates as symbolic capital in modern American mass culture, it cannot be dispensed with so simply. "Paper" may prove to be as enduring as nature's wealth; even as London tries to remove himself from the public, that withdrawal itself becomes yet another public occasion, the subject for a new Jack London novel. Simply put, London the professional can't stop writing or, more accurate, he can't stop publishing—himself as well as his writing. As the epigram to *Burning Daylight* puts it, "Man is made with such large discourse, looking before and after." To keep his life and his discourse circulating in the public domain, London lectures on socialism, travels with Charmian around the world in search of exotic material, grants interviews, cuts movie deals, and, in sum, makes news—publicity that he seeks to control by the only way he knows how, namely, channeling it back into his fiction.[4]

So personal renewal by way of his "dream-ranch" gets cast in terms of a proposed "back to the land" novel (as he writes to editor Brett in 1911)—intimate desire converted into a popular literary genre.[5] As usual, the link between these two dreams is money: London needs cash to build his Wolf mansion, and plans to turn his Sonoma experience into fiction to raise funds. Having vowed to Brett in advance that "I shall absolutely and passionately believe every word" of his story (eventually titled *The Valley of the Moon*), London makes good on his promise by quite literally writing himself into the fiction—or rather the projected "self" that he imagines his readers expect of him, since his belief and his passions have strictly come to depend on that familiar set of public images.

The Valley of the Moon (1913) is a big novel—promoted as London's "longest" (and "finest") in a British advertisement.[6] Rather than rehearse specifics of the back-to-the-land plot, I want simply to look at three small but defining moments that suggest how London is caught in a phantasmagorical recycling act throughout the entire book. This recycling act is most transparent near the end of the novel, when London introduces himself and his wife as the Hastings, a wealthy and carefree peripatetic couple who serve as friendly neighbors helping to orient the working-class hero and heroine to their new Sonoma surroundings. Far more strange and striking, however, is an earlier scene, at the dead center of the novel, during which the heroine, Saxon Brown Roberts, initially decides to leave Oakland to save her marriage. Her decision is triggered by her brief encounter with a young boy named "Jack" (twelve or thirteen years old), who while sailing on a skiff in the San Francisco Bay encourages her to venture forth (like her racial namesakes) beyond the narrow confines of the city. To envision himself as the source of inspiration for his character's epiphany, London thus returns to a prior childhood incarnation crucial for his constructed authorial identity, the figure of a bold, wistful, and poor sailor boy that even today remains firmly part of his readers' screen memories, reinforced by dozens of anecdotes and iconographic representations.

In an illustration from a 1913 advertisement in *Cosmopolitan Magazine*, for example, the iconographic youthful image of "Jack London, Able Seaman" is juxtaposed against a more mature figure representing London's commercial side: the savvy promoter and businessman with a vested interest in keeping his romantic alter ego in the public eye (see figure 2). As London discovered when he dressed up like a bum for *The People of the Abyss*, clothes do indeed make a difference—but a difference that can be negotiated as long as "the London body dimensions" remain constant. In both the 1913 magazine advertisement and *The Valley of the Moon* (which was being serialized in the very same issue of *Cosmopolitan*), redemption for London (and Saxon) means cashing in one's coined image as folk hero, "a child of the people" (262), as Saxon imagines Jack.

Such folk images are quite literally projected onto a screen a few pages later in the book, when Saxon and her husband Billy get the idea of moving to the country by watching a moving picture show filled with bucolic scenes of farm life. Immediately they decide to watch the movie over again, Saxon exclaiming, "I'd just die of happiness in a place like that" (280). Although in this episode London does not represent himself directly, by depicting the movie screen as the locus of Saxon's wish fulfillment he is acknowledging the power of a popular medium akin to his own writing. London, in fact, was one of the first American writers in the new century to recognize the potential of movies to replace print as the cen-

JACK
LONDON
*Royal
Tailored
Man*

JACK LONDON—
Able Seaman

COPYRIGHT 1913, THE ROYAL TAILORS

"It's funny what a difference a few Clothes make!"

When Jack London picked out a Royal Fabric for a 2 piece Fall suit a few weeks ago, the fancy took him that he wanted a hat made of the same material. "Nothing easier!" said the local Royal dealer. And straightway he measured the London head and the London crown—sending those measurements to us along with the London body dimensions.

We cut and tailored the hat just as we did the suit, to exactly dovetail the specifications given us. Perhaps it may, or it may not be to your taste to wear a hat that matches your suit. But the point is:

We pay $1 A Day For every Day of Delay When A Royal Garment isn't Finished on time.

Royal Service gives you exactly what you want—exactly as you order it. There is no such thing as "partial satisfaction" in a Royal Tailor transaction. A Royal deal means *complete* satisfaction or no sale.

You select the fabric you want. You pick out the style and cut you want—and if any little individualities are wanted, not shown in the fashion plate you select, you dictate the desired changes to your local dealer—and we edit them into your suit. The Royal Tailored Man is the type of man who appreciates exact perfection—and gets it in his clothes.

This Guarantee comes buttoned onto the Garment.

"Get that Royal Tailored Look"

The Royal Tailors

Chicago   *Joseph Nelson* President   New York

Figure 2. An advertisement for Royal Tailors.

tral vehicle for mass culture—a change that quickly also led to a shift from New York to California as the center of cultural power.

London was interested in Hollywood's culture industry as early as 1911, when he began to deal for the movie rights to *The Sea-Wolf*. By 1913 (when *Valley of the Moon* was published) he had begun negotiations with the Balboa Amusement Company to produce a series of movies based on his books. Although these dealings soon led to a copyright battle that was eventually settled in London's favor (with the help of the Authors League of America), the head of Balboa (named H. M. Horkheimer, ironically enough) was sufficiently encouraged at one point to pass along an astonishing bit of news from the "horse's mouth," quoting London as promising, "I shall appear as the leading actor in all my own short stories and novels characterized into motion pictures." The logic is clear: if movies are "characterized" novels, then who better to play the role of star than the author himself? London quickly disavowed this misinformation/publicity stunt by insisting that he would not act but serve "solely as author." But as if he just could not help himself, he then added (perhaps a bit playfully), "Although I may pose at my desk."[7]

Sitka Charley's pictured man glimpsed from the trail in the act of writing has thus become the famous writer deliberately posing at his desk for the cameras. In this scenario little difference exists between leading actor and star author or between characterized movie and cinematized character, for as Billy says to Saxon near the end of *The Valley of the Moon*, "We're livin' movin' pictures these days" (418)—a line right out of a Don DeLillo novel. But what DeLillo treats with wry mockery, London takes straight, too much an Ernest Everhard, too firm a believer in himself, to abandon his faith in the power of personality. Unable to embrace his various publicized images as postmodern caricatures, London simply grows self-conscious about them as he continues in book after book to impersonate himself.

High-minded London loyalists are inclined to find something affirmative in this sort of self-consciousness by pointing to the discovery of Carl Jung by London late in his career. For these critics (and for London himself), the psychology of the collective unconscious helps to unify disparate strains running through his writing into a coherent set of archetypes. The influence of Jung, in this view, helps explain the bold, experimental nature of London's later fictions, many of which were difficult to place in the market despite the writer's great celebrity.[8] The novel *The Star Rover* (1915), for example, offers a harrowing, graphic, claustrophobic account of the intense torture of a prisoner, who learns to escape from his painful torment by a kind of out-of-body astral projection that enables him to live other lives in the past: French count, young Western pioneer, Roman legionnaire, and so on. Exerting enormous pressure on his alter ego, London thus probes the possibility of a common human experience through time, inventing a striking narrative structure somewhat akin to the crosscutting structure of D. W. Griffith's blockbuster film *Intolerance* (1916).

But the collectivity of this reincarnated consciousness by which the body is left behind may be as much commercial as spiritual, affording London an opportunity to attract readers with a variety of highly popular genres or literary styles: historical costume drama, Zane Grey novel, *Ben Hur* imitation. It doesn't really matter that such recycled styles often seem so at odds with one another or at odds with the grim realism of the prison torture scenes; as in *The Iron Heel*, London is working to make ideas appealing. If he wrote the book mainly to expose "our horrible prison conditions," as he wrote to one correspondent, he also included "good accessible stuff," "pseudo-scientific and pseudo-philosophic" material as well as "romantic love" to "make it most palatable to most of the rest of the folk who will read it," as he wrote to another friend. The book "cuts various ways," as London shrewdly assessed it, because its quantifying logic of "most"—adding one type of story to another, "all mixed up with passion and love and unphilosophic brass tackism of the uneducated" means that continuity counts less than a sheer barrage of popular pastiche. Most readers of this novel are bound to like something in it, reasons London, and that should be enough. What may look like a confusion of motives from a biographical perspective, or stylistic incongruity from a formalist one, turns out to be an experiment in marketing designed to gain the widest possible audience when viewed in the light of late capitalism's postmodern culture.[9]

The last novel published during London's lifetime, *The Little Lady of the Big House* (1916), returns to a more intimate, single setting, confronting the key question of marital infidelity more through the perspective of Freud than Jung. Despite the novel's embarrassingly formulaic representations of sexual desire (rearing stallions and so on), London manages to break the producer/consumer feedback loop by shifting the burden of celebrity from himself onto his wife Charmian—the transparent source for the novel's heroine who acts throughout the narrative as a magnificent "hostess with the mostest" for an entourage of hangers-on and guests visiting Sonoma's "big house." In other words, while he maintains the same triangulated configuration on which he relied in *The Sea-Wolf*, it is now the woman-mate (Paula Forrest), not the men (husband Dick Forrest and rival Evan Graham), who takes on grandiose superhuman dimensions. Realizing that the role of publicist (hostess Charmian) might now be more interesting than the front man, London thus frees himself to explore his masculinity with a bit less hyperbole than did he in his previous decade's productions.

The result is a troubled, uneasy book in which London finally tries to come to terms with his public personality. Nuanced party games are played with subtle innuendo and stylized gestures, roles are assumed and then discarded, and barbs are exchanged, all with a disturbing air of decadence. Surrounding themselves with constant diversion, Dick and Paula socialize nonstop, we come to suspect, because they are afraid to be alone with each other or, even worse, simply alone. As Dick explains, their "one magic formula" remains "Damn the expense when fun is selling. And it doesn't matter whether the price is in dollars, hide, or life." [10] London's characters are still plagued with the fatal facility of self-advertisement, but now they know it and act to expose it in each other. Dick's pretentious racial theories, for example, are dismissed by his wife as sheer mystification—"words, words, words" (259), while her own presumed philosophical alienation amounts to little more than "boredom and nervousness" (270). Paula is "too diversely talented" to have done anything big, except, her husband says, "to be herself," to which a character replies, "Which *is* the big thing" (221). But such efforts at verbal wit hardly disguise the more painful examination of celebrity at work throughout the novel. Unable to resolve the novel's love triangle, London chooses to kill off Paula (by suicide).

So sacrificing his plot's source of glamour, London closes the book on his own twenty-year drive for recognition, which began when he first asked, "Who am I?" in his high school literary magazine (February 1895) and answered, "Why I'm de 'Frisco Kid.'" That book of life would literally close for London a few months after he published *The Little Lady of the Big House*—a pity considering the promising direction the novel had opened up. London's notorious death, like his birth, is filled with controversy, but unlike the case of the missing father, here the mystery centers on the question of volition—whether London overdosed himself by accident or not. But as I have been suggesting all along, London's autonomous agency is always at issue in his writing and life, whether it be the decision to (trade)mark "the White Silence," tour the slums of the East End, or serialize a sea epic. His death can therefore perhaps simply stand as the final, supreme expression of a self made in public. After all, it matters little whether or not he committed suicide, as long as in so sensationally dying, Elvis-style, his name would continue to circulate past his bodily demise. In the end, Jack London still could not resist playing himself.

Notes

Introduction

1 This claim for London's worldwide readership is frequently made by London specialists. For a nonspecialist who has recently confirmed, to his surprise, the same absolute claim, see Hank Gutman, ed., *How Others Read Us: International Perspectives on American Literature* (Amherst: University of Massachusetts Press, 1991), pp. 5–6.

2 Undated (late 1903), unsigned book review in *The Guard and Tackle*, Jack London Scrapbooks, vol. 3, Jack London Collection (JL), Henry E. Huntington Library, San Marino, California (HEH). Subsequent references to the scrapbooks (on microfilm) will identify articles by date, whenever possible, because pagination is inconsistent.

3 The terms "cultural capital" and "symbolic capital" are taken from Pierre Bourdieu, *The Field of Cultural Production: Essays on Art and Literature* (New York: Columbia University Press, 1993).

4 John London, "Story of a Typhoon Off the Coast of Japan," *Morning Call* (San Francisco), 12 November 1893, p. 11.

5 Alfred Kazin, *On Native Grounds* (New York: Doubleday, 1942), p. 85.

6 Most biographers open their accounts by pointing out that the most basic facts of London's start and finish are both shrouded in mystery, raising in each case questions of authority: an illegitimate birth (with the presumed father denying his son) and a drug-induced death at the age of forty—by accident, willed suicide, or something in between. A better script could not have been imagined for a writer intent on keeping his life rather than his writing at the center of his readers' attention. For an excellent discussion that analyzes the problematic operative assumptions of London's biographers, see Clarice Stasz, "The Social Construction of Biography: The Case of Jack London," *Modern Fiction Studies* 22 (1976): 51–71. For a similar sort of metacommentary that examines the reasons for London's shaky status among academic critics, see Christopher Gair, "London Calling: The Importance of Jack London to Contemporary Cultural Studies," *Works and Days 22*, 11, no. 2 (1993): 27–43.

7 Analyzing how the author-function operates critically, Michel Foucault memorably calls the author "the principle of thrift in the proliferation of meaning" in "What Is an Author?" in *Textual Strategies: Perspectives in Post-Structuralist Criticism*, ed. Josué Harari (Ithaca: Cornell University Press, 1979), p. 159.

8 June Howard, *Form and History in American Literary Naturalism* (Chapel Hill: University of North Carolina Press, 1985), particularly chaps. 3 and 4.

9 Walter Benn Michaels, *The Gold Standard and the Logic of Naturalism: American Literature at the Turn of the Century* (Berkeley: University of California, 1987), esp. "The Writer's Mark."

10 Mark Seltzer, *Bodies and Machines* (New York: Routledge, 1992), p. 167. Two other important books on American naturalism should be mentioned here, both more general in scope and more narrow in methodology than the provocative cultural studies of Seltzer and Michaels: Lee Clark Mitchell, *Determined Fictions: American Literary Naturalism* (New York: Columbia University Press, 1989), and Christopher Wilson, *The Labor of Words: Literary Professionalism in the Progressive Era* (Athens: University of Georgia Press, 1985). Mitchell sees naturalism as radically undermining fundamental philosophical assumptions about agency and personal identity, but relies primarily on traditional stylistic analysis (an extended close reading of a single London story, for example). Wilson, on the other hand, eschews literary analysis altogether to focus on turn-of-the-century American publishing practice. This excellent institutional history, in conjunction with Wilson's previous article "American Naturalism and the Problem of Sincerity," *American Literature* 54 (December 1982): 511–27, crucially informs my understanding of how authenticity is privileged in naturalist writing.

11 Letter to Mabel Applegarth, 28 November 1898, *The Letters of Jack London*, ed. Earle Labor, Robert C. Leitz III, and I. Milo Shepard, 3 vols. (Stanford: Stanford University Press, 1988), 1:26. Subsequent references to London letters cited by correspondent and date will be taken from this edition, unless otherwise noted. Varying practices of prostitution, we have recently come to see, are themselves historically and culturally contingent in very specific ways that can help us to appreciate how London's literary ambitions likewise emerged in particular ways at a specific time and place.

12 This tension is closely examined in the excellent study by Joan D. Hedrick, *Solitary Comrade: Jack London and His Work* (Chapel Hill: University of North Carolina Press, 1982). See also Andrew Sinclair, *Jack: A Biography of Jack London* (New York: Harper and Row, 1977), p. 92. Also relevant is a line from Rudyard Kipling's poem "The Law of the Jungle" in *The Second Jungle Book* (1895): "For the strength of the Pack is the Wolf, and the strength of the Wolf is the Pack." For a discussion of the wolf that emphasizes its archetypal function for London, see

Ann Upton, "The Wolf in London's Mirror," *Jack London Newsletter* 6 (September–December 1973): 111–18.

13 Richard Brodhead, *Cultures of Letters* (Chicago: University of Chicago Press, 1993), p. 115. The book's sole specific reference to Jack London is immensely suggestive in this regard: "But to note the poverty of the literary resources London's writing knows how to command is not only to engage in social or literary snobbery. It is to identify the specific difference in seized competence and realized power (every author possesses such a difference) that is his mark" (109).

14 Letter to Johns, 12 June 1899. Although it has no independent source of verification, Joan London's often-repeated anecdote about her father's apprenticeship, during which he laboriously copied Kipling stories in longhand, word for word, is pertinent here, suggesting that for the aspiring author this manual, mechanical reproducton of writing, under the logic of naturalism's machine culture, could in and of itself convey and confer literary style. See Joan London, *Jack London and His Times*, 2d ed. (Seattle: University of Washington Press, 1968), p. 170.

15 See, for example, letters to Ida M. Strobridge and Elwyn Hoffman, 17 June 1900, and to George Brett, 2 September 1903.

16 Letter to Cloudesley Johns, 2 May 1900.

17 Letter to Johns, 12 June 1899. See also letters to Johns dated 28 May 1899 and 7 June 1899.

18 Russ Kingman, *A Pictorial Life of Jack London* (New York: Crown, 1979), p. 97.

19 For a detailed account of such trailing, see Jack London, "Editorial Crimes" (1901), *No Mentor but Myself: A Collection of Articles, Essays, Reviews, and Letters on Writing and Writers*, ed. Dale L. Walker (Port Washington, N.Y.: Kennikat, 1979), pp. 30–31.

20 The first rejection slip saved by London on file in the Huntington Libary (JL box 584) actually dates from 23 November 1894 (from the *Youth's Companion*). But this is an isolated case; not until spring 1897 did London begin to save such slips en masse. Although Appendix A ("Publication History") of *The Complete Short Stories of Jack London*, ed. Earle Labor, Robert C. Leitz III, and I. Milo Shepard (Stanford: Stanford University Press, 1993), p. 2497, indicates that London began keeping detailed submission records in Sept. 1898 (two months after he returned from the Klondike), an early notebook organized by magazine title (HEH, JL 933) lists over a dozen entries dating from May and June of 1897.

21 Letter to Strunsky, 10 February 1900. As an indication of how the circulation of letters for London functioned to embody a professional community, I would point out that London used the mails to act informally as Strunsky's literary agent

by sending one of her stories, accompanied by a personal letter, to Bliss Perry, editor of the *Atlantic Monthly*. See letter to Strunsky, May 1900, ibid., p. 186. I will have much more to say about London's relation with Strunsky in Chapter 5.

22 The connection between turn-of-the-century American writing and masculinity is by now a critical commonplace. In addition to the various recent studies of literary naturalism that I have already cited, see T. J. Jackson Lears, *No Place of Grace* (New York: Pantheon, 1981), for one version focusing on high culture.

23 Jack London, *A Daughter of the Snows* (New York: Macmillan, 1902), p. 275 and p. 55. London's first boys' novel *The Cruise of the Dazzler* (New York: Century, 1902) follows a similar scheme, with the orphaned rogue The Frisco Kid discovering that his bay pirating is immoral only once he learns how to read books (p. 189); his friend Joe Bronson (the novel's protagonist) likewise must learn the symbolic law of the letter. After a series of adventures with The Frisco Kid that serve to prove Joe's manhood, the prodigal son returns to find his businessman father dictating business correspondence. Their reconciliation is conducted as a legal, commercial transaction. The relations between father, son, and writing in London's early fiction will be more fully examined in my second chapter.

24 For London's trouble with plot origination, see his letters to Johns dated 24 August 1899, 6 September 1899, and 31 October 1899. Christopher Wilson in *Labor of Words* suggests that London's later travels became "a global quest for new material" (102), a perspective similar to the argument made about another American naturalist by Christopher Benfey in his biography *The Double Life of Stephen Crane* (New York: Knopf, 1992).

25 Throughout this volume, I occasionally use the problematic adjective "red" to refer to Native Americans. I do this for two reasons: to dramatize London's own symbolic construction of race by way of binaries of color; and to suggest the relation between London's thinking on race and his socialist politics, in which "red" stands for revolutionary activity.

26 Tom Lutz, *American Nervousness, 1903: An Anecdotal History* (Ithaca: Cornell University Press, 1991). Unfortunately Lutz's discussion of London and his works is a bit cursory and factually inaccurate in spots.

27 By "fixed" I don't mean "ruined." Challenging the still pervasive critical misconception that London's later work is a clear sign of his artistic and psychic decline, Earle Labor and Jeanne Campbell Reesman have argued vigorously for the importance of this writing by focusing on its powerful archetypal patterns, in their *Jack London*, rev. ed. (New York: Twayne, 1994), esp. chaps. 5 and 6. But in so defending London's later work, they tend to reaffirm a romantic notion of the heroic author questing "beyond the literary marketplace" to explore, in relation to Jung, an authentic collective consciousness within. For London, I would argue that from the author's start, such a "self" is measured strictly by the field of

publishing—standards for success that became only more entrenched once he became famous, despite his best efforts to turn his back on the market.

Yet emphasizing London's endeavors to get past his fame does have the advantage of reminding us that individual writers can position themselves in different ways to the culture at large. Using the case of Jack London to examine the relation between American naturalism and celebrity, my own work seeks to mediate between critics (such as Mark Seltzer and Lee Clark Mitchell) who treat turn-of-the-century texts as precursors to postmodernism, and traditional devotees such as Labor and Reesman who tend to accept London's self-definitions as the basis for their own evaluations.

I The Question of a Name

1 Cited in *The Letters of Jack London*, ed. Earle Labor, Robert C. Leitz III, and I. Milo Shepard (Stanford: Stanford University Press, 1988), 1:42 n. Subsequent references to London letters cited by correspondent and date are from this collection unless otherwise noted.

2 Letter dated 6 September 1899. Jack London's personal copy of Reeve's book, with penciled corrections and notes to himself about where to submit stories, is on file in the Jack London Collection (hereafter JL), Henry E. Huntington Library (hereafter HEH), San Marino, California (JL 600). By 1905 Reeve had doubled his list to 1,001 places—an expansion that helps measure the explosive growth in mass-market publishing in the years during which London first rose to fame.

3 Christopher Wilson, *The Labor of Words: Literary Professionalism in the Progressive Era* (Athens: University of Georgia Press, 1985). Wilson offers the best general account of writing and publishing during this period, as well as the most detailed analysis of London's professional labor as a writer, but he only briefly considers how London's sense of his vocation informs the writing itself. See also Daniel H. Borus, *Writing Realism* (Chapel Hill: University of North Carolina Press, 1989), for a similar excellent treatment of late-nineteenth-century American publication practice, especially chapter 5, in which Borus discusses the significance of the author as mass-marketed celebrity.

4 Clifton S. Wady, "My Record of Manuscripts," *The Writer* 8 (April 1895): 47–48. The bound copy of *The Writer* at the Huntington Library has London's wolf logo bookplate pasted in it, which indicates that he owned this particular set of early volumes.

5 Jack London, "On the Writer's Philosophy of Life," *No Mentor but Myself: A Collection of Articles, Essays, Reviews, and Letters on Writing and Writers*, ed. Dale L.

Walker (Port Washington, N.Y.: Kennikat, 1979), pp. 7 and 8, respectively. Cited parenthetically, subsequent references to this and other early advice essays will be taken from this valuable collection of London's comments on writing rather than from the less available magazine sources of initial publication. Borrowed from one of London's many autobiographical musings, the title of Walker's book needs to be interrogated and not simply accepted as an entirely accurate description of London's apprenticeship, if "mentorship" can be defined to include trade journals such as *The Writer.*

6 See, for example, Jerome McGann, "Byron and 'The Truth in Masquerade,'" and Peter J. Manning, "*Don Juan* and the Revisionary Self," in *Romantic Revisions*, ed. Robert Brinkley and Keith Hanley (Cambridge: Cambridge University Press, 1992), pp. 191–209 and 210–26.

7 The fact that I have included Fanny Fern in this list of antebellum authors suggests that my study's operative pun on mail/male delivery should not be taken too broadly, since women writers in the 1840s and 1850s were also seeking to promote themselves aggressively in a changing commercial market. See, for instance, Susan Coultrap-McQuin, *Doing Literary Business: American Women Writers in the Nineteenth Century* (Chapel Hill: University of North Carolina Press, 1990). Coultrap-McQuin's emphasis on the paternalism displayed toward women novelists by gentlemen publishers during the antebellum period certainly suggests quite a different commerce in belles lettres than the publishing industry that London sought to master in the late 1890s.

Like the question of gender, the problem of periodization is equally vexed, with some critics locating in the 1840s key transformations in publishing that others locate in the 1890s. For an important discussion of authorship models and institutions of publishing that spans the Civil War, see Richard Brodhead, *Cultures of Letters* (Chicago: University of Chicago Press, 1993). I would maintain that material conditions such as the circulation of Reeve's trade directory made available for an outsider like London certain points of entry into publishing that would have been far more difficult in an antebellum culture driven less by professionalism and mass-market production. One small way to gauge the difference is (pace Seltzer's arguments about the technology of writing) to contrast Poe's interest in reading the penned signatures of authors as expressions of their personal style against London's emphasis on authorial style as "stamped." For a discussion of Poe's relation to a different sort of market, see Jonathan Auerbach, *The Romance of Failure: First-Person Fictions of Poe, Hawthorne, and James* (New York: Oxford University Press, 1989), pp. 51–70.

8 Information about Twain's trademarking can be found in Louis J. Budd, "A 'Talent for Posturing': The Achievement of Mark Twain's Public Personality," in *The Mythologizing of Mark Twain*, ed. Sara deSaussure Davis and Philip D. Beidler

(Tuscaloosa: University of Alabama Press, 1984), p. 79. Hank Morgan's remark in *A Connecticut Yankee* is cited in an excellent volume by Randall Knoper, *Acting Naturally: Mark Twain in the Culture of Performance* (Berkeley: University of California Press, 1995), p. 160.

9 For a discussion of turn-of-the-century American trademark law, see Susan Strasser, *Satisfaction Guaranteed* (New York: Pantheon, 1989), pp. 44–57. For a provocative discussion of the relation between corporations and persons in the 1880s, see Howard Horwitz, *By the Law of Nature* (New York: Oxford University Press, 1991), pp. 181–91.

10 Dime-novel production methods are discussed by Michael Denning, *Mechanic Accents: Dime Novels and Working-Class Culture in America* (London: Verso, 1987). A letter from London to Cloudesley Johns dated 18 May 1899 refers to a newspaper article entitled "Machine-Made Fame" that reviews James Lauren Ford's *The Literary Shop, and Other Tales* (1894)—a book that satirically connects such factory-like production to the practices of apparently more respectable editors and publishers.

11 See the series of letters from J. B. Walker to Jack London starting 13 December 1900, HEH, JL 19828–33. In a letter to Cloudesley Johns dated 4 February 1901, London enclosed one of these *Cosmopolitan* letters, remarking: "I stood off first one & wrote to *McClure's*. They have agreed to go with me, giving me utter freedom. So you see, at least they have not bought *me* body & soul."

12 William Dean Howells, "The Man of Letters as a Man of Business," *Scribner's Magazine* 14 (October 1893); subsequent references are cited parenthetically. For an important discussion linking Howells's models of authorship to his notions of realism, see Amy Kaplan, *The Social Construction of American Realism* (Chicago: University of Chicago Press, 1988), pp. 15–43.

13 The number of rejections for these years is cited in Russ Kingman, *A Pictorial Life of Jack London* (New York: Crown, 1979), p. 97.

14 Letter to Johns dated 10 February 1900.

15 See, for instance, letter to Houghton Mifflin, 31 January 1900; letters to Cloudesley Johns, 6 September and 26 September 1899; and letter to Maitland L. Osborne, 24 March 1900, in which he disparages his forthcoming first volume of short stories (*The Son of the Wolf*) as "written to supply a pressing need for cash."

16 London, *No Mentor but Myself*, p. 29.

17 Following Pierre Bourdieu, I prefer to use the term literary "field" instead of "market" because it allows for a more expansive notion of what counts for cultural capital, the symbolic importance of prestige and status (in the market but not identical to it) that London himself understands as the value of a name. See Pierre Bourdieu, "Intellectual Field and Creative Project," trans. Sian France, *Social Science Information* 8 (April 1969): 89–119; Bourdieu, "The Genesis of the

Concepts of *Habitus* and *Field*," trans. Channa Newman, *Sociocriticism* 1 no. 2 (December 1985): 11–24; Bourdieu, "Flaubert's Point of View," trans. Priscilla Parkhurst Ferguson, *Literature and Social Practice*, ed. Philippe Desan, Priscilla Parkhurst Ferguson, and Wendy Griswold (Chicago: University of Chicago Press, 1988), pp. 211–34; and Bourdieu, *The Field of Cultural Production: Essays on Art and Literature*, ed. and intro., Randal Johnson (New York: Columbia University Press, 1993), esp. "The Production of Belief: Contribution to an Economy of Symbolic Goods." Unfortunately, beyond this general concept of field (on which I will rely in my next chapter), Bourdieu's work is not especially helpful for understanding London, whose efforts to reach a *mass* audience in turn-of-the-century America have little to do with Bourdieu's Gallic analysis of taste (as a form of snobbery, in effect)—an analysis that tends to reinscribe the opposition between high and low culture.

18 *The Complete Short Stories of Jack London*, ed. Earle Labor, Robert C. Leitz III, and I. Milo Shepard (Stanford: Stanford University Press, 1993), pp. 55–74. See also Appendix A ("Publication History"), p. 2500. In London's earliest surviving notebook (HEH, JL 1004), he records his idea for this suggestive story as follows: "The 'Mysiogonist' [*sic*] Men choosing different ways of ceasing to propagate, industrial, economic, and political conditions which lead to a national tragedy, and also same as it works itself out—don't forget the idea of the one child born in opposition to the collective will, etc." Later in this study I will have occasion to examine London's tendency to collapse the distinction between public and sexual politics, as well as his continuing autobiographical interest in "one child born" against the collective will.

19 Quoted in James Hepburn, *The Author's Empty Purse and the Rise of the Literary Agent* (New York: Oxford University Press, 1968), p. 72.

20 See Labor, Leitz, and Shepard, *The Complete Short Stories of Jack London*, p. 2507. For London's own assessment of the tale as "ambitious," see his letter to Johns dated 11 November 1899. For the differences between these various magazines, see Frank Luther Mott, *A History of American Magazines* (Cambridge: Harvard University Press, 1957), 4:1–56, 480–99, 589–611, 633–38.

21 For an interesting discussion of the multiple institutional venues available to nineteenth-century American authors, see Brodhead, *Cultures of Letters*, pp. 1–12 and passim.

22 London, *No Mentor but Myself*, p. 24.

23 HEH, JL 572 (handwritten notes); typed version, JL 780.

24 In this connection London's comparison of Kipling with Stevenson is revealing: Stevenson is a better writer, London remarks early on to his friend Cloudesley Johns, because he "never had to worry about ways and means," whereas Kipling, "a mere journalist," sacrificed "posthumous fame" to earn a living.

London thus directly ties the quality of their work to the material conditions under which each writer labored. See letter dated 15 March 1899. But beyond "means" were "ways," which London understood in relation to the symbolic value of his circulated name. On 28 February 1899 he writes to Mabel Applegarth, for example, that despite getting such low pay for his first *Overland* stories, such exposure, according to his editor, would lead to "valuable returns" by virtue of the "boom" created "to put my name before the public." Later that same year (11 November 1899) he writes (to Johns) that a law suit to get money owed him by a recalcitrant publisher would be worth pursuing, for "advertisement, if nothing else."

25 London, *No Mentor but Myself*, p. 18.

26 Jerome McGann, *The Textual Condition* (Princeton: Princeton University Press, 1991), p. 21; McGann uses the phrase while discussing the scholarly editing of texts, but it can be applied more generally to the selecting, cutting, rejecting, and revising done by those editors (mostly magazine editors in London's case) who initially receive an author's submissions for publication. Ibid., p. 21.

27 See, for example, Theodor W. Adorno and Max Horkheimer, *Dialectic of Enlightenment* (New York: Seabury, 1972).

28 "The Star System in Literature," *Dial* 28 (16 May 1900): 389–91.

29 It is interesting to note that London's line of reasoning closely resembles the argument pursued by Stanley Fish in 1979 against the policy of blind submissions instituted by *PMLA*. See Stanley Fish, "No Bias, No Merit," in *Doing What Comes Naturally* (Durham: Duke University Press, 1989), pp. 163–79. Intensely professional, both Fish and London challenge the assumption that merit resides intrinsically in writing apart from the institutionalized position of the writer. But unlike Fish, London then goes on to relocate "intrinsic value" in the magic authorial name itself. The provocative significance of London's argument was not entirely lost on his contemporaries. See, for instance, the review of his "Question of a Name" in *Town Talk*, 19 June 1901 (HEH, JL Scrapbooks, vol. 2).

30 Headline cited in *Letters of Jack London*, ed. Labor, Leitz, and Shepard, pp. 274–75. To some extent, the prominence of London's name is a function of turn-of-the-century newspaper conventions that tended to write the byline into the headline. Yet the newspaper's decision to highlight London suggests a local interest in the figure of the writer that would seem to outweigh the subject of his interview.

31 For a discussion of this hierarchy see Wilson, *Labor of Words*, pp. 17–91. Even though he had submitted his writing to newspapers from the very start of his career, in his official autobiography submitted to Houghton Mifflin in early 1900 (to be discussed shortly), London maintained that he had "done no newspaper work," presumably to emphasize his isolation from the profession's usual means

of ascent. In an earlier article discussing Progressive Era publishing practice, Wilson offers an excellent analysis of the construction of sincerity in naturalist writing, but concludes his essay with an overtly moralistic attack on these writers' commodification of personality, as if there were some utopian alternative to the marketplace for London and other professionals. See Christopher Wilson, "American Naturalism and the Problem of Sincerity," *American Literature* 54 (December 1982): 511–27. HEH, JL Scrapbooks, vol. 1.

32 HEH, JL Scrapbooks, vol. 2. Samuel J. Steinberg claimed that he wrote his John Liverpool parody eighteen months earlier (soon after the April 1900 publication of *The Son of the Wolf*). The parody is reprinted (but without the key opening authorial jokes) in Robert C. Woodward, *Jack London and the Amateur Press* (Grand Rapids, Mich.: Wolf House Books, 1983), "Appendix B," pp. 43–45. This appendix also reprints Anna Strunsky's key February 1901 review of *The Son of the Wolf* (see Chapter 5 in this volume).

33 Two letters by the *Atlantic Monthly*'s powerful editor in chief Bliss Perry to London make this connection between magazine and book publishing explicit. On 7 November 1899 he praised "An Odyssey" as a strong story that will "be of service in calling attention to the book," whereas on 18 February 1902 he wrote to ask if London's current novel in progress would be suitable for serialization in his magazine, promising that book publication by Houghton Mifflin "would naturally follow." See HEH, JL 16431–36. For a discussion of the acceptance of *The Son of the Wolf* from the publisher's perspective, see Ellen Ballou, *The Building of the House* (Boston: Houghton Mifflin, 1970), pp. 482–84. London actually first submitted "An Odyssey of the North" in May to *McClure's*, which rejected it. I should point out that on 10 July 1899, while still waiting to hear from the *Atlantic Monthly*, London sent a letter of inquiry to Macmillan offering his untitled Klondike volume of "interlac[ing]" short stories, which he had already conceived as a single unit of nine stories, even though two (including "An Odyssey") were still "hunting publication." Subsequent letters from Parker suggest a falling out between London and the *Atlantic Monthly*, which began to reject most of his submissions. In one letter dated 14 March 1901, Parker responded to London's complaints by saying that the author's financial hardships were "needless" and that Houghton Mifflin would have forwarded him an advance on his first collection (as *McClure's* was doing for his second volume) if he had only known. See HEH, JL 16238–49.

34 See letters in HEH, JL 7652–71. The letter asking for "hints" about "special reviewers" is dated 5 February 1900.

35 Budd, "A 'Talent for Posturing,' " p. 83.

36 The letter from S. S. McClure (HEH, JL 14198–203) asking "send me all you write" is dated 6 February 1900. London was so proud of this letter that he

mentioned it to Anna Strunsky (letter dated 13 February 1900, in *Letters of Jack London*), actually enclosing a copy in a letter sent to Cloudesley Johns a few days later (17 February 1900). Presumably London acted as his own agent to deliver McClure's letter to *The Oakland Enquirer*; neither Strunsky nor Johns could have mailed it to the newspaper, whose article appeared on 13 February 1900. See HEH, JL Scrapbooks, vol. 1.

37 Letter reprinted in *Letters of Jack London*, pp. 148–50.

38 These reviews can be found in HEH, JL Scrapbooks, vol. 1. For the dating of book review syndication in newspapers, see Elmo Scott Watson, *History of Newspaper Syndicates in the United States* (Chicago, 1935), p. 57. Dated 15 July 1903, a letter from Macmillan's marketing department about *The Call of the Wild* illuminates this practice by alerting London that "a stereotype" of a (positive) "review" by Hamilton Mabie has been inserted in the review copies sent to 250 "special" newspapers and that London should therefore expect to see copies of this review show up in these various papers. A survey of book reviewing and reviewers that appeared in *The Publisher's Weekly* 62, no. 1596 (30 August 1902): 299–300, condemned the practice by which "papers of a lower grade" reprinted the "prepared notice sent by the publishers."

39 Letter to Johns dated 8 April 1901.

40 London, *No Mentor but Myself*, p. 49. This paradox is also discussed by Joan D. Hedrick, *Solitary Comrade: Jack London and His Work* (Chapel Hill: University of North Carolina Press, 1982), pp. 154–55.

41 London, *No Mentor but Myself*, p. 55.

42 Letter to McClure dated 10 April 1906, and letter to the editor of the *Independent* dated January 1907, in *Letters of Jack London*, pp. 569 and 667, respectively.

2 The (White) Man on Trail: London's Northland Stories

1 Letter to Mabel Applegarth, 6 December 1898, in *The Letters of Jack London*, ed. Earle Labor, Robert C. Leitz III, and I. Milo Shepard, vol. 1 (Stanford: Stanford University Press, 1988). Subsequent references to London letters cited by correspondent and date are from this collection unless otherwise noted.

2 Letters to Cloudesley Johns, 10 August 1899 and 22 April 1899.

3 Letter to George Brett, 21 November 1902. By the end of 1902 London had also published two novels: *A Daughter of the Snows* (set in the Yukon) and *The Cruise of the "Dazzler,"* a boys' adventure novel set in San Francisco. My focus here on London's apprenticeship magazine work precludes me from discussing in any detail these early novels, which I have briefly mentioned in my introduction.

4 See Earle Labor, "Jack London's Symbolic Wilderness: Four Versions," *Nine-*

teenth Century Fiction 17 (Summer 1962): 149–61; and Earl J. Wilcox, "The Kipling of the Klondike: Naturalism in Jack London's Early Fiction," *Jack London Newsletter* 6 (January–April 1973): 1–12. Against those who might assume that London's naturalism works as a reasonably transparent rendering of his experience in nature, I would point out that the diaries he kept during his brief stay in the Yukon are relatively uninteresting and bland, especially when it comes to describing encounters with native peoples, whose squalor and half-breed status most occupy London's attention in his diary—two issues frequently found in travel accounts that he hardly touches in his imaginary tales of the Northland.

5 See letter to the *San Francisco Bulletin*, 17 September 1898, p. 18 n. 2.

6 Letter to Johns, 22 February 1899.

7 Jack London Scrapbooks, vol. 1, in Jack London Collection (hereafter JL), Henry E. Huntington Library (hereafter HEH), San Marino, California.

8 Lauren Berlant, "National Brands/National Body: Imitation of Life," in *Comparative American Identities: Race, Sex, and Nationality in the Modern Text*, ed. Hortense J. Spillers (New York: Routledge, 1991), pp. 110–40.

9 Owen Wister, *Red Man and White* (New York: Harper and Brothers, 1896), p. v.

10 Richard Brodhead, *Cultures of Letters* (Chicago: University of Chicago Press, 1993), "The Reading of Regions," pp. 115–41.

11 Repeatedly referring in his early correspondence to the discipline of professional short story publishing as requiring "digging," London drew the obvious connection between prospecting in goldfields and working the "magazine field" in a November 1900 letter to one of his Yukon buddies: "No; I never realized a cent from any properties I had interest in up there; Still, I have been managing to pan out a living ever since on the strength of the trip." See letter to Cornelius Gepfert, 5 November 1900. The phrase "magazine field" can be found in a letter dated 28 February 1899 to Mabel Applegarth. For "digging" comments, see letters to Johns, 7 March, 24 October, and 12 December 1899, and his first letter to Ann Strunsky, 19 December 1899.

12 Letter dated 10 July 1899.

13 Letter to Edward Applegarth, 31 December 1898. One of London's very early notebooks (HEH, JL 1004), filled with typed plot ideas pasted over penciled jotting (and therefore difficult to date precisely), contains numerous references to various short story "series" of one sort or another, again confirming the centrality of this unifying principle for London.

14 See letter to Johns dated 18 May 1899. Although the subheading of "The Men of Forty-Mile" does refer to the "Malemute Kid," it is not numbered.

15 For discussions of the role of the Kid, see Earle Labor, *Jack London* (New York: Twayne, 1974), p. 51, and James McClintock, *White Logic: Jack London's Short Stories* (Grand Rapids, Mich.: Wolf House Books, 1975), pp. 57–78.

16 See Michael Denning, *Mechanic Accents: Dime Novels and Working-Class Culture in America* (London: Verso, 1987), chap. 2.

17 Letters to Mabel Applegarth, 28 January 1899, and to Johns, 17 April 1899 and 18 May 1899.

18 For definitions and examples of the short story cycle, see Forrest Ingram, *Representative Short Story Cycles of the Twentieth Century* (The Hague: Mouton, 1971), and Susan Garland Mann, *The Short Story Cycle* (Westport, Conn.: Greenwood, 1989). The best discussion of the terrific rise in popularity and status of American short story writers at the turn of the century remains Fred Lewis Pattee, *The Development of the American Short Story* (New York: Harper and Brothers, 1923).

19 The tables of contents for London's first three volumes of stories are:

The Son of the Wolf	*The God of His Fathers and Other Stories*
The White Silence	The God of His Fathers
The Son of the Wolf	The Great Interrogation
The Men of Forty-Mile	Which Make Men Remember
In a Far Country	Siwash
To the Man on Trail	The Man with the Gash
The Priestly Prerogative	Jan, the Unrepentant
The Wisdom of the Trail	Grit of Women
The Wife of a King	Where the Trail Forks
An Odyssey of the North	A Daughter of the Aurora
	At the Rainbow's End
	The Scorn of Women

Children of the Frost
In the Forests of the North
The Law of Life
Nam-Bok the Unveracious
The Master of Mystery
The Sunlanders
The Sickness of Lone Chief
Keesh, the Son of Keesh
The Death of Ligoun
Li Wan, the Fair
The League of the Old Men

For dates of magazine submission and presumed dates of composition, see *The Complete Short Stories of Jack London*, ed. Earle Labor, Robert C. Leitz III, and I. Milo Shepard, 3 vols. (Stanford: Stanford University Press, 1993), Appendix A ("Publishing History"). For an interesting discussion of London's compositional dates and practices that argues against packaging his work into neat thematic categories, see James Williams, "The Composition of Jack London's Writings," *American Literary Realism, 1870–1910* 23 (1991): 64–86.

20 Jack London, *The Son of the Wolf* (New York: Houghton Mifflin, 1900), pp. 19–20. Since I am interested in how London organized his short stories in his published books, throughout this chapter I will also be using the first editions of his two subsequent Northland collections—*The God of His Fathers and Other Stories* (New York: McClure, Phillips, 1901), and *Children of the Frost* (New York: Macmillan, 1902)—as opposed to the individual stories as they appear in the more readily accessible *Complete Short Stories of Jack London*, ed. Labor, Leitz, and Shepard. Subsequent page references to all three first editions are cited parenthetically.

21 For some other references to "the White Silence" in *Son of the Wolf*, see pp. 36, 40, 239, 246. London recognized the atmospheric significance of this phrase early on, remarking in a letter to Ted Applegarth (31 December 1898) that "the White Silence seems to strike you." In a letter to Johns dated 15 March 1899, London praises his friend for adding "a few hints of atmosphere" to one of his stories—an ingredient that London deems "essential" for readers. Another rather browbeating letter to Johns dated 16 June 1900 insists that "atmosphere stands for the elimination of the artist, that is to say, the atmosphere is the artist." While flirting with a modernist notion of impersonality, London doesn't seem quite willing to dispense with his authorial stamp of self altogether.

"White Silence" shows up in that early notebook of penciled jotting (HEH, JL 1004) in the following passage: "Since first the Northland stirred with life, this knell has rung—to the pinch of famine, to the quick death midst forming[?] ice, to the roar of the avalanche, to the hunter beneath the bald-faced grizzly, to the frozen grave beside the river, and always to the pitiless White Silence which never answers back." As I mention in chapter 1, in a letter to London dated 3 January 1900, Houghton Mifflin recognized the value of the phrase as well, recommending it for the volume's subtitle, which would be a "distinct help to the book in a commercial sense" (HEH, JL 7652).

22 Letter to Edward Applegarth, 31 December 1898. McClintock, *White Logic*, chapter 1, offers a valuable analysis of the relation between London's emphasis on literary technique and the technical expertise displayed (as content) in the Yukon stories themselves.

23 For London's complaints about this "editorial censor," see letter to Edward Applegarth, 31 December 1898, as well as letter to Cloudesley Johns, 27 February 1899.

24 For two key studies connecting a thematics of American naturalist writing at the turn of the century with the material production of marks, see my discussion

of studies by Walter Benn Michaels and Mark Seltzer in the introduction to this volume.

25 In the same early letter to Mabel Applegarth that announces his first magazine sale (6 December 1898), London also expressed dread that his other mailed articles had "vanished utterly" from view, never to be seen or heard of again, despite his many trailing letters. London's very first letter to Johns (10 February 1899) similarly responds to the young man's fan mail by confessing that as a beginning writer, London has been "groping in the dark on strange trails." For a graphic dramatization depicting how the landscape can obliterate persons, see London's story "At the Rainbow's End" (in *The God of His Fathers*), which ends: "A great wall of white [a breaking ice jam] flung itself upon the island. Trees, dogs, men, were blotted out, as though the hand of God wiped the face of nature clean" (251).

26 London's early notebook (HEH, JL 1004) records an earlier draft of this dedication: "To my brother adventurers of the Northland—toils—some of who[m] may recognize familiar strains and ancient comrades in these pages." The rather pedestrian quality of this version suggests how London was still in the process of discovering the deeper implications of his own stories as he was collecting them together for his first book.

27 There is a rapidly growing body of scholarship on this masculinity crisis. See, for instance, Gail Bederman, *Manliness and Civilization* (Chicago: University of Chicago Press, 1995). Demonstrating how Americans sought to counteract the overcivilizing tendencies of modernity by seeking refuge in a certain kind of muscular primitivism, Bederman insists, as I have done, on linking issues of race and gender, but in a way less vexed and complex than my reading of London's totemism suggests. See also E. Anthony Rotundo, *American Manhood* (New York: Basic, 1993), chaps. 10 and 11; Joe L. Dubbert, "Progressivism and the Masculinity Crisis," *The American Man*, ed. Elizabeth H. Pleck and Joseph H. Pleck (Englewood Cliffs, N.J.: Prentice-Hall, 1980), pp. 303–20; and Amy Kaplan, "Romancing the Empire: The Embodiment of American Masculinity in the Popular Historical Novel of the 1890s," *American Literary History* 2, no. 4 (Winter 1990): 659–90.

28 On the socially constructed nature of the totem, see Emile Durkheim, *Elementary Forms of the Religious Life* (New York: Free Press, 1965), pp. 121–215, but particularly p. 122. From a psychoanalytic perspective, see also Sigmund Freud, *Totem and Taboo* (New York: Norton, 1950), especially Freud's quotation (p. 158) from Goethe's *Faust*: "Was du ererbt von deinen Vatern hast, / Erwirb es, um es zu besitzen" ["What thou hast inherited from thy fathers, / Acquire it to make it thine"].

29 Walter Benn Michaels, "The Souls of White Folks," *Literature and the Body:*

Essays on Populations and Persons, ed. Elaine Scarry (Baltimore: Johns Hopkins University Press, 1988), pp. 185–209; and Michaels, "Anti-Imperial American-ism," in *Cultures of United States Imperialism*, ed. Amy Kaplan and Donald E. Pease (Durham: Duke University Press, 1993), pp. 365–91. Michaels's argu-ments have been elaborated and expanded in his book *Our America: Nativism, Modernism, and Pluralism* (Durham: Duke University Press, 1995).

30 For one more recent charge of racism, see William Cain, "Socialism, Power, and the Fate of Style: Jack London in His Letters," *American Literary History* 3, no. 3 (Fall 1991): 603–13. Although Cain concentrates on London's letters, he gives little indication that he would view London's fictional writing any differ-ently. For a defense that focuses on showing London's sympathetic treatment of individual nonwhite characters in his fiction, see Andrew Furer, " 'Zone Con-querors' and 'White Devils': The Contradictions of Race in the Fiction of Jack London," in *Rereading Jack London* (Stanford: Stanford University Press, 1996). Such an approach that assumes London's overt attitude toward his protagonists as the basis for comparison (American Indians versus Hawaiians, primarily) over-looks the more complex intersections in London's writing between race and gen-der as ideological systems.

31 For an overview of this modern fascination with the primitive, see Marianna Torgovnick, *Gone Primitive* (Chicago: University of Chicago Press, 1990), esp. chaps. 1 and 10.

32 Freud, *Totem and Taboo*, pp. 115, 118.

33 Herbert Spencer, *Principles of Sociology* (New York: D. Appleton, 1923), 1: 329–54. On pages 346–47 Spencer specifically mentions the "raven" clan and the "wolf" clan as the two founding gods of the (Northwest Coast) Tlingit Indians.

34 In more recent years many feminists examining patriarchy have sought to articulate the relation between psychoanalytic theories (focused on the family and the construction of the subject) and large-scale social structures such as kinship systems. For one admirably lucid discussion, see Gayle Rubin, "The Traffic in Women," in *Toward an Anthropology of Women*, ed. Rayna Reiter (New York: Monthly Review Press, 1975), pp. 157–210.

35 Letter dated 23 June 1899.

36 In "The Son of the Wolf" Ruth and her half-breed child are briefly mentioned (*Son of the Wolf*, p. 32) living now on the Outside, as the dying Mason wished, and therefore are conveniently exempt from participating in London's Northland racial configurations. The only significant half-breed we discover Inside is the bitter Baptiste the Red, who triumphs over the white man in "The God of His Fathers."

37 I will have occasion to examine this sort of homoerotic triangle in subsequent chapters of this volume, particularly when I discuss *Sea-Wolf*.

38 As I discuss in the previous chapter, London himself shrewdly recognized his opportunity, sending out *The Son of the Wolf* to Houghton Mifflin directly after he had shortened and resubmitted "An Odyssey of the North" at the request of the *Atlantic Monthly*. See his letter to Johns dated 10 August 1899.

39 Brodhead, *Cultures of Letters*, pp. 132–141.

40 McClintock, *White Logic*, pp. 69–70.

41 Sylvia Van Kirk, *Many Tender Ties: Women in Fur-Trade Society, 1670–1870* (Norman: University of Oklahoma Press, 1980). In the novel *A Daughter of the Snows* (1902), London's heroine Frona Welse expresses white supremacist sentiments far more dogmatically than the men in the novel—a clear sign that although daughters of the snow closely resemble daughters of the soil as "natural" women, snow and soil represent the two opposite sides of London's racial line.

42 Building on the insights of Freud, a host of feminist theorists have examined the implications of paternity as invisible. For one summarizing discussion, see Jonathan Culler, *On Deconstruction* (Ithaca: Cornell University Press, 1982), pp. 58–61. Freud points out in *Totem and Taboo* that totems can be "inherited only through the female line" (107), presumably because of the same kind of invisibility of the (white) father that haunts London's Northland.

43 See Durkheim, *Elementary Forms of the Religious Life*, p. 162. London's theologizing of the white "wolf" race was singled out for comment by Anna Strunsky in her review of *The Son of the Wolf*, published in *Dilettante* 7, no. 8 (February 1901): 179–84, and of *The God of His Fathers*, published in *Impressions* 2, no. 4 (October 1901): 59–60. See also Chapter 5 for Strunsky's views on race.

44 For one such standard argument that assumes London's fiction endorses imperialist expansion, see Amy Kaplan, "Nation, Region, and Empire," in *The Columbia History of the American Novel*, ed. Emory Elliot (New York: Columbia University Press, 1991), pp. 263–66.

45 Letter dated 30 January 1902.

46 An interesting tale published in *The Faith of Men and Other Stories* (New York: Macmillan, 1904), London's fourth collection of Northland narratives, "The Story of Jees Uck" takes a daughter of the soil and her half-breed son to San Francisco, where she briefly confronts her former husband and his new (white) wife. In summing up Jees Uck's own genealogy, London allows for a remarkable mixing that defies essentialist categories of race: "Her lineage has been traced at length to show that she was neither Indian, nor Eskimo, no Innuit, nor much of anything else; also to show what waifs of the generations we are, all of us, and the strange meanderings of the seed from which we spring" (241).

But lest we jump on this passage to show how progressive and antiessentialist London was, Walter Benn Michaels has warned how such fashionable antiessentialism is easier to assert than to make work as a way of understanding racial identity. See his "Anti-Imperial Americanism," pp. 390–91 n. 27. More germane here is that London can allow for such a liberal sentiment only in a story set outside his Northland. I have chosen not to discuss other stories from this fourth collection because the majority were published together as a book two years or more after their initial composition. The volume thus lacks the internal coherence found in each of London's first three Northland collections.

47 Given the story's emphasis on graphic violence, it is hard to know how seriously to take London's representation of the potlatch ceremony. But framed by white commerce, Palitlum's story does suggest how London understands the potlatch as an alternative to rationalized market economy, a contrast along the lines of Marcel Mauss's highly influential *The Gift* (New York: Norton, 1967). For a more recent anthropological interrogation of the effects of global capitalism on traditional society, see Michael T. Taussing, *The Devil and Commodity Fetishism in South America* (Chapel Hill: University of North Carolina Press, 1980).

48 See Jack London, "My Best Short Story," *The Grand Magazine*, August 1906. See also letters to George Brett, 2 May 1902 and 26 December 1904.

49 For a summary of such theories, see Freud, *Totem and Taboo*, p. 110. London's fearful account of writing as an instrument of subjugation closely resembles the famous parable offered by Claude Lévi-Strauss in *Tristes Tropiques* (New York: Atheneum, 1974). In the chapter "A Writing Lesson," Lévi-Strauss follows up his historical claim that writing "was perhaps indispensable for the strengthening of dominion" by remarking: "The fight against illiteracy is therefore connected with an increase in governmental authority over the citizens. Everyone must be able to read, so that the government can say: Ignorance of the law is no excuse" (300). See Jacques Derrida, *Of Grammatology* (Baltimore: Johns Hopkins University Press, 1976), pp. 118–40, for a careful dismantling of Lévi-Strauss's assumptions about writing and the pristine nature of primitive cultures.

50 Here I am specificallly thinking of the photographs of Indians as "Vanishing Americans" which Edward S. Curtis took and which began to appear in *Scribner's* by 1905. See, for instance, Curtis, "Vanishing Indian Types," *Scribner's Magazine* 39 (May 1906): 513–29. For an interesting, if one-sided, discussion of how Remington and other turn-of-the-century American painters represented Indians, see Alex Nemerov, "Doing the 'Old America,' " *The West as America*, ed. William Truettner (Washington, D.C.: Smithsonian Institution Press, 1991). For an analysis of how the trope is appropriated by various writers in the 1920s, see Walter Benn Michaels, "The Vanishing American," *American Literary History* 2, no. 2 (Summer 1990): 220–41.

51 Always attentive to the material conditions of his publishing, London appended a note to the essay when it appeared in his collection *War of the Classes* (1905) that insisted that the essay was accepted, paid for, but left unpublished out

of an editor's fear of its radical nature. London delivered the lecture on 25 November 1899. See *Letters of Jack London*, p. 126 n. 8. I should point out that as in all London's fiction (*White Fang*, for instance), some ambiguity exists in "The League of the Old Men" about the meaning of "meat," which can be both a natural resource and a product for consumption. The fact that the Indians in the story sell "meat" to the whites complicates my comparison between the analysis of imperialism in "The Question of the Maximum" and the role of commerce in the tale.

3 *"Congested Mails": Buck and Jack's "Call"*

1 Letters to Marshall Bond and Merle Maddern dated 17 December 1903 and 28 August 1903, respectively, in *The Letters of Jack London*, ed. Earle Labor, Robert C. Leitz III, and I. Milo Shepard, vol. 1 (Stanford: Stanford University Press, 1988). Subsequent references to London letters cited by correspondent and date are from this collection unless otherwise noted. Two dogs named "Buck" and "Bright" first appear in London's story "Jan, the Unrepentant" (*Outing*, August 1900).

2 Cited in Franklin Walker, *Jack London and the Klondike: The Genesis of an American Writer* (San Marino, Calif.: Henry E. Huntington Library, 1966), p. 218. What Walker calls a "notebook" may in fact have been a loose folder with a series of individual jottings, so that these plot ideas may have been separate entries in close proximity rather than on a continuous page, as Walker's citation suggests. I have not been able to locate this "notebook" but have identified these two jottings, filed individually in the Jack London Collection (hereafter JL) at the Henry E. Huntington Library (hereafter HEH), San Marino, California, as items JL 858 and JL 1289, respectively. Many of London's notes for plot ideas exist in multiple versions, so it is quite possible that the Indian "buck" idea and the dog story were in fact conceived together.

3 Jack London, "A Relic of the Pliocene," *The Complete Short Stories of Jack London*, ed. Earle Labor, Robert C. Leitz III, and I. Milo Shepard, vol. 1 (Stanford: Stanford University Press, 1993), p. 493.

4 HEH, JL Scrapbooks, 2:40. Several other textual sources for Buck deserve to be mentioned: first, London's sketch "Husky—The Wolf Dog," published 30 June 1900 in *Harper's Weekly* (pp. 611–12); second, his short story "Bâtard" (published as "Diable, a Dog" in *Cosmopolitan* [June 1902]), which spurred him to write *The Call of the Wild* as a "companion" piece, as he explained to Anna Strunsky (letter dated 13 March 1903); third, an article by London in the *San Francisco Examiner* (14 October 1901) interviewing a Klondike explorer who was exhibiting a "new Animal from the Polar Zone" purportedly with the body of a bear-wolf and the head of a dog; fourth, those instances in early letters to Johns (such as 24 October

1899) where he urges him to "buck" against publishers to make his reputation, and similarly to Strunsky (2 May 1900) urging her to "shout" as a writer to make the world heed her "call." See JL Scrapbooks, 2:110, and more generally Walker, *Jack London and the Klondike*, pp. 230–63, for a discussion of London's textual borrowing for his Yukon writing, particularly his habit of using clippings from newspapers for his Klondike plot ideas.

5   Edward B. Clark, "Roosevelt on the Nature-Fakirs," *Everybody's Magazine* 16 (June 1907): 770–74, supplemented by Theodore Roosevelt, "Nature Fakers," *Everybody's Magazine* 17 (September 1907): 427–30. Calling Roosevelt a member of the Ananias Club (a liar), London replies in "The Other Animals," *Collier's* 41 (5 September 1908): 10–11, 25–26. See also Roosevelt's letter to his friend and fellow target of attack John Burroughs (12 March 1907), as well as his subsequent angry response to *Collier's* editor Mark Sullivan (9 September 1908) in *The Letters of Theodore Roosevelt*, ed. Elting E. Morison (Cambridge: Harvard University Press, 1952), 5:617, and 6:1220–23. Roosevelt ends his letter to Sullivan by saying that he would no sooner enter into a serious controversy with London about his fiction than he would seriously engage the writer's views on social or political reform.

6   More recently there has been a rash of popular accounts of this still controversial issue. See, for example, Marian Stamp Dawkins, *Through Our Eyes Only: The Search for Animal Consciousness* (Oxford: Freeman, 1993); Elizabeth Marshall Thomas, *The Hidden Life of Dogs* (Boston: Houghton Mifflin, 1993); Vicki Hearne, *Animal Happiness* (New York: HarperCollins, 1994); Stanley Coren, *The Intelligence of Dogs: Canine Consciousness and Capabilities* (New York: Free Press, 1994); and Jeffrey Moussaieff Masson and Susan McCarthy, *When Elephants Weep: The Emotional Lives of Animals* (New York: Delacorte, 1995). That a renowned opponent of psychoanalysis (Masson) would turn his attention to the inner lives of animals bears consideration in relation to London's own efforts to turn psychoanalysis inside out via naturalism, as I will suggest near the end of this chapter. For a highly original view interrogating the way modern science has historically construed the relationship between humans and animals, see Donna Haraway, *Primate Visions* (New York: Routledge, 1989).

7   Frederic Taber Cooper, cited in C. C. Walcutt, *American Literary Naturalism: A Divided Stream* (Minneapolis: University of Minnesota Press, 1956), pp. 96–97.

8   Christopher Wilson, *The Labor of Words: Literary Professionalism in the Progressive Era* (Athens: University of Georgia Press, 1985).

9   Walter Benn Michaels, *The Gold Standard and the Logic of Naturalism: American Literature at the Turn of the Century* (Berkeley: University of California, 1987); Mark Seltzer, *Bodies and Machines* (New York: Routledge, 1992).

10   Page references are to Jack London, *The Call of the Wild* (New York: Mac-

millan, 1903). Subsequent page citations are also to this edition and are given parenthetically.

11 The comparison with Kipling and Seton is frequently made, but often in rather general terms. See, for instance, James Lundquist, *Jack London* (New York: Ungar, 1987), p. 100. Two additional contemporaneous dog stories are also worth noting at this point: Richard Harding Davis, "The Bar Sinister," in *The Bar Sinister* (New York: Scribner's 1903), which explicitly uses dogs to treat race relations; and Mark Twain, "A Dog's Tale," *Harper's Monthly* 108 (December 1903): 11–19, which introduces race as well via a first-person narrator—a talking dog—whose story playfully flaunts the sort of active anthropomorphic consciousness that London's narrative barely represses. The publication date of Twain's story likely makes it an overt parody of *The Call of the Wild*.

12 Seltzer, *Bodies and Machines*, p. 166.

13 London claimed, with perhaps some real justification, that he was "unconscious" while writing the novel. See Joan London, *Jack London and His Times*, 2d ed. (Seattle: University of Washington Press, 1968), p. 252. See also HEH, JL Scrapbooks, vol. 4, for a letter written by London which was published 21 October 1903 in the *Stockton Evening Mail* and in which he interceded in a debate between two other critics about *The Call of the Wild*'s meaning, with London claiming that he was unaware of his story's allegorical implications.

14 Christopher Wilson briefly notes the same paradox but perhaps too optimistically claims that the two plots work in "counterpoint." See *The Labor of Words*, p. 104.

15 For an important discussion of naturalist plotting, see June Howard, *Form and History in American Literary Naturalism* (Chapel Hill: University of North Carolina Press, 1985). Emphasizing the binary opposition between nature and culture, Howard admits that such antinomies are "unstable" (53) in London's *White Fang*. Yet she goes on to rely on such a structuralist model (Greimas's semiotic rectangle) in a way that too readily accepts London's constructed oppositions as givens.

16 In a note, Walcutt briefly ponders the same sorts of questions, which he leaves unanswered. See Walcutt, *American Literary Naturalism*, p. 311 n. 22. It might be argued that Social Darwinism would work precisely to naturalize the notion of human mastery, but Buck's atavistic reversion to savagery would more logically remove him from the human realm entirely.

17 Ibid., p. 106.

18 This striking phrase is used in a series of 1880s essays on the relation of human and animal psychology that were written by George John Romanes, a professor and popular explicator of Darwin whom London cites in his *Collier's* reply to Roosevelt. See Romanes, *Essays* (London: Longmans, Green, 1897), pp. 71, 75.

19 June Howard, *Form and History in American Literary Naturalism*, chaps. 3 and 4. The (parodic) resemblance between Buck's plot and a classic bildungsroman has also been noted by E. L. Doctorow, *Jack London, Hemingway, and the Constitution* (New York: Random House, 1993), p. 18.

20 This brief summary of Hegel's master/slave dialectic is based on Alexandre Kojève, *Introduction to the Reading of Hegel* (Ithaca: Cornell University Press, 1980), pp. 3–70. The quoted passage can be found on page 42. By seeing Hegel (as read by Kojève) as the source for London's Nietzsche and Marx, I am not making claims for direct influence; while to my knowledge Hegel is not mentioned by London in his letters or essays, Hegel powerfully informs American literature's conceptual foundations, as has been suggested in a recent collection of essays. See Bainard Coward and Joseph G. Kronick, eds., *Theorizing American Literature: Hegel, the Sign, and History* (Baton Rouge: Louisiana State University Press, 1991). For a fleeting allusion to Hegel pertaining to London, see Joan D. Hedrick, *Solitary Comrade: Jack London and His Work* (Chapel Hill: University of North Carolina Press, 1982), p. 138.

21 Kojève, *Reading of Hegel*, pp. 52, 64.

22 London's joke is even more pointed in the serialized version of the story, which was first published in the *Saturday Evening Post*, a mass-circulation magazine with a large format closely resembling that of a daily newspaper. We thus begin the story by reading the news of Buck reading the news—presumably the very same way London got the idea to write the story in the first place, as I have already suggested. I should also point out that American newspapers at the turn of the century commonly contained the name "Mail" in their title, which suggests yet another link between Buck's reading and letter delivery conceived as the mass circulation of print.

In an early note to himself for a plot idea that anticipates Faulkner's Benjy, London imagines the "autobiography of an idiot who has learned to read and write a bit—or else devise some other way of getting this autobiographical sketch" (HEH, JL 461). That other way was to figure himself as a working dog.

23 Seltzer, *Bodies and Machines*, pp. 224–25 n. 37. Michaels, *The Gold Standard*, "The Writer's Mark."

24 Jack London, "How I Became a Socialist," *War of the Classes* (New York: Macmillan, 1905), pp. 267–78. Further page references to this essay will be provided parenthetically in the text.

25 According to his records (HEH, JL 483) London started writing *The Call of the Wild* during the first week of December 1902 and was finished by the middle of January 1903; the novel was serialized the following summer (beginning June 1903) in the *Saturday Evening Post*. In addition to writing the novel and the essay on socialism as well as preparing *The People of the Abyss* for publication the follow-

ing fall, during this remarkably concentrated and intense six-month period London also published the novel *The Kempton-Wace Letters* (published anonymously and coauthored by Anna Strunsky), bought the sloop *Spray* to sail around San Francisco Bay, began writing *The Sea-Wolf* (virtually completed by the end of the year), separated from his wife and children, and fell in love with Charmian Kittredge, his future wife.

26 Kojève, *Reading of Hegel*, p. 65. Basing class distinctions on the difference between mental and manual labor, London uncharacteristically falls prey to a vulgar Marxism, an argument all the more surprising since his essay was published by the prominent socialist editor John Spargo, who in other contexts criticized such confused and unscientific thinking. See Daniel T. Rodgers, *The Work Ethic in Industrial America, 1850–1920* (Chicago: University of Chicago Press, 1978), pp. 219–20, 229. Presumably, securing London's famous name for the socialist cause would be more important than the depth of his analysis itself.

27 See Charles N. Watson, *The Novels of Jack London* (Madison: University of Wisconsin Press, 1983), p. 36, for a brief comparison of *Black Beauty* with *The Call of the Wild*. Watson also offers an interesting comparison between *The Call* and *White Fang* (p. 85) that shows the structural similarities of these two plots, despite the latter's ostensible reversal of direction. For the suggestion that *The Call of the Wild* functions in some ways as a slave narrative, I am indebted to my student Benjamin Diamond.

28 Earlier in the narrative (pp. 75–76) Spitz falls through the ice, leaving Buck on the slippery edge, straining in a panic along with Dave and François to pull the dog back up and thereby save themselves, all linked together to the sled by the traces. The writing of these two fictional abyss passages is clearly informed by London's terror of falling into the social pit.

29 Later in the narrative, in describing Buck's newly found "pride in himself" as a killer, London remarks that in Buck's physical swagger this pride "advertised itself . . . as plain as speech" (77). The shift from pride in work to pride in killing is thus matched by the shift from writing to public (advertised) speaking.

30 Letters to George Brett dated 21 November 1902 and 11 December 1902. Letter to Cloudesley Johns, dated 27 January 1903. Like Thornton, London too was wounded, maimed during the writing of *The Call of the Wild* in a manner almost too good to be true: "A heavy box of books fell on me, striking me in a vital place" (letter to Anna Strunsky dated 20 January 1903). Here the hazards of a career in letters take on a physical dimension. See *The Letters of Jack London*, ed. Labor, Leitz, and Shepard, vol. 1. I should also point out that the autobiographical dimensions of the novel are apparent from the start of the narrative, when London dates Buck's capture and transportation as taking place in "the fall of 1897" (18)—coinciding with his own stay in the Yukon, a time period "four years

since his puppyhood" (18)—an implicit reference to London's first piece of writing published four years earlier in 1893. In my chapter on *The Sea-Wolf* I will discuss how London uses this seminal 1893 story to begin to retell his professional writing career retrospectively.

31 See Earle Labor, *Jack London* (New York: Twayne, 1974), pp. 57–81. Watson, *Novels of Jack London*, pp. 47–48, offers a similar reading, focusing on Buck's killing of Spitz in terms of Freud's totemic parricide but glossing over the subsequent murder of the Yeehats.

32 See his 27 June 1900 letter to Senator Hanna in Roosevelt, *Letters*, 2:1342.

33 Letter to Johns dated 16 February 1900. London was quite taken with this poem mailed to him by Johns, repeatedly pondering the interpretation of its wolf and dwarf, as his queries suggest. See his other letters to Johns dated 30 January 1900 and 1 March 1900.

34 See, for example, his references to "wolfish" capitalists in *The Iron Heel* (New York: Macmillan, 1908), pp. 359 and 370. In *The Kempton-Wace Letters* (see Chapter 5), Dane Kempton (Anna Strunsky) argues that if a man writes simply for the sake of money, then the "the wolf of despair" (195) must be at his door. The "Roosevelt's Biggest Game" cartoon, along with many others dramatizing Progressive Era politics in terms of animals, can be found in Albert Shaw, *A Cartoon History of Roosevelt's Career* (New York: Review of Reviews, 1910), p. 78. For the insight that the political rhetoric of the "wolf" can at once encompass both capital and labor, I am indebted to Donald Pease. For a more general discussion of the wolf in Western culture and Native American mythology, see Barry Holstun Lopez, *Of Wolves and Men* (New York: Scribner's, 1978), esp. chaps. 5 and 10. Lopez points out that associations between wolves and famine, as well as between wolves and avaricious landlords, date back to the Middle Ages.

4 *The Subject of Socialism: Postcards from London's* Abyss

1 Jack London, *The People of the Abyss* (New York: Macmillan, 1903), p. 313. Subsequent references to this edition are cited parenthetically.

2 See, for example, Leonard Cassuto, "Jack London's Class-Based Grotesques," *Literature and the Grotesque*, ed. Michael J. Meyer (Amsterdam: Rodopi, 1995), pp. 113–28.

3 An early plot idea for a "San Francisco Slum Study" invokes capitalism explicitly to link the cultural with the natural, as London contemplates: "A study of natural selection under capitalism, or in other words, of commercial selection." See the Jack London Collection (hereafter JL), Henry E. Huntington Library (hereafter HEH), San Marino, California, item JL 1150. London's inability to write such a

study of "The American Abyss," as he imagined yet another plot (JL 437), suggests that the subject was too close to home, as I will be indicating in this chapter.

4 Letters to Brett dated 21 November 1902, 11 December 1902, and 29 September 1902, respectively, in *The Letters of Jack London*, ed. Earle Labor, Robert C. Leitz III, and I. Milo Shepard, vol. 1 (Stanford: Stanford University Press, 1988). Subsequent references to London letters cited by correspondent and date are from this collection unless otherwise noted. Letter to Strunsky dated 28 August 1902. In a subsequent 30 January 1903 letter to Brett, London changed his opinion on serialization, worrying about the lack of time to make such arrangements and confiding that his opinions in the book might be too radical to be published in most mass-circulation magazines.

5 For an interesting discussion of *The People of the Abyss* in relation to contemporaneous British and American tropes of social reform, including General William Booth's *In Darkest England and the Way Out* (1890), see Andrew Sinclair, "A View of the Abyss," *Jack London Newsletter* 9 (1976): 86–95. Sinclair points out that the exoticizing of London (the city) as an African jungle was a standard comparison frequently invoked by late-nineteenth-century reformers. Another interesting discussion downplays literary precursors to argue that London's narrative stance as engaged nonfiction novelist anticipates the "New Journalism" of American writers such as Mailer, Capote, and Tom Wolfe. See Marie L. Ahearn, "*The People of the Abyss*: Jack London as New Journalist," *Modern Fiction Studies* 22, no. 1 (Spring 1976): 73–83.

6 Letter to Brett dated 21 November 1902.

7 Letter to John Spargo dated 28 July 1902. This is the same letter, interestingly enough, in which he agrees to write for Spargo's magazine "How I Became a Socialist," an essay I discussed in terms of London's aspirations as a writer.

8 For an excellent essay examining in detail how London's patriotism functions ideologically in the book, see Robert Peluso, "Gazing at Royalty: Jack London's *The People of the Abyss* and the Emergence of American Imperialism," in *Rereading Jack London*, ed. Leonard Cassuto and Jeanne Reesman (Stanford: Stanford University Press, 1996). Although my arguments and Peluso's overlap at several points when we consider how London aims to distance himself from his British subjects, Peluso's interesting emphasis on London's subject position as a colonizer tends to downplay the role of the body—a source of authorial integrity and anxiety for London, one not always totally contained by categories of nationality. In making his case for London's implicit endorsement of American expansionist policy, Peluso may also be overestimating London's investment in the new science of efficient management—a conclusion London added to the book at Brett's urging that is quite uncharacteristic when viewed in the light of London's entire corpus of political writing.

9 Letter to Anna Strunsky dated 31 July 1902.

10 This is basically the argument of Joan D. Hedrick, *Solitary Comrade: Jack London and His Work* (Chapel Hill: University of North Carolina Press, 1982). Other critics interested in London's politics who deploy a primarily biographical approach include Phillip S. Foner, *Jack London: American Rebel* (New York: Citadel, 1947), pp. 1–130, as well as Carolyn Johnston, *Jack London—An American Radical?* (Westport, Conn.: Greenwood, 1984). The titles of this pair of books suggest how London's thinking on political matters tends to be pigeonholed. See also Eric Homberger, *American Writers and Radical Politics, 1900–39: Equivocal Commitments* (London: Macmillan, 1986), pp. 1–33, for another general assessment of London's politics based more directly on his novels and on *The People of the Abyss*.

11 In a letter to Philo M. Buck Jr. dated 5 November 1912, London remarked, "I was a socialist before I was a writer." By "writer" London presumably meant a professional, since his initial (amateur) appearance in print as a contest winner dates from 1893. But then again, his definition of "socialist" is also open to interpretation, perhaps referring to his brutal work experience and not his official membership in the Socialist Labor Party beginning in 1896.

12 Those of us a hundred years later who are inclined to make strong claims about the upcoming twenty-first century would do well to consider how such talk may come perilously close to the *Examiner*'s sort of sloganeering prophecies.

13 London is first sketched in the *Morning Call* (San Francisco), 12 November 1893, alongside his winning "Story of a Typhoon Off the Coast of Japan." These two Bay Area "Boy Socialist" articles represent London's next appearances in print after this 1893 sketch and after a series of stories published February ("'Frisco Kid's' Story") through December ("'One More Unfortunate'") of 1895 in his Oakland yearbook *The High School Aegis* (reprinted in *The Complete Short Stories of Jack London*, ed. Earle Labor, Robert C. Leitz III, and I. Milo Shepard, 3 vols. [Stanford: Stanford University Press, 1993]). An attribution for the *San Francisco Chronicle*, 16 December 1894, pp. 11–20, about a "Pastor Kid" (otherwise unnamed and unidentified by illustration) is probably incorrect, since the dates and places of his tramping do not strictly coincide with London's accounts in his tramp diary. See William McDevitt, *Jack London's First* (San Francisco: Recorder-Sunset, 1946). Whether this particular article refers to London or not, it is interesting to note that London is presumably only one among many such youthful "tramps" written up by the local press during the 1890s. For another valuable resource see Tony Bubka, "A Jack London Bibliography: A Selection of Reports Printed in the San Francisco Bay Area Newspapers, 1896–1967" (master's thesis, San Jose State College, 1968).

14 William Dean Howells, "My First Visit to New England," *Literary Friends and Acquaintances* (Bloomington: Indiana University Press, 1968). I am indebted to Martha Banta for suggesting this comparison.

15 Jack London, "The Minions of Midas," *The Complete Short Stories of Jack London*, p. 435. Additional page references will be cited parenthetically.

16 See Irving Stone, *Jack London: Sailor on Horseback* (Boston: Houghton Mifflin, 1938), pp. 154–55, and Foner, *Jack London: American Rebel*, p. 46. Johnston, *Jack London—An American Radical?* avoids the story altogether, despite its obvious political content.

17 Letter to Cloudesley Johns dated 24 March 1900.

18 Convinced that London's "hack" fantasies are sometimes more revealing than his "serious" literature, I will be discussing another such important early potboiler—"A Thousand Deaths"—in my chapter on *The Sea-Wolf*.

19 Joan London quotes Anna Strunsky to that effect in her *Jack London and His Times*, 2d ed. (Seattle: University of Washington Press, 1968), p. 217.

20 In a letter to Johns dated 24 March 1900, London emphasizes the clever title of his story. In his introduction to London's *The Assassination Bureau* (New York: Penguin, 1994), Donald Pease suggestively analyzes London's "erasure of the differences between violent crime and the law" (xxvi) along similar lines to my discussion in this chapter of "The Minions of Midas."

21 Jack London, "The Scab," *War of the Classes* (New York: Macmillan, 1905), pp. 102–3. Subsequent references to other socialist essays from this edition will be cited parenthetically.

22 Johnston, *Jack London—An American Radical?* pp. 67–68. For a letter indicating London's own shift to the Socialist Democratic Party, see his 29 January 1901 acceptance of the party's nomination for mayor of Oakland.

23 "The Scab" was delivered by London many times as a lecture. Although London is most active in socialist causes after 1905 (beyond the frame of my study), many of his early essays were presented before audiences. For a discussion of London's career as a public speaker, see Mark Zamen, *Standing Room Only: Jack London's Controversial Career as a Public Speaker* (New York: Peter Lang, 1990).

24 Letter to Brett dated 8 December 1904.

25 For an interesting discussion of the role of tramps in 1870s American dime novels, read as social allegory, see Michael Denning, *Mechanic Accents: Dime Novels and Working-Class Culture in America* (London: Verso, 1987), pp. 149–57.

26 Jack London, " 'Frisco Kid's' Story," *The Complete Short Stories of Jack London*, p. 6. For the story's *Atlantic Monthly* date of submission, see Jack London's handwritten notebook in HEH, JL 933.

27 For a discussion of interpellation, see Louis Althusser, *Lenin and Philosophy and Other Essays*, trans. Ben Brewster (London: New Left Books, 1971), p. 169. Whether updated, qualified, or simply dismissed as outdated, Althusser's basic point remains crucial: subjects do not create themselves out of thin air but occupy preexisting roles that have been fashioned by institutionalized groups with power. As London's representation of the police in his story suggests, these roles need not be fixed and unchanging or defined strictly in terms of social class.

28 London would continue to write a number of local color stories in colloquial idiom about tramps, including one entitled "Local Color" published in *Ainslee's*, December 1903.

29 London submitted this sketch in 1897 to the *San Francisco Examiner*, which rejected it, as did three others, presumably because they found the contents objectionable.

30 Bliss Perry quotation in Richard Etulain, ed., *Jack London on the Road* (Logan: Utah State University Press, 1979), p. 121; Etulain offers a very useful annotated anthology of this body of London's writing. Letter to Brett dated 16 April 1902.

31 Reprinted by Etulain, in *Jack London on the Road*, the version of the essay that appeared in 1904 differs markedly from "The Tramp" as it appears in London's *War of the Classes*, which actually represents a prior version with subheadings removed (including "The Call of 'The Road' "), footnotes added, and statistics not brought up to date. Parenthetical page references are from *War of the Classes*.

32 Letter from George Brett dated 2 October 1902 (HEH, JL 2973), and letter from S. S. McClure dated 6 March 1900 (HEH, JL 14205).

33 Jacob Riis, *How the Other Half Lives* (New York: Scribner's, 1890). Walter A. Wyckoff, *The Workers: The West* (New York: Scribner's, 1898), p. 83.

34 See Riis, *How the Other Half Lives*, and Walter A. Wyckoff, *The Workers: The East* (New York: Scribner's, 1898). These books are part of a tradition emerging in Britain by midcentury aimed at ameliorating social ills from a technical, professional perspective. This loose affiliation of medical officers, sanitation experts, social workers, academics, ministers, and newspaper writers covering crime produced a wide range of work, from technical reports, to journalistic exposés, and to popular narratives such as Riis's, all designed to drum up support for housing and labor reform.

Crucial for many such texts was the accompanying visual representation of poverty. Although I will only briefly discuss the photographs in *The People of the Abyss* in the next chapter, they are worth analyzing more thoroughly in relation to London's writing, especially as he took and selected most of them for publication. For two interesting discussions of the role of photographs in turn-of-the-century social reform texts, see Alan Trachtenberg, *Reading American Photographers* (New York: Hill and Wang, 1989), chap. 4 ("Camera Work/Social Work"), pp. 164–

230, and John Tragg, *The Burden of Representation* (Minneapolis: University of Minnesota Press, 1993), pp. 117–52.

35 In his introduction to *The Assassination Bureau*, Pease argues that during London's stay in the East End he "reenacted Buck's regressive evolution" (xx), but this reverses the time scheme, since *The Call of the Wild* was written a few months after London's return from England as a kind of purified rewriting of his East End experience. Joan London, *Jack London and His Times*, was the first to argue that her father's stay in London informed the writing of *The Call of the Wild*.

36 Joan London, *Jack London and His Times*, pp. 247–48.

37 It might be argued, drawing on narrative theory, that this oscillation stems from the tendency of first-person narration to collapse the distinction between narrating teller and narrated character. See, for example, Jonathan Auerbach, *The Romance of Failure* (New York: Oxford University Press, 1989). This tendency would be all the more acute given London's impulse to write up his experience in the East End mostly as he was living it and not retrospectively on his return to America, so that his double identities as discouraged worker and publishing author would be continually blurred on a daily basis. But I would prefer to see such formal issues as symptoms of the larger question of how London writes himself in relation to other subjects.

London's photographs can also serve to expose the problematic relationship between identity and perspective in the text, in that he sometimes abandons his documentary position behind the camera to include himself in his photos of the poor, as a visitor might seek to be shot alongside the natives. A (seemingly staged) photograph of a policeman rousing a homeless man shows up between pages 114 and 115 of *The People of the Abyss*.

38 Although there is no evidence to suggest that London has read much of Emerson at this point, *The People of the Abyss* takes quite an ironic turn on *English Traits* (1856), which emphasizes the English as "a rude race, all masculine, with brutish strength." See Ralph Waldo Emerson, *Essays and Lectures*, ed. Joel Porte (New York: Library of America, 1983), p. 788. Fifty years of industrial capitalism has clearly taken its toll, or perhaps it is just that Waldo and Jack happened to travel in different circles.

39 HEH, JL 1048. These notes for *People of the Abyss* also include London's intense wish (reprinted in Russ Kingman, *A Pictorial Life of Jack London* [New York: Crown, 1979], p. 115) to be "God one hour" in order to "blot out all London and its 6,000,000 people, as Sodom and Gomorrah were blotted out, and look upon my work and call it good." I wonder if the "London" of such a powerful genocidal desire might extend to the author himself, given his state of misery in the East End.

40 The postcard is reprinted in Kingman, *Pictorial Life of Jack London*, p. 114.

For a photograph of Bert and Jack posing together as hop pickers, see *The People of the Abyss*, p. 172.

5 *Collaborating Love in and out of* The Kempton-Wace Letters

1 Jack London Collection (hereafter JL), Henry E. Huntington Library (hereafter HEH), San Marino, California, JL 1222. The typeface and typing paper of this note correspond closely to other notes for plot ideas which London typed up and which date from between 1900 and 1902.

2 Wayne Koestenbaum, *Double Talk* (New York: Routledge, 1989), p. 2.

3 Jack London, *The People of the Abyss* (New York: Macmillan, 1903), p. 192. Further page references will be cited parenthetically.

4 HEH, JL Scrapbooks, vol. 2.

5 For a discussion of the ambiguous status of Jews in nineteenth-century American culture, see Louise A. Mayo, *The Ambivalent Image* (Rutherford, N.J.: Fairleigh Dickinson University Press, 1988). Mayo points out that the immigration of Eastern European Jews late in the century further complicated ambivalent attitudes by setting up a contrast between previously assimilated German-American Jews and these recent, poorer arrivals. Although born in Russia, Strunsky and her family, unlike the majority of Eastern European Jews, were relatively affluent members of a small circle of turn-of-the-century socialist intellectuals and professionals living in the Bay Area. Strunsky introduced London to Emma Goldman, for example.

I should note, as perhaps yet another sign of his inclination to repress Jewish subjects in *The People of the Abyss*, that in London's personal copy of the book (HEH, 337689), the chapter with by far the most passages crossed out in pencil is "The Ghetto."

6 Bryan Cheyette, *Constructions of "the Jew" in English Literature and Society* (Cambridge: Cambridge University Press, 1993). For a particularly interesting analysis of an English writer whose race theories most closely resemble London's, see the discussion on Kipling, pp. 72–93. The association between Jews and cosmopolitanism that I have been stressing represents something of a special case, since many Jews carried (or were presumed to carry) their own cultural traditions along with them in exile. For an interesting discussion of the concept in light of its more recent critical currency, see Bruce Robbins, "Comparative Cosmopolitanism," *Social Text* 31, no. 2 (1992): 169–86.

7 Slavoj Žižek, *The Sublime Object of Ideology* (Verso: London, 1989), pp. 48, 125–28; emphasis in original (p. 126). Žižek's analysis of ideology bears a certain

resemblance to Kenneth Burke's emphasis on the dialectics of scapegoating, especially his reading of *Mein Kampf*, in his "The Rhetoric of Hitler's 'Battle,' " in *The Philosophy of Literary Form*, rev. ed. (New York: Vintage, 1957), pp. 164–89.

8 HEH, JL 1048.

9 In a letter to Strunsky dated 5 February 1902, London addresses her as "you proud-breasted woman," a phrase that resembles the "firm white breast" that "Li Wan, the Fair" exposes at the end of that story, which was first submitted to a publisher in August 1901, in *The Letters of Jack London*, ed. Earle Labor, Robert C. Leitz III, and I. Milo Shepard, vol. 1 (Stanford: Stanford University Press, 1988). Subsequent references to London letters cited by correspondent and date are from this collection unless otherwise noted. I would also note a series of typed, unpublished short story ideas (HEH, JL 781) dating from 1900–1902 (based on paper watermarks and internal references) that begin at the top of one page with the story of a writer in the habit of "vivisecting psychologically countless women" who meets his match by falling in love with a woman "who vivisects him." At the bottom of the same page are two more notes: "Title of old maid suckling infant— 'The Eternal Feminine' " (with this title crossed out), and, finally, "Story of Anna Strunsky's Big Chest." Paired with the previous note (which reappears in other unpublished jottings), the reference to Strunsky's "Big Chest" is less ambiguous than it first may appear. As we will see, the phrase "proud-breasted" will turn up in *The Kempton-Wace Letters* itself.

10 Letter to Anna Strunsky dated 26 December 1900, and letter to Johns dated 17 October 1900.

11 Letter to Elwyn Hoffman dated 6 January 1901, and letter to George Brett dated 9 November 1902.

12 According to the index of *The Letters of Jack London*, London's initial reference to Jews (a complaint about a publisher) occurs in a letter dated 20 November 1910, although there is a passing reference to Ferdinand Lassalle as a "brilliant German Jew" in an early letter to Johns dated 17 April 1899. See also London's 27 August 1911 letter to the *American Hebrew and Jewish Messenger* in which he calls himself "a terrific admirer of the Jews," who are "some of my finest and noblest friends"—surely a cliché for racial condescension even back then. Identifying Jews as composing both a "race" and a "nationality," London goes on to associate his fondness for them with his socialist beliefs in brotherhood. A similar uncertainty about the status of Jews—as members of an alien race or an assimilated superior culture—marks his relationship with Strunsky. For an interesting early reference to Jews, published a month or so before he first met Strunsky, see London's October 1899 advice essay "On the Writer's Philosophy of Life" (discussed in Chapter 1), in which he enthusiastically recommends that aspiring

authors study "all the varied traits which form collectively the character of the Jew, his beliefs and ideals, his passions and his pleasures, his hopes and fears!" in *No Mentor But Myself: A Collection of Articles, Essays, Reviews, and Letters on Writing and Writers*, ed. Dale L. Walker (Port Washington, N.Y.: Kennikat, 1979), p. 9.

For a suggestive comparison between "the Jew" as modernism's radically indeterminate signifier and earlier constructions of "the Noble Savage," see Cheyette, *Constructions of "the Jew,"* p. 5 n. 9. Stoddard Martin, *California Writers* (New York: St. Martins, 1983), briefly discusses London's attitude toward Jews (pp. 46–47) but unfortunately mistakes the title and publication date for *The Kempton-Wace Letters*.

13   The character of "Jaky" shows up in a fragment of a story entitled "Class Consciousness" (HEH, JL 535), which is perhaps a version of "The Children of Israel," another unpublished story to which London refers in his letters but which no longer survives as far as we know. The letter to Strunsky quoting her criticism of Jaky is dated 29 December 1899, and the letter listing London's influences is dated 21 January 1900.

14   The best discussion of London's nativist politics remains Joan London, *Jack London and His Times*, 2d ed. (Seattle: University of Washington Press, 1968). London's daughter also is one of the few commentators to appreciate the importance of Strunsky in London's life and writing. For London's nativism, see also Carolyn Johnston, *Jack London—An American Radical?* (Westport, Conn.: Greenwood, 1984).

15   Anna Strunsky, " 'The Son of the Wolf.' A Review of Jack London's Book," *Dilettante* 7, no. 8 (February 1901), 179–84, rpt. in Robert A. Woodward, *Jack London and the Amateur Press* (Grand Rapids: Wolf House Books, 1983), pp. 39–43.

16   As is the case with London's initial correspondence with Cloudesley Johns, unfortunately no letters from Strunsky written prior to their 1902 breakup are known to have survived, presumably because he did not bother to keep them. But as in the instance of Johns, the sheer quantity and intimacy of his mail to her enables us to infer a great deal about her responses to him. For an interesting discussion of a similar epistolary collaboration between Viktor Shklovsky and Elsa Triolet that more deliberately and ironically blurs the line between reality and fiction, see Linda S. Kauffman, *Special Delivery: Epistolary Modes in Modern Fiction* (Chicago: University of Chicago Press, 1992), pp. 44–51.

17   One notable exception is an ebullient 15 October 1902 letter (written on the letterhead of a Roman hotel) which London sent her soon after their breakup and which details his meetings with European socialists. In HEH, Walling Collection (Box 3A), this interesting letter is not printed in *The Letters of Jack London*.

18 This negative review from the *New York City Tribune* (14 June 1903) can be found in HEH, JL Scrapbooks, vol. 3.

19 Niklas Luhmann, *Love as Passion: The Codification of Intimacy* (Cambridge: Polity, 1986), p. 147.

20 Ibid., p. 165.

21 [Anna Strunsky and Jack London], *The Kempton-Wace Letters* (New York: Macmillan, 1903). Subsequent references to this edition are also cited parenthetically. For the second edition of the book, London agreed to have his name and Strunsky's on the title page.

22 This information is contained in a letter from Jack London to George Brett dated 9 November 1902.

23 See HEH, JL 863, for the novel's penultimate draft, with corrections by both London (in pencil) and Strunsky (in pen).

24 Perhaps to get back at Strunsky/Kempton for showing such passion, London cruelly emphasized in a paragraph he deleted from the novel's final draft (HEH, JL 863, p. 92) that Kempton was without progeny—his manhood biologically unfulfilled—and that he was therefore "abnormal."

25 Unfortunately we can only surmise the contents of Strunsky's "Dear Jack" letter, which presumably no longer survives. Particularly tantalizing in London's pair of replies are his repeated references to the "W.C.T.U.," which he associates with an "orgy" in the 28 August letter. It seems that Strunsky gathered strength to reject London by attending a Woman's Christian Temperance Union meeting, during which she was encouraged to break off their relationship—an unlikely source of support for a Jewish socialist.

Strunsky was informed of Bessie Maddern's pregnancy by London's mother Flora, as indicated in her letter to Anna (addressed "my dear daughter") dated 20 August 1902 (HEH, Walling Collection, Box 3A). Referring to Bessie as her "persistent enemy," Flora's letter immediately triggered Anna's letter to Jack. Flora's fondness for Anna, as well as the warmth and affection expressed by close friends of London (including Charmian Kittredge and the socialist publisher Gaylord Wilshire, among other correspondents), suggest that Strunsky was indeed a very special, charismatic person. Given the enormous attention paid to London's life and work over the years, surely his remarkable coauthor deserves a biography of her own.

26 See Joan D. Hedrick, *Solitary Comrade: Jack London and His Work* (Chapel Hill: University of North Carolina Press, 1982), p. 69, and Andrew Sinclair, *Jack: A Biography of Jack London* (New York: Harper and Row, 1977), p. 90.

27 See Strunsky's autograph manuscript, entitled "Prologue," in HEH, JL 1705. Penciling it across the top of the first page, George Brett had written, "I am very doubtful about this prologue." In 1958 Strunsky (by now Strunsky-Walling, hav-

ing married William English Walling in 1906) penned her own note on a manilla folder (JL 1706) saying how "greatly relieved" she felt that Brett and London rejected the prologue, which "would have spoiled the book had it been used." A letter from Strunsky-Walling to Hilda Abel dated 16 June 1958 in the Strunsky-Walling Collection of the Bancroft Library describes her efforts to track down the *Kempton-Wace* manuscript some fifty-five years after its initial publication.

28 London's desire to "exploit" Strunsky clearly parallels his understanding of the Yukon as a "field" for "exploitation." The editors of *The Letters of Jack London* have inadvertently transposed the final two paragraphs of the third page of London's first letter (dated 19 December 1899) to Strunsky (beginning, "Pardon me") with the final two paragraphs of the second page of a subsequent letter dated 27 December 1899 (beginning, "Let me see"), as revealed by a careful examination of the originals (especially paper creases and consecutive page numbering) in HEH, Walling Collection, Box 3A. The puzzling past-tense reference to "New's Year Day" in the 27 December letter (as the Hendricks and Shepard edition noted [see *Letters from Jack London*, ed. King Hendricks and Irving Shepard (London: MacGibbon and Kee, 1966), p. 75]) indicates a transposition in the originals that suggests an as-yet-unidentified third letter (presumably sent in early January 1900) as a more likely attribution for this unnumbered page, which closes with a handwritten "P.S." London's tendency to begin new paragraphs on separate pages, as well as the somewhat disjointed nature of his epistolary associations, makes putting these letters together in their original state a rather challenging task.

29 HEH, JL Scrapbooks, vol. 3, July and August 1903.

30 Ibid.

31 See letters to Fannie K. Hamilton and George Brett dated 14 August 1903 and 2 September 1903, respectively.

32 HEH, 337693. The poem is noted but not reprinted in David Mike Hamilton, *"The Tools of My Trade": The Annotated Books in Jack London's Library* (Seattle: University of Washington Press, 1985), p. 191. The poem is clearly aimed at Anna and not Charmian, who was addressed by London with an affectionate inscription in her presentation copy of the novel. See Labor, Leitz, and Shepard, *Letters of Jack London*, vol. 1, photographs between page 218 and page 219. "The Passionate Author to His Love" is probably a response to a poem that Strunsky wrote entitled "Ambition" (HEH, JL 1704) during the height of their relationship (14 March 1902). This poem recounts the desire of a woman for a man (unnamed) who she hopes will love her by virtue of her hard work as a writer. Whereas Strunsky's poem conceives of the toil of authorship as a means to prove the woman's love, the poem in London's book turns desire into a means of professional fulfillment, the raw material for publishing.

6 Between Men of Letters: Homoerotic Agon in The Sea-Wolf

1 George Chauncey, *Gay New York: Gender, Urban Culture, and the Making of the Gay Male World* (New York: Basic, 1994), pp. 80, 47, and 96, respectively.

2 Ibid., p. 88.

3 For London's "meat" comment, see his *The Road* (New York: Macmillan, 1907), p. 83. Andrew Sinclair cites this passage while briefly speculating on London's early sexual experiences. See Andrew Sinclair, *Jack: A Biography of Jack London* (New York: Harper and Row, 1977), pp. 22–26. Like most commentators, Sinclair narrowly treats sexual orientation as an either/or proposition that divides gender performance strictly along biological lines.

4 *The Letters of Jack London*, ed. Earle Labor, Robert C. Leitz III, and I. Milo Shepard, 3 vols. (Stanford: Stanford University Press, 1988), vol. 1. Subsequent references to London letters cited by correspondent and date are from this collection unless otherwise noted.

5 Jack London, *The Sea-Wolf* (New York: Macmillan, 1904), p. 40. Subsequent references to this edition will be cited parenthetically.

6 The earliest piece of correspondence in the Jack London Collection (hereafter JL) at the Henry E. Huntington Library (hereafter HEH), San Marino, California, this handwritten letter from Russell, addressed simply "Dear Sir" and dated 1 December 1892, offers tantalizing grounds for speculation: we can surmise from it that London (age sixteen) had written the well-known author asking permission to reprint or use an early short story of Russell's entitled "Perplexity" that he had published under a pseudonym. Calling attention to his "legal rights," Russell denied London's request, claiming that such a poor story would harm the career of a man "to whom reputation is capital"—an uncanny anticipation of the lessons that London would soon be mastering as a writer. I have not been able to locate Russell's story or to determine the precise circumstances surrounding London's presumed request. See HEH, JL 17399.

7 Jack London, *The Sea-Wolf*, ed. John Sutherland (Oxford: Oxford University Press, 1992), esp. the Introduction, Appendix A, and Notes.

8 See, for example, Joan D. Hedrick, *Solitary Comrade: Jack London and His Work* (Chapel Hill: University of North Carolina Press, 1982), p. 114.

9 Earle Labor, for instance, simply calls the story "mediocre" in retelling how its acceptance saved London. See Earle Labor and Jeanne Campbell Reesman, *Jack London*, rev. ed. (New York: Twayne, 1994), p. 21.

10 Jack London, "A Thousand Deaths," in *The Complete Short Stories of Jack London*, ed. Earle Labor, Robert C. Leitz III, and I. Milo Shepard (Stanford: Stanford University Press, 1993), p. 75. Subsequent references to this story are from this edition and are cited parenthetically in the text.

11 Chaney's remarkable pair of letters are reprinted in Russ Kingman, *A Pictorial Life of Jack London* (New York: Crown, 1979), pp. 18–21.

12 Jack London's notebook *Magazine Sales No. 1* (reprinted in edited form as Appendix A of *The Complete Short Stories of Jack London*) does not list the date of the submission to *Scribner's*. But an earlier unpublished notebook (HEH, JL 933) gives the submission date as 27 June 1897, with the "7" penciled over the second "8" in 1898. The date 1897 is far more likely than 1898, because on 27 June 1898, London was still making his way by boat from Dawson to St. Michael on the Bering Sea. The autobiographical implications of the story are discussed briefly by Edwin B. Erbentraut, "'A Thousand Deaths': Hyperbolic Anger," *Jack London Newsletter* 4 (1971): 125–29.

13 Devoting almost as much space to Poe as to Emerson, Wendell sensibly reads him as a marginalized "Bohemian" (206) whose writing carries high, if problematic, international interest. See Barrett Wendell, *A Literary History of America* (New York: Scribner's, 1900), pp. 204–18. London's fascination with Poe's problematic status in American letters at the turn of the century is worth pursuing, since unlike Hawthorne or Melville, he is neither openly canonized nor relegated to obscurity but exists instead in a twilight zone, popular enough but not considered great or worthy of a school, dwelling somewhere between high and low culture in ways that would illuminate turn-of-the-century publishing institutions. London expresses his misgivings about *The Black Cat* in letters to Cloudesley Johns dated 27 October 1900 and 23 February 1902, respectively.

14 Jack London, "The Terrible and Tragic in Fiction," in *No Mentor but Myself: A Collection of Articles, Essays, Reviews, and Letters on Writing and Writers*, ed. Dale L. Walker (Port Washington, N.Y.: Kennikat, 1979), pp. 59–60. Further references are cited parenthetically in the text.

15 For a discussion of Poe's encoding, see Jonathan Auerbach, *The Romance of Failure: First-Person Fictions of Poe, Hawthorne, and James* (New York: Oxford University Press, 1989), pp. 51–70.

16 The significance of Charley Furuseth extends beyond the novel to resonate autobiographically, since this character is clearly a thinly veiled version of London's close friend George Sterling. I will not be pursuing this particular autobiographical dimension, which has occasioned some speculation (by biographers Joan London and Andrew Sinclair, for instance) about the nature of London's intense affection for Sterling, whom he called "Greek," signing himself "Wolf" in return. London's self-identification as "Wolf" in relation to Sterling's "Greek" suggests his interest in playing Larsen's part—the man's role—in the novel's homoerotic economy, although I am not interested in specifically identifying the "real" or "latent" "homosexual" object underlying *The Sea-Wolf*. I would point out, however, that the Sterling-London friendship heats up just about the time the

novel is being written, as indicated by an intimate letter sent by London to Sterling on 11 July 1903.

17 Jack London, "The Strange Experience of a Misogynist," in *The Complete Short Stories of Jack London*, pp. 55, 58, 65, and 71, respectively. An address change from 25th Ave. to E. 16th Street on the original typescript (HEH, JL 1270) indicates that the story predates his summer 1897 departure for the Yukon. A cryptic note for this story that emphasizes "the idea of the one child born in opposition to the collective will" can be found in an early notebook, HEH, JL 1004. The story was published for the first time in 1993, as part of *The Complete Short Stories of Jack London*.

18 Two other early cabin tales are worth mentioning here in the context of homoerotic attachment: "The Handsome Cabin Boy (1898), which details a double cross-dressing on board ship, and "In a Far Country" (1899), which describes the fatal relationship between two men pent up alone together in a Northland cabin. For an interesting discussion focusing on London's fear of homosexual/underclass contamination, see Scott Derrick, "Making a Heterosexual Man: Gender, Sexuality, and Narrative in the Fiction of Jack London," in *Rereading Jack London*, ed. Leonard Cassuto and Jeanne Campbell Reesman (Stanford: Stanford University Press, 1996). Discussing London's representations of interactions between men, Derrick is apt to focus on scenes of homophobic panic, whereas I am more inclined to see affection, however brutally expressed, underlying London's fears.

19 See, for example, the John Sutherland edition of *The Sea-Wolf.*

20 The swelling leg episode clearly recalls the protagonist's similar predicament in Melville's *Typee: A Real Romance of the South Seas* (1846), a novel London knew from boyhood, as noted by Charles N. Watson, *The Novels of Jack London* (Madison: University of Wisconsin Press, 1983), p. 161. Watson (pp. 58–74) also usefully provides the most detailed and intelligent comparisons between *Moby-Dick* and *The Sea-Wolf.*

21 For an interesting analysis of sadomasochism that attempts to break free of Freud's emphasis on the father, see Giles Deleuze, *Sacher-Masoch: An Interpretation*, trans. Jean McNeil (London: Faber and Faber, 1971), esp. chap. 5, "Father and Mother."

22 I am indebted here to Michael Warner, "Homo-Narcissism; or, Heterosexuality," in *Engendering Men: The Question of Male Feminist Criticism*, ed. Joseph Boone and Michael Cadden (New York: Routledge, 1990), pp. 190–206.

23 Chauncey, *Gay New York*, pp. 86–87. Most dictionaries of American slang fix the 1910s as the first appearance of "wolf" to refer to an aggressive male seducer of men, although Eric Partridge, *Slang To-Day and Yesterday* (New York: Barnes and Noble, 1970), dates this meaning at "ca. 1900" (p. 467). I am assuming that

well before "wolf" showed up in the mainstream print media to refer to gay predators, this slang would have been available, via oral circulation, to persons such as London familiar with the subcultures of sailors, tramps, and prisoners. But beyond the presence or absence of the slang word "wolf" in 1900, Larsen's activity marks him as a sexual predator. As Michael Warner has suggested in another context, "historians may have given too much credit to the power of merely lexical changes. The genealogy of the modern vocabulary of hetero/ homosexuality can be seen already in Thoreau's framing of the problem." See Michael Warner, "Thoreau's Bottom," *Raritan* 11 (Winter 1992): 55.

24 D. A. Miller, "Anal Rope," *Representations* 32 (Fall 1990): 121.

25 There is another way to view Larsen's cigar sucking: as a kind of infantile, masturbatory self-fellatio, a self-absorbed sexuality. But this interpretation ignores the performative, social aspects of Larsen's phallic displays of power, which are intended to intimidate his fellow crewmen. Focusing briefly on the practice of oral intercourse as described in the Kinsey report, George Chauncey remarks that "while homosexually active middle-class men were almost equally likely to play either the active or passive role in fellation, a much higher percentage of lower-status men restricted their participation to the 'masculine' role" (*Gay New York*, p. 119). Hence the class implications of these early scenes, where the "Wolf" tries to insist on playing the man's part, even as the cigar seems to be thrust in him.

26 It is worth pondering how and why the orifice of the mouth tends to be relatively neglected in recent queer theory. D. A. Miller ("Anal Rope"), for instance, after arguing that homosexuality in our culture is relegated to sheer connotation, then goes on to accept as a given "the popularly privileged site of gay male sex" (127) in his focus on the anus in Hitchcock's *Rope*, a discussion that cites Lee Edelman's analysis of "the sodomitical scene." In seeking to revise Freud's case study *The Wolf Man* (another turn-of-the-century "Wolf" text), Edelman likewise dwells on the anal intercourse that fuels Freud's imaginative reconstruction of the primal scene, as if other sites for sodomy were not available. Similarly, Leo Bersani gives only a passing mention to "fellatio and sodomy" (220), as if the two were mutually exclusive categories, in "Is the Rectum a Grave?" *October*, no. 43 (1987): 197–222. Guy Hocquenghem, *Homosexual Desire* (Durham: Duke University Press, 1993), offers a theoretical justification for this privileging by arguing in anticipation of Bersani that anal intercourse encourages a liberating loss or dissolution of identity, particularly identities based on gender, with the assumption that faces are more easily categorized than behinds. But London's representations of orality in *The Sea-Wolf* suggest how the mouth can also work as a transgressive site of pleasure between men.

27 This split in narrative perspective between Wolf and Larsen is complicated by another sort of temporal split as London moves back and forth in his novel

(beginning in chapter 6) between present and past tenses in an attempt to achieve the effect of immediacy that can be found in some of Poe's sea tales such as "MS Found in a Bottle." For the serialized version the editors of *Century* magazine standardized tenses, but London restored his shifts into present tense for the book publication.

28 For a complex rereading of Lacan that argues for a more dynamic construction of the male gaze than tends to be assumed by film theorists such as Laura Mulvey, see Kaja Silverman, *Male Subjectivity at the Margins* (New York: Routledge, 1992), chap. 3, pp. 125–57.

29 In so downplaying the intellectual content of these debates, I am taking my lead from Gordon Mills, who recognized long ago how London "was too ready to call an emotion by the name of a philosophical point of view" (9), although I am less interested in simply faulting the author than closely analyzing the particular emotions that underlie his philosophizing. Mills was also one of the first critics to call attention to the divided plot structure that patterns many of London's novels, which midway through suddenly turn from adventure/violence to love. See Gordon Mills, "Jack London's Quest for Salvation," *American Quarterly* 7 (1955): 3–14.

30 For a recent discussion of the novel that emphasizes this naturalizing but doesn't consider how for London the concept of nature itself is gendered, see Christopher Gair, "Gender and Genre: Nature, Naturalism, and Authority in *The Sea-Wolf*," *Studies in American Fiction* 22, no. 2 (Autumn 1994): 131–47. Gair has also noticed the novel's scandalous pun on "mate."

31 Portentously signaling an impending crisis on ship, the prophetic sailor Louis prepares for Maud's arrival by cryptically muttering "she's close, she's close" (126).

32 Sam S. Baskett, "Sea Change in *The Sea-Wolf*," *American Literary Realism* 24, no. 2 (1992): 5–22. Three other influential readings of London's gender constructions are worth mentioning here: Robert Forrey, "Male and Female in London's *The Sea-Wolf*," *Literature and Psychology* 24, no. 4 (1974): 135–43, who brings up many of the key passages in the novel in arguing, somewhat reductively, for London's latent homosexual drives; Clarice Stasz, "Androgyny in the Novels of Jack London," *Western American Literature* 11 (1976): 121–33, who argues, like Baskett, for a relatively static model of internalized difference; and Joseph Boone, "Male Independence and the American Quest Genre: Hidden Sexual Politics in the All-Male Worlds of Melville, Twain, and London," in *Gender Studies: New Directions in Feminist Criticism*, ed. Judith Spector (Bowling Green: Bowling Green State University Press, 1986), pp. 187–217, who focuses on the novel's divided structure but does not fully consider the Hump-Wolf relationship as a kind of homoerotic mating, as I do.

For my interrogation of the concept of androgyny, I am indebted to similar theoretical critiques leveled by Jonathan Goldberg, *Sodometries* (Stanford: Stanford University Press, 1992), and Lee Edelman, *Homographesis* (New York: Routledge, 1994), pp. 24–41. Beyond simply the title of this chapter, my thinking on homoerotic economies has also been greatly influenced by Eve Kosofsky Sedgwick, *Between Men: English Literature and Male Homosocial Desire* (New York: Columbia University Press, 1985), and Sedgwick, *Epistemology of the Closet* (Berkeley: University of California Press, 1990).

33 Van Weyden himself registers the absolutely conventional nature of Maud's arrival when he observes, "I had read sea-romances in my time, wherein figured, as a matter of course, the lone woman in the midst of a shipload of men," although he goes on to admit that "I had never comprehended the deeper significance of such a situation" (212).

34 Chauncey, *Gay New York*, p. 120. See also Jonathan Ned Katz, *The Invention of Heterosexuality* (New York: Dutton, 1995). To make their point, both Chauncey and Katz may be overestimating the degree to which heterosexuality since the 1920s has simply become entrenched as normative. For an earlier discussion that calls heterosexuality into question from a somewhat different perspective emphasizing the role of patriarchy, see Adrienne Rich, "Compulsory Heterosexuality and Lesbian Existence" (1980), reprinted in *Blood, Bread, and Poetry* (New York: Norton, 1986).

35 London's shift from working-class to middle-class values is the overriding thesis of Hedrick, *Solitary Comrade*, although she does not precisely locate this change in such a decisive moment midway through a single novel, as I have done. It is tempting, in fact, to locate two such crucial moments linked in London's early writing: Buck's staged sled pull for the love of Thornton in *The Call of the Wild*, when London realized he preferred to be mastered by fame than by hard work; and Maud's dramatic arrival in *The Sea-Wolf*, when London realized he preferred respectability (afforded in part by heterosexuality) than to remain at the service of a powerful man.

36 As in the case of *The Call of the Wild*, this particular sum of money matches the advance Jack London requested and received from his publisher Macmillan at the end of 1902.

37 Their doubling as comrades is matched by Wolf Larsen's increasing association with his brother Death, who is introduced early in the novel (the end of chapter 10) but who takes on significance only near the conclusion as a kind of mock enemy, an evil shadow of his brother. Doubling Wolf, Death serves to underscore the break between captain and mate by reasserting more "natural" bonds between brothers.

38 Later in his narrative Van Weyden does allow for Maud's bodily attraction,

focusing on the hair of this "one woman in the world" (283), but even this "physical characteristic of love" (259) pales in comparison with the furry pelt that Van Weyden first spies on the dying mate's chest near the beginning of his adventure. Like the vast majority of critics, I too find the second half of the novel unconvincing, although I am less interested in faulting London's characterization of Maud than in analyzing how the woman structurally functions to uphold heterosexuality. For one notable exception to this critical disparagement of Maud, see Forrest Robinson, "The Eyes Have It: An Essay on Jack London's *The Sea-Wolf*," *American Literary Realism* 18 (1985): 178–95. Robinson sees how Maud deflects Hump from his attraction to Wolf but then argues, in a dubious New Critical throwback to assumptions about unreliable narrators, that this deflection shows Hump's limited and ironized view of Maud, who for Robinson is far more interesting and powerful than Van Weyden's narration would allow. In a subsequent version of this article reprinted in *Having It Both Ways: Self-Subversion in Western Popular Classics* (Albuquerque: University of New Mexico Press, 1993), pp. 55–78, Robinson no longer tries to save Maud at the expense of Hump but instead argues, a bit more persuasively, that her assertiveness is "inadvertent" on London's part, although he still insists on taking seriously Maud and Wolf's mutual sexual attraction. Robinson also notes the novel's fixation with eyes (seeing) but does not register London's even more obsessively literal rendering of mouths (speaking).

39 Hedrick, *Solitary Comrade*, p. 124. The literal cause of Hump's headaches turns out to be a massive brain tumor.

40 Letter dated 23 October 1911 in *The Letters of Jack London*, vol. 2. One might assume that the only reason London inserted early in his novel the detail (narrated secondhand) about Larsen and his crew ravishing a group of Japanese women (pp. 56–57) would be to make his subsequent attack of Maud seem more plausible.

41 Hedrick also makes this comparison with Poe; see *Solitary Comrade*, p. 130.

42 That Larsen is to be punished for reveling in his body is clear from a comment London made in a synopsis for the novel in which he refers to the captain's "soul walled up by flesh" (see n. 48, this chapter, for a fuller discussion of this synopsis). Two very different contexts for Van Weyden's allusion to large "doses" of Larsen are worth considering here. First is the notorious initiation rites of the Sambia of New Guinea, who require young men to perform ritual "homosexual" fellatio on elders in order to gain the patriarchal power invested in sperm. See David D. Gilmore, *Manhood in the Making* (New Haven: Yale University Press, 1990), pp. 146–68. Without pressing the play on words, the pun semen/seaman might be seen to operate in London's novel. The second context concerns the cultural centrality throughout nineteenth-century America of patent medicines, which

functioned as magic tonics or elixirs promising self-transformation and renewal, as Jackson Lears discusses in his history of advertising, *Fables of Abundance* (New York: Basic, 1994), pp. 142–53.

43 Van Weyden's immediate reaction on discovering Wolf and his dismasted *Ghost* had washed up on their Endeavor Island—the final return of the repressed—is worth contemplating as perhaps the last sign of the narrator's most intense affections: "It was impossible, impossible. A wild thought of rushing in and killing her as she slept rose in my mind" (300). London is so fascinating and wonderful a writer precisely for allowing such a stray thought to stand. Van Weyden quickly thinks better of murdering Maud and decides to kill Larsen instead.

44 Mark Seltzer also singles out this "fulcrum" passage but reads it (incorrectly, in my view) as celebrating self-reproduction via a machine-body complex, thus ignoring London's quite traditional (and nonmechanical) emphasis on gender: the woman as the fulcrum that makes the man self-reliant. See Mark Seltzer, *Bodies and Machines* (New York: Routledge, 1992), p. 171.

45 The editors of *The Letters of Jack London* put this letter (1: 370–71) fourth in the sequence beginning 18 June 1903.

46 Warner, "Homo-Narcissism."

47 Letter from Gilder to Brett dated 26 August 1903 (HEH, JL 6683) that Brett apparently enclosed alongside his own caution to London sent a day later (HEH, JL 3001). However gentle, patient, and sympathetic, Brett's moderation of Gilder's veiled threats still represents a doubling of editorial pressure on London—two fathers instead of one. The crucial encouraging role played by Brett throughout London's literary career remains to be analyzed, especially since it could be argued that Brett, not London, was the hero of the writer's life, seizing his potential in ways that London himself could not. For informative discussions of Gilder's pivotal role in turn-of-the-century publishing, see Arthur John, *The Best Years of the Century* (Urbana: University of Illinois Press, 1981), and Herbert F. Smith, *Richard Watson Gilder* (New York: Twayne, 1970). Both Smith and John point out that by the late 1890s the genteel *Century Magazine* was losing preeminence (measured in terms of circulation)—a loss that Gilder's serialization of London and his brand of muscular naturalism was intended to reverse, despite Gilder's editorial reservations. Smith (pp. 125–39) intelligently assesses Gilder's infamous blue penciling of *Huck Finn* with more sympathy and balance than my own brief allusion would allow.

48 Agreeing to editorial changes, London sent his reassuring note to Brett one day after sending Charmian his letter about their essential masculinity and femininity. Charmian Kittredge (and George Sterling) quite literally fulfilled the role of editor in the case of the serialized version of *The Sea-Wolf* when London left for Korea in January 1904 to work as a war correspondent for Hearst newspapers.

Unfortunately, the original manuscript was destroyed in the 1906 San Francisco earthquake, so that we cannot know the extent of their editing or the extent to which the many differences between the book and magazine versions were introduced by London himself when he returned in the summer of 1904 to prepare the book for publication. Given to George Sterling on 16 August 1913 (see letter from London) and then subsequently donated to the University of Virginia, the corrected typescript for the Macmillan publication reveals only relatively minor revisions.

For a discussion of London's concessions to Gilder for the sake of securing popularity, see Susan Ward, "Social Philosophy as Best-Seller: Jack London's *The Sea-Wolf*," *Western American Literature* 17 (1983): 321–32. Ward refers to a four-page pair of documents, "Synopsis of Sea Novel" and "Amplification of Synopsis of Last Half of Sea Novel" (#6240E, Jack London Collection, Clifton Walker Barrett Library, University of Virginia), in which London reassures his editors that "with the arrival of Maud on the schooner, the key in which the story is written will at once begin to change, and in no time the key will be wholly changed. Up to this point, Humphrey Van Weyden has been singing another man's song. . . . From this point and to the end he will sing his own song the warm and glowing song of love triumphant." In keeping with the novel's fixation on oral intercourse, singing songs becomes London's metaphor for control, with self-mastery now coinciding with the author's willingness to change his tune to meet the expectations of his editors, even as he assumes that very tune is his own. Hence London's closing invitation to his editors: "Free hand with the blue pencil."

49 Jack's love for Charmian would also seem to have resolved the problem of the Law or social mastery that had troubled London from the start of his career, allowing him to conclude simply that "We ARE the Law," presumably as long as the ship they copiloted in marriage conformed to the surrounding ocean. See his letter to Charmian dated "Monday June 1903" in *The Letters of Jack London*, 1:369. Two other documents offer telling glimpses into the dynamics of Jack and Charmian's mutual (self-)worship specifically in relation to *The Sea-Wolf*. In a letter dated 10 November 1903, London writes Charmian: "Know, sweet love, that I never knew how greatly you loved me until there came the free and utter abandonment, the consent of you and your love and of every fibre of you. . . . It was *after* you gave greatly that I became your 'slave,' expressed willingness to die for you" (London's emphasis). This interesting letter is not reprinted in *The Letters of Jack London* but can be found in Irving Stone, *Sailor on Horseback: The Biography of Jack London* (Cambridge, Mass.: Houghton Mifflin, 1938), p. 188. Charmian herself commented thusly on their relationship: "It is a privilege to serve under a great captain; and I sat at his feet and endeavored with all my womanhood to come up to his fine, sane standard of companionship, the thing he

had missed even with men, it would seem." See Charmian London, *The Book of Jack London* (New York: Century, 1921), 2:52. For a detailed and sympathetic account of their marriage, see Clarice Stasz, *American Dreamers: Charmian and Jack London* (New York: St. Martin's, 1988).

50 These sales numbers are given by Kingman, *Pictorial Life of Jack London*, p. 126. Kingman points out that some of these advance purchases came from *The Ladies' Home Journal*, which used the book for a promotional premium—a clear sign of how respectable London's work had become.

Epilogue: Celebrity

1 Jack London, "The Sun-Dog Trail," in *The Complete Short Stories of Jack London*, ed. Earle Labor, Robert C. Leitz III, and I. Milo Shepard (Stanford: Stanford University Press, 1993), pp. 969–85. For a more extended reading of this story that resembles my own, see Leonard Cassuto, "Chasing the Lost Signifier Down 'The Sun-Dog Trail,'" *Jack London Journal*, no. 2 (1995): 64–72.

2 Letter to George Brett dated 5 December 1904, in *The Letters of Jack London*, ed. Earle Labor, Robert C. Leitz III, and I. Milo Shepard, vol. 1 (Stanford: Stanford University Press, 1988).

3 Jack London, *Burning Daylight* (New York: Macmillan, 1910), p. 10. Subsequent references are cited parenthetically.

4 Here I must register one important exception to my broad generalizations: London's Hawaii stories, an important body of writing that enabled him to dislodge himself from the center of his work. Hawaii and its people offered London an alterity powerful enough to resist the author's appropriation by way of autobiography. These Hawaii tales are sufficiently complex and interesting to merit a more extensive analysis in their own right.

5 Letter dated 30 May 1911, in Labor, Leitz, and Shepard, *Letters of Jack London*.

6 Russ Kingman, *A Pictorial Life of Jack London* (New York: Crown, 1979), p. 241. Jack London, *The Valley of the Moon* (New York: Macmillan, 1913). Subsequent references are cited parenthetically. For an interesting discussion of the novel focusing on its racialism, see Christopher Gair, "'The Way Our People Came': Citizenship, Capitalism, and Racial Difference in *The Valley of the Moon*," *Studies in the Novel* 25, no. 4 (Winter 1993): 418–35.

7 Kingman, *Pictorial Life of Jack London*, p. 240. For a useful discussion of London's relation with Hollywood, see Tony Williams, *Jack London—The Movies* (Middletown, Calif.: Rejl, 1992), pp. 1–68. Williams's book is mainly descriptive; what remains to be done is an analytic study showing how from 1904 to 1916 London in effect predicts and helps prepare the way for Hollywood's global cul-

tural ascendancy by virtue of his appreciation of publishing as collective and profit-driven, his goodwill worldwide travels exporting himself, and his fictions themselves. Starting with *The Sea-Wolf*, London's novels embody narrative structures and characterizations that could fruitfully be compared with analogous formal features of early Hollywood movies. The degree to which these movies influenced literary production in the twentieth century has not yet been fully appreciated.

8 Arguing for the importance of later works such as "Samuel" and "Told in the Drooling Ward," Earle Labor and Jeanne Campbell Reesman support their claims for this writing's experimental power by stressing London's difficulties in getting it published. See *Jack London*, rev. ed. (New York: Twayne, 1994), p. 136. Perhaps, but an alternative explanation offers itself: that by the 1910s London, as the highest-paid living author of his time, had virtually priced himself out of the market, such that many magazines could not afford his work.

9 Letters dated 17 November 1915, 26 March 1914, and 3 April 1915, respectively, in Labor, Leitz, and Shepard, *Letters of Jack London*.

10 Jack London, *The Little Lady of the Big House* (New York: Macmillan, 1916), p. 107. Subsequent references are cited parenthetically.

Index

Eames, Ninetta, 39
Edward VII, 117, 139, 141
Eliot, T. S., 151
Emerson, Ralph Waldo, 24, 122, 267
    n.38
Engels, Friedrich, 101

Fern, Fanny, 26
Foner, Phillip, 125, 130
Franklin, Ben, 26
Frazer, James, 60
Freud, Sigmund, 59–60, 110, 201, 236

Ghent, William J., 131
Gilder, Richard Watson, 221, 225
Griffith, D. W., 236

Harte, Bret, 47
Hawthorne, Nathaniel, 122, 190
Hedrick, Joan, 219, 260 n.20, 278
    n.35, 278 n.41
Hegel, G. W. F., 95–97, 102, 105
Hemingway, Ernest, 53, 55
Hills, William H., 31
Hoffman, Elwyn: correspondence
    with Jack London, 154
Homosexuality, 170, 199–200, 214,
    216, 219, 224, 276 n.26
Howard, June, 6–7, 94–95, 259 n.15
Howells, William Dean, 28, 34, 122
Huxley, Thomas, 114

Imperialism, 59, 74–75, 82, 210, 263
    n.8
Irving, Washington, 122

James, Henry, 28, 32
Johns, Cloudesley: correspondence
    with Jack London, 11, 13, 20, 21,
    29, 42, 47, 49, 52, 54, 61, 112, 153,
    157, 171, 189

Johnston, Carolyn, 130
Joyce, James, 53
Jung, Carl, 20, 111, 235

Katz, Jonathan, 216
Kazin, Alfred, 5
Kelly's Army of the Unemployed,
    122–23, 134, 179
Khayyám, Omar, See Omar
    Khayyám
Kipling, Rudyard, 90–91, 137, 151,
    158, 181–82, 240 n.12, 241 n.14,
    246 n.24, 268 n.6
Kittredge, Charmian, 9, 157, 176,
    181, 221–26, 231–32, 236–37, 281
    n.49
Koestenbaum, Wayne, 149
Kojève, Alexandre, 97, 102

Labor, Earle, 48, 242 n.27
Lacan, Jacques, 109, 151
Laurie, Annie, 138
Lévi-Strauss, Claude, 60
London, Jack, Identities of: as Ameri-
    can, 118, 130, 153; as "Boy Social-
    ist of Oakland," 121–24, 132–34,
    147; as dog, 84–85; as journalist,
    28, 36–37, 116, 139; as literary
    critic, 182, 207; as mail carrier, 12–
    13, 69, 88, 227–28; as mate, 167,
    198–99, 209, 223; as professor,
    162; as sailor, 4, 145, 183, 233; as
    "Wolf," 9–10, 56–57, 112, 156,
    198. See also Authorship
London, Jack, Works of: "Again the
    Literary Aspirant," 42; Burning
    Daylight, 229–32; The Call of the
    Wild, 12, 18–19, 37, 43, 45, 84–
    113, 114, 118–19, 139, 141, 143,
    159, 162, 166, 170, 173, 175, 176,
    178, 180–81, 183, 185, 194, 196,

Jonathan Auerbach is Professor of English
at the University of Maryland.

Library of Congress Cataloging-in-Publication Data

Auerbach, Jonathan, 1954–

Male call : becoming Jack London / Jonathan Auerbach.

p.   cm. — (New Americanists)

Includes index.

ISBN 0-8223-1827-X (cloth : alk. paper). —

ISBN 0-8223-1820-2 (paper : alk. paper)

1. London, Jack, 1876–1916—Criticism and interpretation.

2. Autobiographical fiction, American—History and criticism.

3. Masculinity (Psychology) in literature.   4. Self in literature.

5. Men in literature.   I. Title.

PS3523.046Z53   1996

813'.52—dc20   96-14682   CIP